PERRY
BOYS

PERRY BOYS

IAN HOUGH

MILO BOOKS

First published in April 2007 by Milo Books

Copyright © 2007 Ian Hough

ISBN 978 1 903854 65 5

Typeset by e-type

Printed in Great Britain by CPD

MILO BOOKS LTD
The Old Weighbridge
Station Road
Wrea Green
Lancs PR4 2PH
www.milobooks.com

For Kimberly

P.S. – you too.

He who fights and runs away
Lives to fight another day
He who fights and stands his ground
Gets his bleedin' head knocked round

—Uncle Bernard

CONTENTS

ABOUT THE AUTHOR

Ian Hough was born and raised in Salford and North Manchester. He has a degree in Environmental Toxicology and Chemistry from the University of Massachusetts, Amherst, and lives in the USA, where he continues to write non-fiction. *Perry Boys* is his first book.

PROLOGUE

BRITISH YOUTH movements tend to emerge and remain popular for little more than three or four years, at most. Typically they are documented in real time by the London-based media, and fashion styles are tightly coupled to certain forms of music, whose proponents, propagandists and superstars champion them wildly through that same media, boosting the economy and encouraging scandal while the nation looks on in glee. When teddy boys ripped and slashed cinema seats in 1957, when beatniks refused to seek jobs in the early 1960s, when mods and rockers rioted at the seaside in 1964, the Establishment grumpily voiced its disdain. When hippies took LSD in 1967, when glam rockers wore make-up and glitter in 1972, when punk rockers wore safety-pins and spat on each other in 1976, and when football hooligans wrecked stadiums and fought with police through the early to mid-1970s, many tutted contentedly, and discussed bringing back National Service. Each of these new phases had been fed directly by the momentum provided by the dissolution of the previous one, and young people were able to jump ship and ride each strange new vehicle without missing stride, amid the indignation. Each of these phases was comparable in duration and in the extent to which it deviated from what the older generation considered to be 'proper'. In short, the momentum, the energy, was not dissipating; it was a constant, a perpetual self-renewing process that couldn't be stopped. The scale of the momentum transfer between each phase was the same, and consequently each phase was roughly equal in magnitude.

Magnitude, scale and energy are subject to change, however.

By 1978, the evolving, mutating body that was Britain's youth appeared to have entered an energy crisis: nothing was happening; 'New Wave' had largely replaced punk rock, and its heroes wallowed uncertainly in the weak swirls and eddies of a fashionless cultural landscape. Various underground and over-ground factors had contributed to the sudden death of flared trousers, and drainpipes were worn for the first time since the late 1950s. The blockbuster movie *Grease* and the 1979 release of the Who album/film *Quadrophenia* were certainly contribu-tors to this development. Things were languid, disconnected and confused. Where had the momentum for the ideas gone?

Something happened around 1979. The magnitude and the impetus of ideas, and the energy with which young people pursued the evolution of those ideas, underwent a considerable shift, both in character and in scale; a cloaked youth movement emerged which outfoxed the radar of the London media, which possessed no musical definition and whose 'superstars' were non-existent, and which, above all, has endured to the present day. It had no rules, it had no name and it had no outline, save a geographical one. It began in the north-west of England in a weird resonance between the cities of Liverpool and Manchester. Its materials were vastly more obtainable in the latter, but the application of them initially belonged largely to the former. Its appearance did not betray its intensity – devia-tion from what the older generation considered proper was not evident in its styles at all. Unlike previous youth movements, this one did not seek to shock, or to appear different simply as an end in itself; in fact its main purpose was to *camouflage* its propo-nents as they went about their business.

The region is no stranger to innovation; from Southport to Stockport once lay the engine room of the British Empire, a hub of invention and industry that attracted visitors from all corners of the globe, creating cosmopolitanism unrivalled outside London and a world centre for textiles, especially cotton. Unlike the south-east, the north-west was subject to tremendous local rivalries, as the similarities between its two cities generated a powerful repulsive force. There were other differences from the south-east, too; in the 1830s, while Londoners rode a tiny toy train around Piccadilly Circus, imagining they were sampling a novel form of transport, the world's first inter-city passenger railway was already operating between Liverpool and Manchester. Despite this early-developed connectivity, denizens of the two cities never did see eye to eye. It was a tribal thing, born deep in time, probably at the end of the Ice Age. In the absence of environmental stressors we fail to grow as people, and ten thousand years of rivalry had us well primed. This inter-city stress created selection pressures on those caught in its sway, forcing the evolution of ideas to gather pace, to outrun the other in the race for improved adaptations, and so the Boys were born.

The story of humankind is one of beginnings, mutations and evolutionary endpoints. Beginnings throughout history have arisen from the confluence of seemingly unrelated factors, and the phenomenon of the Perry Boy is no exception. Several disparate pieces dovetailed to create something novel and unexpected in youth culture. Just as Ice Age hunters travelled great distances to acquire rare (and therefore valuable) pelts, pottery and jewellery, the proponents of this movement did the same. Continental Europe was their destination, and shoes and clothing their target. Many of the youngsters participating in the hunt were natives of the inner cities of Manchester and Liverpool. These were people accustomed to poverty. Large numbers of them had been displaced as children during the slum clearance projects of the early 1970s, and a deep sense of exhilaration and fear had accompanied their evacuations from terraced streets to high-rise towers. The cosy webs of established communities were ripped apart, and their occupants randomly assigned space in this or that tower, on this or that estate. This had several effects on those caught up in the concrete tide: it created a need to be around like-minded people, namely those who felt alienated and dissatisfied; it created relatively long-distance communication between former neighbours who had been separated; and it fostered a sense of victimhood, which replaced the comfortable feeling of familiarity with the old faces from the terraced streets now gone.

As a result, a new age of urbanite evolved in the inner cities,
one in need of satisfaction, determined to obtain it by hook or by
crook. They wanted *more*, and they decided to take it. Where their
ancestors had been excluded by those in the higher social strata,
the natives from these smashed communities themselves rejected
contact with those who didn't understand, and a culture of its
own was born. This culture was not confined to the very poorest
in the high-rises, though. Its participants came from all over the
two cities, but it is true to say that most had somehow descended
from those ancient cobbled cores. They did what they did, and it
never occurred to them that what they did was actually anything.
In time, it became truly something. This thing without name,
driven by the inter-city dynamism of north-west England, was
forced to rapidly mutate, as have other human vehicles and mind-
sets, eventually settling into its lowest energy configuration; the
essence of what it is to be young and hip. That the final product,
hatched like an alien being from an unknown egg in 1979, constituted an evolutionary endpoint that is glaringly obvious in the way
young people in 2007 continue to prize the same styles and brand
names coveted by those youngsters almost three decades ago.

What began as roving bands of young men pillaging, hunting
and gathering the materials they needed to survive in a
changing world, morphed into a full-blown consumer culture
that no longer needed searching out. The rest of the country had
finally cottoned on, and the sports shops of all England were
suddenly stocked to the gills with identikits of the north-west
template. This was the point when the phenomenon had
reached London and was promptly given an official name. This
shift in public visibility and general application parallels the shift
from hunting and gathering to agriculturalism over 10,000 years
ago. When the tribe learned to corral the object of the hunt, and
sew the seed of their bread, within walking distance of their
camp, the world was forever transformed.

The new lifestyle was irresistible, and vastly superior to that
which came before. It spread like wildfire. The Perry Boy was
no longer a unique creature, confined to the slopes of north-
west England's grey and plundered land. He was everywhere.

Journalists finally began to report on his 'movements', by now ironically constrained to the auspices of the local sporting goods shop and the stadium of his favourite football team, wherever that may be. The thrill of the hunt may have gone, replaced by an unadventurous ramble down the local high street, but the other side, the dark side, remained. The violence of the football terraces, essentially an addiction to the molecule called adrenalin, was stoked up by the novelty of this ultra-cool new look. Every city and town in Britain was viciously made aware of the phenomenon, now referred to as the Casual movement. The lager lout era had begun.

At this point, some time in 1983, the individuals responsible for the creation of the movement grew jaded and bored, even as the rest of the country was set alight by the 'new' styles. They sought substitutes for the rush of a dangerous day out at the football. These substitutes were rapidly determined to be molecules other than adrenalin, which themselves provided their own unique and irresistible effects. Hallucinogenic drugs offered a challenge all of their own, this time from within. The need for thrills focussed on novel inner landscapes, and once more the fun and games began. Manchester became Madchester, and happiness became Ecstasy, as the mutation again found that lowest energy configuration. A new essence of being young and hip was born, the ageless cycle of repetition having orbited around itself more speedily than ever before. The mechanical transports of the hunt mutated into the chemical transports of the trip, but the clothes remained essentially the same. The constant re-colouring of the human path received a particularly vivid coat of paint, as young people began launching themselves off on voyages of discovery around the globe, and the whole game became a feedback loop, coming and going, going and coming. Those youngsters, exiled as children from cobbled streets to high-rise flats, witnessed first-hand the systematic transformation of other countries, often in the name of tourism, much of it British. Ancestral dwellings and authentic artefacts were replaced by high-rise hotels and counterfeit designer sportswear. Working-class Brits were now able to afford foreign travel like never before, and the irony of what they wrought was not lost on them. The clothes, the footwear, the music, the chemicals, the travel, *the irony*, all were now locked in equilibrium, an orbit that touched the deepest crannies of the mind and spanned the planet.

I am about to tell you that story. Open up a cold one, light up a smoke and curl up with me, deep in the sedimentary matrix, in the machinations of the seed, where the new breed was forged – in tower-blocks, European *de luxe* sweatshops and, of course, on the terraces of you-know-where, you-know-when. The history of youth movements in the UK has been told and retold, and recently even the history of what emerged in 1979 has been related, in hooligan memoirs, and more thoroughly by Phil Thornton in *Casuals* and David Hewitson in *The Liverpool Boys are in Town*. This book seeks to add to those accounts, with humour and prose. This is not a hooligan memoir, nor a rundown of what came into fashion in 1983 in London, or in 1986 somewhere else. It is simply the account of a normal lad, alive and young, in Manchester, during a special time. It will become obvious to the reader that there are pirates and there are Vikings here, and that some individuals belong in both camps. The story is set in a pre-mobile phone, pre-computer world, for the most part, and in this lies much of the magic. The chronology behind the emergence of an entire lifestyle will be described to you, from the viewpoint of those who invented it.

I was not a gang leader or a glory hunter, just a Perry lad living in a new time, and I write this book for all of you who were the same. We are the faceless drones, those who worked hard to make life worth living, and to have fun, but we weren't just there for the fun of it. I won't go into endless detail about the stealing, drug-taking or fighting, which we all did at times – but you'll understand what's going on, believe me. I am neither one thing nor another; I am the cross-section. I bring to you the tale of the many, embodied in the tale of the one: me. There is no cure for the English disease, because the English disease is a virus. Herein lie the accounts of the final, deciding pandemic, the Big One that infected the world. In short, it's a fucking good read.

PART 1

THE THING IS BORN

1

CHAOS AND CHEMISTRY

I've been in more courts than Bjorn Borg.
—Tommy Docherty

MAN IS AN egg-and-bollocks-based life-form. We all love a good fry-up on a Sunday morning, a bubble-and-squeak on a Monday night, some good chinwag and a leg-over just about anytime. It is the stuff of life: grease, oil, spuds and protein. It's all about texture. But we forget there's a lot of DNA in there, too. It's not all just *structural* material, sprung from the soil like bamboo, overnight in a monsoon, rigid and unfeeling. Inside everything that ever lived there lurked a trillion little identical *informational* molecules responsible for evolving your meal into the meal it was, via billions of years of mutations. The life-form that is your egg-and-bollocks brekkie may once have been your worst enemy, but is now your sustenance. Are you a herbivore or a carnivore? Breakfast is the most important meal of the day, and what you eat often determines how the rest of the day will proceed. Some eat Cornflakes, some eat Rice Krispies, some eat toast and some eat West Ham. With brown sauce on and two eggs, if they've got any sense.

I was born towards the end of 1965, so in 1975 I was nine, going on ten. In 1985 I was nineteen, going on twenty. These were changing times for my cohorts and me, on the streets of north-west Manchester. As kids, back in the dinosaur 70s, we spent a goodly amount of time being legged by older lads in flares and blue, white and purple football scarves, lads who wanted to do us harm when we just wanted to *be*. When playing footy, we would spot them, skulking around the gates at the other end of the local park, *their* end, eyeing us like hyenas, making sure we were young enough for them to get away with it. Often, even though they didn't know me at all, they instinctively knew I was a red. The older kids were rotten, nasty bullying bastards in those days. They could break up a friendly neighbourhood football game by steaming the players and going for the United fans, sending them scattering in all directions, to take the long way home, shaking with adrenalin. Perhaps because I was never the target of older reds I developed an idea that City fans alone were of this character. I don't recall ever seeing United fans doing the same to young blues. Perhaps it was just an unfortunate geographic twist that placed me in a neighbourhood somewhat divided between red and blue, and that we hung out in a park that was right on the physical border between the two sides. Perhaps I learned to avoid older lads wearing City scarves, unless they lived down in my neighbourhood, where they were personal acquaintances rather than faceless assailants.

Kezz was one kid who lived just down the street from me. Back then he was a blue, but we hung around together all the time, climbing trees and riding our bikes. One Thursday evening in the early 70s, I'd stayed a bit later than usual at Kezz's house, and was astonished at the sight of the gold, red and blue 'kits' of the Starship Enterprise personnel. We had a black and white telly when everyone else had colour, and this was a major revelation to me. I watched *Star Trek* at Kezz's house every week from then on.

The unbridled and merciless bullying by the strong against the weak during those barbaric years forged powerful allegiances between developing kids on the streets, and the population became genetically selected for the ability to take a kicking, as well as give one. This was a handy trait. City had relegated United at Old Trafford, and the resultant pitch invasion would become a legendary event, as Dennis Law took that long, sad walk to the tunnel, ashamed of himself, ashamed of that gift.

We forgave him. This was the age when Man United went everywhere and fought to take every end in the country, on a weekly basis. An age when banners on poles were still allowed in football grounds, when riot police fought to save Norwich City's ground as it was half-wrecked by a rampaging mob after Norwich knocked United out of the FA Cup. When the older reds started to actually acknowledge our existence and to relate exciting stories of their adventures off around the country with United, it was a warm welcome that fostered meaning in a bewildering, glittering era, apparently dictated by big, tough peacocks who emulated hermaphroditic pop stars whilst wearing high-heeled shoes, Doc Martens and tartan scarves.

We all have our story of the day we first set eyes on hallowed ground, be it Upton Park, Villa Park, Ayresome Park, Roker Park, Filbert Street or Maine Road. Even the lowliest hovels become tinged with supernatural powers in the eyes of a child, so you can imagine what the grandest, most modern stadium in Britain looked like to an over-imaginative little scamp. My first glimpse of Old Trafford came one Saturday in the early 70s. It was the first time I'd accompanied my cousin Roy on his regular car-minding voyage, among the swarming thoroughfares and thunderous atmosphere of a typical Saturday in Old Trafford's adjacent Salford neighbourhood, Ordsall. Car-minding was an attractive source of income for the local kids from the ancient terraced houses, now gone forever. Thinly-veiled threats of what might happen to owners' cars should they refuse to hand over 'payments' guaranteed no argument – most were buzzed to be going to the match and this was just the cost of attending United games. The kids who minded cars at United were all ages, and Roy was one of Ordsall's youngest. Those shark-infested cobbled streets were thick with older lads, who'd give you a vicious bang on the nose and take your money in a second. Roy was already a seasoned urchin, and we made a rapid, commando-like zigzag from one victim to the next, while the thunder ricocheted from the houses all around us.

But money was the last thing on my mind. My only thoughts were of the Devil's Tower, which was drawing all into its orbit,

like a black hole. I'd seen it on telly, read about it in the papers.
This was where the bad boys went to run wild, under a vast,
silver cantilever, or on the evil pile that was the Stretford End.
As we ran from street to street towards the ground, my cousin
asking blokes, 'D'yer want yer car minded, mister?' and taking
tons of shrapnel, I could feel every fibre of my being quaking,
knowing that around the next corner I might actually see it –
the cauldron from where most of the noise was emanating.

Finally, I knew in my bones we were there. I stopped at the
corner. My cousin, puzzled, asked, 'What's wrong? *Come on!*'
How could I tell him, a year younger than me, that I was actually frightened of seeing it? I was afraid it would be too much,
like a glimpse of a real flying saucer, or an oncoming tsunami. I
leaned around the corner, peering, straining – and suddenly
caught sight of an immense, curving wall, topped with enormous, terrifying steel brackets that rose from the rim and
plunged hazily inward, holding up the roof of that awesome
pressure-cooker. To this day, I swear I saw the roof lined with flags
on poles, and glass turnstiles far down below, and the walls
moulded from some smooth and seamless white concrete, which
angled outward as it rose up to meet those giant supports, while
a series of rectangular, space-age slot-windows arranged themselves around the top. I was delirious, and could go no further.

A year or so later, myself and Dave Roberts, a pal at primary
school, hatched a plan to stow away on a ship bound for America.
We talked about it for a couple of days, and one Wednesday night
we set off for Manchester Docks under a dark, drizzling sky. We
pretended we were going to the swimming baths. He was
carrying clothes for the voyage in a clean, white pillowcase, stolen
from his mother's airing cupboard. Apparently he'd hid the bundle
somewhere near his house. The first thing he did as we set off was
to pull the pillowcase off the clothes and launch it into some
nearby bushes, putting the clothes into his swimming bag.

'I won't be needin' *that*!' he said.

My stomach lurched at the realisation we really were going
to try to stow away on a ship.

We never reached the docks. United were at home to

Sunderland that night and the crowd was somewhere in the region of 66,000. Floodlights bathed the entire area in a dazzling purple gleam and the air was full of smoke, chewing gum, beer and noise. We were waylaid by the general melee somewhere near White City dog stadium, and carried in a flowing mass onto the Old Trafford forecourt. With all thought of America forgotten, we made several laps of the stadium, round and round, with a lot of people giving us quizzed looks: *what were a pair of nine-year-olds doing, unescorted, at a place like this?* We pushed through the queuing crowds, hugging the vast wall, and lads said things like, 'Who are you two, the fucking mascots?' We didn't go in – our parents thought we were at the local swimming baths and we lived two buses away – we had to get home, quick, as it was past our bedtime. When it came out where we'd been, I didn't feel that bad, as the truth of our plan to run away to America wasn't out of the bag, and the resultant bollocking was cushioned by this. I was actually more afraid of offending my parents by suggesting their hospitality wasn't up to my expectations.

The fashions and the music of the time overlapped. The 1970s saw flared trousers and big collars assume the role of 'cool' and the bands making the records certainly kept abreast of developments. The sound of Slade, Sweet, Gary Glitter, The Osmonds, The Partridge Family and the Bay City Rollers was always somewhere, and most people seemed to tolerate it. T-Rex, Free, Clapton, Bachman Turner Overdrive, Rod Stewart, Peter Frampton, Wings, Elton John, Queen, Carly Simon, Chicago, Lynyrd Skynyrd, Stevie Wonder and Led Zeppelin were slightly better appreciated, it seemed, though all wore the platform shoes and the centre-parting haircut. But one name towered above all others. Even then, I was astute enough to discern the talent margin between David Bowie and the rest of glam rock and pop; while Glam Rock Central was slapstick, Bowie more resembled a form of style-workshop, dedicated to impressing and frightening his admirers in equal measure. He was an original. Even his name conjured the image of a knife. It was a quality I wanted to emulate, alone in my psychedelic childhood consciousness, little realising there were many more like me, all around me, clustered in an invisible colony like ticking time-bombs. Tracks like 'Up the Hill Backwards', 'Sound and Vision' and 'Ashes to Ashes' were to become marrowbone favourites of the resultant explosion, several years in the future.

In Prestwich, north Manchester, there were gaggles of centre-parted, denim/long leather jacket-wearing lads and girls in wide flares and platform shoes, hanging out on every corner. As they migrated from place to place, their little patches would be sequentially festooned with spray-painted graffiti, 'MUFC' or 'MCFC' being the prerequisite brands, sprayed like a cat's territorial pheromone. It was like living among a lot of tiny, nomadic Stone Age tribes, each incestuously keeping to itself, until Saturday came along. Then, it was like Stonehenge on the summer equinox around 5,000 years ago. And it was every week, the Meeting of the Tribes. Kenny, one of the Lewis twins, remembers those Saturday afternoons, and here describes them as a Tetley Bittermens' weekly riot: 'Just walking down the street outside your house, it was immediately obvious who was at home that day, either red or blue. Walking past a pub, or riding past one on a bus, you'd see a massive display of loads of blokes, all decked out in the 70s gear, swilling pint pots full of Younger's Tartan and Watney's Bitter. Football scarves and flared trousers and centre-partings a-plenty, the look of the time. Lads used to carry George Best penknives and combs to give it the big one with the centre-partings.'

The town would be full of lads in star jumpers and 'skinners' – flared, ever-so-slightly shortened jeans with very narrow, well-sewn turn-ups, worn with cherry red Doc Martens, or insane steelies – and sporting feathered hair. If it was United, there'd be silk tartan scarves with white tassels at the end, tied around their necks like actual ties, sometimes even placed under the large collars of the star jumpers. These lads were considered rock hard, or 'rocko', and were named skinners after the pants they wore, which weren't necessarily jeans but Northern Soul-style 'bags'. Of course, many also wore scarves around their wrists and hanging from the belt loops of their flares. The real skinners seemed to favour just the one red, white and black silk tartan job, their hard faces peering out from under those feathered haircuts, daring you to just fucking glance at them, even for a second, in their brown Birmingham bags, made from smooth, almost silky material, with the patch pockets down the sides and the high waistband, with three buttons studded on the facets of each outer-pelvis. There was a distant suggestion of some androgynous, glittery eroticism, as the Bowie influence enabled these lads to make even those styles look good. You hear a lot of stories about certain football clubs in the 70s being nutters and so on, but I don't think there was any doubt as to who the boys really were. They were the notorious Red Army.

Some time in the mid-70s, beetle-crusher shoes came in fashion; that is, crepe soles, with no heel, just flat bottoms. My mate Dave Roberts had them for months before I did, but I lied to him, saying I had a pair but didn't want to wear mine for school. When my parents eventually got me a pair, I wore them with pride, but realised they looked brand new while Dave's looked much cooler; the vertical grooves in his side soles were worn smooth around the front and back, the legacy of many adventures on the estate he lived on, while mine looked sparklingly untrod. The night before I was due to debut them at school, aged eight or nine, I took my dad's razor blade and retired discreetly to my room. There I began to attempt to sculpt the soles so that they appeared well worn, to support my claims of having owned a pair for months. As the first sliver of plastic sole fell, I gasped at an unexpected sight – the material beneath the incision was a weird and wonderful shining array of oily hues. Totally not what I wanted. Stupidly, I pressed on, slicing away at the heels and frontal soles, sweating anxiously, and basically butchering a brand new pair of beetle-crushers in the cause of trying to be 'with-it'. By the time I'd finished, they looked utterly fucked; a mass of peculiarly configured aspects of shining, angled micro-truncations bejewelled the front and back soles of these now lacerated shoes. The handiwork of a complete oddball – me. My parents were utterly skint, and buying me the shoes was like giving me a million pounds. Now I'd shat on them by cutting the shoes to bits. I suffered a couple of days of total terror, waiting for my crime to be discovered. Funnily enough, they let me off with a soft warning; they were well with-it Teds back in the day, and knew what sort of pressure I was under.

I remember, listening to the patter of the times, that this glam rock, skinner culture was highly stratified, just like all others, and the chief object of ridicule was the 'woe merchant'. The woe merchant was a young man noted for wearing decent clobber and, most importantly, affecting a particular kind of slow, shoulder-rolling gait, known as 'woeing'. Woe-ers were considered wankers, because, despite all the style and attitude, they weren't too handy with their fists. These woe merchants were an early analogue to what my generation called 'Tonka toys', and you'll read about them in good time, as the years roll by like coloured smoke, my friends.

Despite growing up right on the doorstep of Old Trafford and being a fan, my old feller never was a big match-goer. I had to slowly make my own way, as it were, in this football world. He and my Uncle Dave took me and my cousin Paul to watch Salford play rugby a few times, but the habit didn't take. At this time, we had a neighbour, George Butters, who was a sadly devout City fan. He took me to see City with his son, but my heart was elsewhere — with the famous football hooligans of Salford and their space-age stadium. Another neighbour was a Burnley fan, Dave Raxworthy, in the days when Burnley was a top team. I went with him (and my dad came) to a night match out in the frontier, and saw Burnley demolish some unfortunate saps, with Bryan Flynn scoring a spectacular header in a 3-1 win. But still my heart was elsewhere — with the biggest club in the world, right on the doorstep of where I was born, Salford. Eventually, my Uncle Geoff took me to Old Trafford to actually see a match. The sight of those dizzying cantilever brackets met me again, as we swooped off Trafford Road and into the fantastic realm of the Theatre of Dreams. It was United v Middlesbrough, and we won. We went in United Road Paddock, as my old man had issued strict instructions not to take me on the Stretford End. The Stretford End was not the Kop. It was unlike any other 'end' in England, in that its occupants regu-

larly set upon each other with as much viciousness as they did
the lads in the ends they tried to take every other week at away
games. There were no visiting supporters at Old Trafford in
those days. My Uncle Geoff, who was a lot younger than my
dad, not only gave me my first United scarf (a beautiful red and
white Salford Rugby League lambswool number, which I seem
to have misplaced) but took me to my first-ever match. He filled
me in on the triumphs United enjoyed at various shitholes in
the Second Division, not that I needed any encouragement. I
attended games at OT a few more times, sporadically, until the
1977-78 season. Then I went regularly. Myself and the Lewis
twins would set off in the morning and be queuing up before
they opened the turnstiles. We'd pay into the kids' section of the
Stretford End and race along to claim a spot up on the raised
concrete step, our backs against the railings, halfway up the
Stretford. It was a great view. This was when lumber jackets were
in fashion, those lurid little tartan coats with the thick, furry
trim. Everybody seemed to have one.

'We used to be inside the Stretford at some fuckin' ridiculous
hour, ages before kick-off,' remembered Kenny Lewis. 'Tom
Tyrell from Piccadilly Radio would be coming over the tannoy,
playing sounds like Racey's "Some Girls Do" and Billy Joel's
"My Life", while we talked away the hours. These were the days
when the entire ground would explode with *you're gonna getchur
fuckin' heads kicked in* if a United player got fouled and the away
fans cheered. The evil in the place and the looks on the visitors'
faces was something to treasure, especially when the thunder
echoed down from the top of the Scoreboard Paddock when
the beer monsters bounced on the wooden steps. They used to
be shit scared. One season, against West Brom, December 1978,
it was the coldest fucking day of my life, and I kept threatening
to piss off home for a brew and some biscuits, but our Pete
called me a soft cunt so I stayed. Thank fuck I did, cos it was an
eight-goal thriller, with United getting beat 5-3 in the falling
snow. Excellent game. They used to show Gary Bailey's save
from Laurie Cunningham at the start of *Match of the Day* every
week in the opening credits.'

Indeed. The Lewis twins, back to the DNA, that informational molecule that lurks in all cells, in all we eat, all we are, and all we do, since time immemorial. Evolution has a life of its own, natural selection acting upon all things, driving them to change, to adapt and prosper in new and changing environments. Those of us observant enough to notice something worth a wank were becoming itchy. We were too young or censored by parental guidance to be out-and-out skinners, so we made do with milder flares, with not-quite-so-glam collared jumpers, with monkey boots, even! If our mothers were hip enough, they managed to turn our jeans up just right, showing at most a half-inch of pale inner denim, the turn-up sewn tight with many tiny stitches. In time, around 1977, Adidas T-shirts and black trainers began to encroach, just as punk rock reached the crest of its wave. Punk rockers began to appear some time in 1976, and were initially considered violent, dangerous people by the retarded London media, with their spiked mohawks and tendency to swear and spit at each other and everyone else. In my neighbourhood they were considered a joke, and few naughty boys became punks. Most people were content to enjoy the Stranglers, Jam, Angelic Upstarts, Undertones, Ian Dury, Buzzcocks, Stiff Little Fingers, Clash, Elvis Costello, and of course the Sex Pistols from the more accepted vantage of semi-flares, Adidas T-shirt and decent trainers that people had started wearing purely as a football accessory.

That's football as in playing it, not watching it. Kezz, who lived on my street, got the first pair of real training shoes we ever saw, way back in the early 70s. His parents bought them for him because he was a good runner, but he wore them all the time as they were clearly quality goods. This was the Admiral era for United, when a succession of kit changes meant half your Christmas money was spoken for on a new United kit every year. It started an appetite for branded sports gear, and the colours of our team were suffused with a new significance. I loved the United kit, especially the socks, the red and white striped turnover at the top, and the mysterious all-black bottom bits. Overall, it just looked better than other red kits. It was like

when you went hunting for butterflies; you would see cabbage
whites everywhere, but you ignored them. Then, you'd spy the
one you were after, and your heart leapt – only to be disap-
pointed; it was a painted lady, the orange and brown mimic of
your target – the red admiral. The red admiral butterfly was true
red, white and black, and it looked fantastic, just like the red
Admiral football kits we coveted so much.

'The fact was, when you got a replica United kit for
Christmas, you were just as chuffed by the Admiral logo as you
were by the United crest,' said Kenny Lewis. 'It was like, "God,
this was actually made by the *same people* who make United's
real kits!" The logo took on a meaning of its own. Even the red
and black string that you tied the shorts up with was sacred.'

From the heatwave of 1976 to the Argentinean World Cup in
1978, the styles gradually took a turn for the sunnier and more
continental. I remember having a pair of Gola trainers, as my
parents couldn't afford the Adidas Kick that some of the other
lads were wearing. I had a shirt with a lace-up neck, that my
mum cut the sleeves off, in a zigzag pattern, to make it look like
Huckleberry Finn had been wearing it, definitely a hippie style.
Most of us kids had California long hair at this point, and skate-
boards were coming in. Branded sporting gear was becoming a
thing to quest for. Before we were old enough to travel on
voyages of discovery, lads were forced to actually buy the kits of
other teams, because the Adidas, Admiral and Umbro look had a
contagious grip on us which we couldn't resist. A Bowie-crazy
kid on my street, called Robert Tyrell, seemed to own a million
tracksuits and pairs of trainers from football clubs far and wide.
He even walked about in football boots when he wasn't playing
football, which wasn't often. People were wearing this stuff
simply because they liked its casual, sporty feel, out beyond the
commitment of the trends of the time, which were confused.
One of the few constants was the sight of young lads in tracksuits and trainers, usually Adidas. These were the days when
tracksuits had elasticated stirrups on the bottoms; some kids
wore them inside their trainers, and some wore them right
under their footy boots.

Around this time, a kind of weird, imitation leather shoe with mock wooden soles came into fashion; they were called 'spoonies' due to their opening out in a funny-looking, spoon-shaped toe. You had to have a pair, as they were the death knell of the 70s platform shoes, similar in appearance but possessing some mocking quality due to their bizarre, spoon-like morphology. Then there were Royals and Brogues, which were essentially identical save for the fact that the seam on Brogues tapered down to the sole at the sides about halfway back, as opposed to going all the way to the heel, horizontally along the sides, in the case of Royals. Both shoes had leather soles, which had to be covered in a rubber sole by a local cobbler, and of course the heels had to be 'tipped' with steel so that they wouldn't wear out. Lads would relish walking the long stone corridors of my school, Heys Road in Prestwich, as the sound of their tips echoed all around as a kind of animal call, a warning not unlike the stripes of the wasp or the flamboyant colours of the octopus. The Brown twins, Martin and Billy, with their short black feather-cuts and tipped stylish bovver boots, had started the whole thing off a few years earlier, and were considered dark and shady animals of a most superior breed. As a first-year, I remember asking one of them in the corridor one day (I didn't know which, as they were identical) why he had so many steel tips on the soles and heels of the alarmingly cool boots he was wearing. He put his back against the wall and said, 'So if anyone ever grabs me from behind, I can do this…', promptly back-heeling the concrete wall, from which a frighteningly large chunk of masonry fell. End of chat. Cool as fuck. The Browns and their mates were a few years older than us and went on to direct operations in the future, wearing quite different footwear.

And then there were Gibby's. I had a pair, as did a mate of mine, Dave-B-, who will appear again in this story. Gibby's, or Gibson's, were similar to Royals or Brogues in outline but had no patterning. They were a simple, one-piece leather shoe, available in black or reddish-brown, and they didn't half hurt when you got a boot off one or a back-heel from a tip. Some days I wore my comfortable Clarks Polyveldt (which Dave-B- also had), and some days I wore my Gibby's to school. Gibby's came in very handy when we planned to travel as a crew to fight one or more of the neighbouring schools, as we often did.

There was a sliding scale during these chaotic times, involving a correlation between clothing and toughness, and a kind of league table of the species emerged. The skinners had ruled the roost for years, until the sportswear, Royals and Polyveldt brigade made a serious bid to oust them from what appeared to be the top spot. Most of us were cocky little bastards in the face of what was effectively the end of the skinner era. We felt like we were on the crest of the wave, and nobody could touch us. But on trips into Manchester city centre, we occasionally caught glimpses of another rare and exotic animal. This group was apparently obsessed with Northern Soul music, and despite a mid-70s association with the skinner culture, they wore their hair in an inexplicably feminine style. They reminded me somehow of Frenchmen, in their baggy cords and jeans with narrow belts, Fred Perry T-shirts and chunky-knit jumpers tucked *into* their pants, and black slip-on gym pumps. These pumps were for girls and little boys and the bottoms of their baggy pants were very narrow, but there was a strange appropriateness about their bizarre general appearance. The worst thing was, if they caught you looking at them, they were even more apt to spring into violence than the skinners. It was as if they knew what you were thinking about their poofy hair and funny pumps, and they were angry as fuck about it. These lads were so rare in the mid to late 70s that it was easy to receive a fright from them one day, and to have forgotten about their existence the next. They were like a new kid in the schoolyard, one that kept mostly to himself but secretly terrified the tougher lads, peering through that long fringe, always ready to come at you in a heartbeat. We did our best to pretend they weren't there. There was a name for these Soul-worshippers, but when people spoke it, they spoke it in whispers, even the toughest kids. They were called Perry Boys.

Prestwich housed Heaton Park, the largest municipal park in Europe, and in that park was one of the biggest magic mushroom harvests anywhere. Needless to say, Prestwich lads were fond of a psychedelic night out, something that would set us in great stead for the years ahead. 'By the time most of us were in our late teens, we'd been to the moon, Venus and Mars,' said Paul-L-, one of the rummest characters in the entire school, a City lad with a reputation for being hard as nails [see page 86 for an explanation of the name Paul-L-]. 'We'd seen visual effects that most people only saw on *Top of the Pops*' special effects. Whenever we were watching *Top of the Pops* on telly, and the trails were coming from the arms, and purple and silver would start appearing in peoples' faces, everyone'd shout, "Hey it's just like on mushies!" '

A friend from around the corner, Dave-D-, remembers the tide of madness that hit the high-water mark every year, as the summer sun cooled and the sacred fungoid fever gripped the local heads. 'In late August, early September, everyone would be out in Heaton Park, scouting for mushrooms. We'd be dying to get out of school, to get together and get 'em down our heads. One year Manny-B- picked up a traffic cone, held it to his mouth and walked down the street for about a mile, announcing, "It is now officially the Silly Season," in this fucked-up voice like a brigadier general. All the curtains were twitching. People probably thought their fucking water was being turned off.'

Discos and youth clubs abounded, and every church and community centre hosted some form of evening entertainment once a week. Thursday was the main night, at the Longfield Suite in Prestwich. Hundreds of kids from all over the area would attend the Longfield, which had a bar, so also attracted older lads and girls. I went along with friends to hear the mainly black American disco music, interspersed with the odd six-minute (nine, if you were lucky) punk segment. The B-52's and M had appeared on the television show *Revolver*, hosted by Peter Cook, and New Wave sounds, like the Flying Lizards' 'Money, That's What I Want', were played with increased frequency. The instant a punk tune came on, a sizeable gang of us teenie pseudo-punkers would storm the floor in our Golas, Polyveldt, and Adidas Kick, and pogo and kick-dance ourselves into next week, to the sounds of the Sex Pistols, The Buzzcocks, The Stranglers, Angelic Upstarts, Stiff Little Fingers, Elvis Costello, and many more. We waited for those six minutes all week.

Once in a blue moon, some Northern Soul would go on, and John Clucas would get up and dance, while virtually the entire place, hundreds of people, would stand and observe, transfixed. John was a walking fashion barometer who led us all into the 80s with his trend-setting vision, and he often disappeared for the weekend, to some distant Lancashire outpost, where mysterious new styles were compared and coalesced by that rare and equally mysterious body of trendsetters. Sometimes John would tell us about some coat or trousers that were 'coming in', and when he showed them to us, all we saw was quality, but little else. The styles were definitely cool, but they looked so outlandishly expensive we knew we could never afford them, and assumed it was an ultra-cultish thing for committed disciples. I copied my Clark's Polyveldt from him, and we held regular discussion sessions on the suppleness of the leather uppers and soles of those beautiful shoes. John was the next-door neighbour of Dave Roberts, the kid I planned to run away to America with, and I knew him from a young age. There were times when I honestly suspected he had a time machine hidden in his house, by which he was able to predict the next big thing in jeans, cords, sweaters, coats or shoes; he was always so bang-on. He truly rode the head of the fashion wave, like a skilled culture surfer, with bristling antennae constantly detecting movement up ahead in time. When I looked in John's eyes I saw a brother, not just a friend. When I learned of his untimely death in 2006, from a fall down the stairs in his flat, I was genuinely choked up, and I mourned a true player. If they ever make a film about this era, John should be the star, the Ace Face, as he was in real life.

As a result of Northern Soul, Manchester's tendency towards amphetamine-fuelled all-night dance clubs was already established at this point, while many of the ecstasy generation were still learning how to walk. The clubs and discos were a bewildering broth of half-formed tribal expressions; people in

bondage trousers, RAF jackets and kilts would merge with
heavy rockers, disco merchants and, in time, mods, while in the
shadows and at the bar a streamlined new presence began to
form, week by week its numbers growing steadily, invisibly.
Individuals wearing items belonging to a brand new, razor-sharp
fashion, camouflaged by their conventional appearance, who
confidently winked, nudged, and grinned their secret to each
other, and wallowed in their conviction of rightness. Once in a
while, these interlopers would get up and sway to Roxy Music
or Bowie, but it was a rare and sarcastic show. Many of them
were obviously taking guidance from John Clucas, who would
turn up in massive Northern Soul flares one week, and a Fred
Perry and faded straight Levi's the next, with Hush Puppies or
cool hiking shoes. He knew how to play the herd. My thirteen-
year-old eyes were honed and watchful.

With the advent of the mods, fishtail parkas, two-tone suits
and Fred Perries were everywhere. Very quickly, however, the
suit and tie option was binned, forever, and the two-tone suit
was ridiculed as the stiff and awkward posturing of boys trying
to be men. Mods were challenged to gang fights, and were
confused and beaten by this nameless new foe. Previously something to look forward to, Bank Holidays now became a
nightmare for anyone out-of-it enough to ride a scooter and
wear a suit and loafers. The idea of fastening one's top button
was appealing (it bespoke style), but to then cover the statement
with a tie was not. It was common to see lads walking around
in expensive, thick, cotton shirts, with button-down, small or
round collars, increasingly minus the uncomfortable ties that the
endangered mods had so recently preferred, with the top button
fastened. This was as much a declaration that its perpetrator was
prepared to do violence as it was a fashion statement. The Fred
Perry lingered on when the rest of the mod regalia had been
literally kicked out of the door, worn with jeans and Hush
Puppies, Clark's shoes or trainers. Jeans were either baggy or
straight, but mostly straight, and the hairstyle was slowly being
perfected, a curious short back and sides, cut to a point at the
back of the neck, layered in a girlish manner that would've been

considered worthy of a beating by the ancient skinners, with their Rod Stewart blow-waves. It was the hairstyle of those strange Northern Soul outsiders from the city centre, the Perry Boys, and suddenly it was catching on fast. A very odd hybridi-sation of our thing and theirs seemed to be occurring.

It wasn't as if there were young kids staring at photographs of Bowie in groups, playing with their willies and winking at each other, but a deep-seated appreciation was hurtling from the depths of our young minds, into the light; looking plain and old-fashioned while being stylish was a desirable quality. The crew cuts began to lengthen, and that most weird and dangerous silhouette assumed a concrete presence in our lives – the wedge hairstyle of the Mod Killer. Shops like Stolen From Ivor in town began selling baggy two-tone jeans with narrow, turned-up bottoms; a strange substitution for the two-tone mod suit-pants previously on show there in the purple-lit window. Chunky knit fisherman's jumpers and boat shoes replaced the shirt and tie and loafers. The full ensemble – layered haircut with long fringe, fisherman's jumper, baggy jeans with narrow bottoms and boat shoes – slowly emerged as a sinister alternative to the innocent mod fashions of yesterday. The look was wedded to violence from the very beginning, but only in violence does revolution come.

The music moved from Sex Pistols to B-52's to Blondie to Madness to Teardrop Explodes to Human League towards unknown pastures, like a locomotive shunting down a black tunnel, while its passengers took turns to drive and discuss developments. The chromosome was unfurling, crystallising and coming into view under the scope, beginning to change and enter self-consciousness beyond anything before seen. It began to divide, uncontrollably, as if hijacked by a strange and irre-sistible virus. The minds of the Manchester masses had overshot the end of the runway, and it was alright, we were still alive. *But we were finally free*. Free to take the world on a journey with us, once they got a clue.

2

A GLIMPSE OF THE FUTURE

An invasion of armies can be resisted, but not an idea whose time has come.

—Victor Hugo

IN THE BEGINNING was the formless void, the punk-knackered hillsides of crippled Scotty Road, the concrete new-wave flyovers of Salford Precinct, the smouldering council-house constraints of windjammers, Harrington jackets, fish-tail parkas, Lord Anthony jeans and (God help us!) Levi Dudes! But slowly, silently, they emerged, like primeval prototypes from the ancient slime in the sediments of the Mersey and the Manchester Ship Canal. A fish-tail evolved into something more suited for skiing, and Lord Anthony was ripped apart by the bull terriers of tower-block enlightenment, to be replaced forever by a gleaming pair of jade cords by Razzy. Or was it ice blue cords by Lee? Or was it fabulously home-bleached denim FUs? Lumber jackets were transformed into lumber *shirts*, while suede and corduroy hooded jackets with tassels and tartan lining, myriad Adidas training shoes, all striped and dotted and leathery, rubbery and flexible, sprouted from the woodwork like magic mushrooms in many colours. Acrylic star-jumpers no longer cut the mustard. Enlightenment had come to working-class lads in the north-west; they had been the first ones to acquire the style gene, but this didn't happen overnight. There's a story in it.

Once upon a time, from some tepid little pool emerged a cluster of chemicals called enzymes, which eliminated the chemicals around them and began to dominate the environment of early Earth. These enzymes were in time bonded chemically to other compounds, such as DNA and membrane hydrocarbons, and under the primeval sky the first Life emerged. On and on and on, until billions of years later a cheeky likkle monkey lost all his fur and needed an artificial coat to brave the Ice Age nights. Some fur was better than others. The End.

Now let's take it a little more slowly. Just as the weave of the fabric is all-important, and the animal, plant (or laboratory) from where it was derived determines many physical and commercial factors for the usefulness of garment material, so are the cell membranes of the simplest and most complex organisms officially recognised and entered into the world's biophysical libraries for reference purposes. Animals and plants are held together by connective materials such as protein fibres. Protein molecules have personalities of their own; cotton is alive, as is wool, suede and leather – even plastic. Plastic comes from petrochemicals, which consist of the decomposed remains of plants and animals that died millions of years ago. All living things are made of cells, and all cells have DNA and membranes. The DNA manufactures the protein fibre, and the membrane allows the fibre to exit the cell, where it does its job. It becomes a decent piece of clothing, in many cases.

Membranes are selective little buggers, able to dictate what comes through and what doesn't, like a grizzled turnstile attendant on the 1970s Stretford End fortress; sometimes what comes in is made of metal, because it has to be, and sometimes it's made of fluff. The mind is the same way: if an individual is able to admit certain information, while rejecting other information, and these decisions are true to reality, then the mind that develops from this process of accumulation will be formidable indeed (AKA a success). If what comes in is a load of bollocks, the result is, well, a load of bollocks (AKA a failure). This is the difference between adaptation and extinction. Whether the information concerns the physical structure of reality itself (Einstein), or whether it concerns the physical structure of a tracksuit top made in Italy in 1980 (Fila), doesn't really matter.

The point is, if you are *true to reality*, you shall prosper one way or the other, lad.

Yes, we came from bacteria, billions of years ago, and slowly but surely was the ape-like *Homo sapiens* assembled, in brackish pools, in jungle slime, riding on the scales of larger beasts, creeping about the canopy, and finally there on the African savannah did he stand on two feet and walk. He required some sensible footwear, did he not? And metal.

The flashing blades of Casual culture have been talked to death, so let's go to a place that was real and true, where it all started to congeal: it's prehistory, I'm riding the 264 bus back to town from Old Trafford in Clark's shoes, Wranglers, a green Fred Perry, and a lengthening crew-cut. Some utter divvy a few seats and a few years above us, in hushed tones, is pointing out to his mates, 'There they are! Don't look! Don't look! It's the Perries!' He was pointing out of the bus window, to a stretch of the Deansgate pavement, where a group of eight lads were walking, arms swinging, fully evolved, in two columns of four. *Not a Fred Perry in sight.* Wedge hairstyles, long-sleeved blue and yellow Peter Werth polo shirts, straight jeans. The lad suddenly noticed us young 'uns (or our clothes, hair and facial expressions) and his whisper trailed off in fear. I knew something had at that moment penetrated my soul and burst an illusion, revealing a landscape populated by dynamic struggle in this dream called life. It was 1979. It was only about the fifth time in the past year I'd even heard the word 'Perry'; I was a thirteen-year-old doing my best to turn up in decent gear. I felt that Perries were definitely *something*, while not exactly being whatever it was *I* was trying to be, which had an inextricable football connection. Little did I know how close to the mark I was. I sometimes thought of them as 'Ferry boys', confusing their fondness for Roxy Music with the very T-shirt I wore on the bus that day.

One thing I did know was that the people who'd christened these creatures 'Perry Boys' weren't Perry Boys themselves. In fact, I detected something of unintended irreverence in the term, and so did the creature. This led to people receiving a slap for what appeared to be no apparent reason (Q: 'Are you a Perry

Boy?' A: WALLOP!). This may have had something to do with the fact that the only shred of evidence linking this new species to the mods was the Fred Perry T-shirt. It is ironic that the one item of clothing from the mod era that managed to survive the style holocaust, became the very one which finally burned a brand into their rapidly changing and mysterious identity. Despite being adored for its untouchable coolness, the Fred Perry carried a dark and offensive association in Manchester, and provided the momentum for much violence, as the Boys sought to sever all links with what had come before. While the familiar laurel wreath logo on the breast broadcast the high probability of violence to all who beheld it, few took a moment to ponder the dichotomy behind this threat: these spirits loved what they hated, and hated what they loved. They were a new breed, and were not fond of people who asked too many questions, especially ones that were awkward to answer. Fred Perry, born in Stockport, could never have known the effect his T-shirt, with its stitched-on warning sign, would have on Manchester, back when it was simply for playing tennis in.

The tennis – or polo – style, coupled with the insignia and the stripes with which the collars and cuffs were adorned, functioned as a template for much that came after. Lads busily established what was a 'yes' and what was a 'no', often based on this archetype. Kezz was a year older than me, and consequently present during the meetings of the minds which occurred between the older lads during this period of emergence.

'There were a few lads, normal working–class lads, who were into Bowie and Roxy Music, and they weren't necessarily the naughtiest lads around, but they hung round with us all,' he remembers. 'They never got skinheads when we all did. They had, like, short back and sides from the frigging 1930s or something. It was a Bowie look, and they were skinny fuckers an' all, like Bowie. Then there were some who knocked about with us nutters in the tracksuits who went playing footy all the time, and they also hung around with these 'hipsters', as Martin-B- used to call 'em as a kind of piss-take. They were the sort who'd be smoking herb while we were all on the mad piss, chasing birds and steaming the lads from the area next door. Martin-B- and Dave-D- and other lads they knew were good examples of these double agents. This is where it all come together. They used to travel through Europe in the summer and come back with all sorts of smart clothes made by European companies, then we'd be hanging round with them back home, and wanting this stuff ourselves. One of the lads had a cracking jumper that looked brilliant. I think it was for skiing but I didn't realise that then. I thought it was just a dear jumper what rich cunts in Munich wore. One day I tried it on with a view to buying it. I had just bought a pair of dark blue Adidas Jogger at the time, and I remember wearing the jumper, a pair of straight Lois, and the Jogger, and looking in the mirror that day in my bedroom. It must've been sometime before Christmas, 1979. It sounds daft, but I swear I saw the future. In a split second, I just knew that this was gonna be what people our age were wearing for a long time to come. I was always an athletic type, and recognised that this jumper fit me more like a tracksuit than a sweater, and it was perfect for steaming about in, doing the things we did at that age. It was purpose-built for looking the part and not getting in the way if certain activities were in order.

'The footy lads, the Euro-trippers, and the hipsters, all used to see each other at the Longfield on a Thursday night, and every day at school. They'd be at the Wednesday youth club as well, just hanging round, refusing to play table tennis and definitely not dancing in the back disco, which we nicknamed "Sooty's" after the puppet disco on the telly. At school it was mainly uniforms, with the odd lad trying to come in wearing a jumper or training shoes that had just come out. The teachers clamped down cos they'd never seen people not wearing the dark blue or black uniform before. Thursday nights were a different story. Everyone would be togged up and out to impress. It was a contest to see who could surprise, more than anything, and if you knew the lads coming back from Germany in late summer, you were guaranteed to cop for something decent and different. I don't think we thought of it as being that different from when we got into tracksuits, to be honest. We were just the same people, a bit older, after some territory, a leg-over and a laugh. It took off from there, if you ask me.'

Given the previous few years' chemical broth, centred on football, branded sportswear, and trendy music, it was always bound to happen. There were a fair few Perries in my neigh-bourhood, and many more at the disco we would cram into every Thursday night in Prestwich, north Manchester. Most of them were hard lads, with an eye for verve and style. They ruled, despite having literally exploded from nowhere, in the midst of the mod revival. A major transition between aimless innocence and streamlined dynamism was under way in the streets, and there were casualties aplenty. Young lads were colliding at an important attitude-and-style junction, from several directions. The *Quadrophenia* hangover meant that divvy artefacts were everywhere, not just fishtail parkas and two-tone pants but Adidas four-stripe cagoules (from the underground market in the city centre), Dunlop Green Flash (Stan Smiths *not!*) and acrylic polo shirts. The snide polos were easy to spot; not only was the material inferior, and the thin hoops too numerous and too thick, but most importantly, the seam where the arm met the shoulder was actually at the shoulder. The genuine article, manufactured by Peter Werth, featured a novel seam, very low down across the upper-arm, advertised by the thin hoops that followed it down the arm, for all to see. It was a precursor to the habit of wearing jackets and cardigans slung back low over the shoulders, to advertise the designer label on the breast of the garment beneath.

I was quick to acquire a feel for what this clothing was all about. It came from within. The mod revival definitely spoke to me on some level, but this thing was brand new and loaded with something local, yet alien. The hairstyles were a puzzle to me at the beginning, even as I came to recognise them as a symbol of toughness. Crew-cuts were grown out, and side-partings or old-fashioned short-back-and-sides became more popular. The hair at the nape of the neck became subject to a particularly intense work-up, designed to effect something long but yet short, hard but yet soft. The lads started growing their hair out into an exaggeration of the old sculpted forms, from fairly normalish short-back-and-sides to something more effeminate and strange. The fringe was grown low over one eye, and layered around the side, describing a horizontal line across the ear. Initially, the cut would be quite short. An absolute lack of side-boards was a priority, with the hair cut tight across the top of the ear and round the back to a point. That cut across the top of the ear, excluding all evidence of sideboards, was the original symbol of knowing the score. Those who'd been there the earliest had the telltale layering effect across the ear, in a contin-uous line, coming right back from the fringe to the wedge at the back. The shorter hairstyle naturally grew into this shape, which was the sign of being a mature animal, and a status symbol all its own in 1979 and early 1980.

One of the main proponents at this time was a lad I will call Paul-S-, a tough kid who was known far and wide for his ability to have a fight. He was wearing a V-neck burgundy fisherman's jumper with Fred Perries of various colours, Fruit of the Loom overalls and Pod shoes without socks when most were just coming to their senses. The younger crew that hung around with him and his mates were terrors, buzzing about in black Fred Perries with yellow stripes, instinctively homing in on the mods and skinheads, and applying the knuckle. One of them was Adam-G-.

'We used to go to the Longfield Disco every Thursday or the church youth club on Friday, spruced up to the max,' said Adam. 'All the girls would be there, and it was a way to say, 'Look at me'. But all the time we wanted to look like we'd had the clothes for months. The first thing you did after getting hold of a thirty quid pair of shoes or a coat was wear them day in day out, and hammer the shit out of 'em. Looking like you'd liter-ally started a certain style at this time was what it was all about, as we all knew it was a new thing and nobody was taking it for granted. This was 1979, going into 1980. Anyone could have spent a few hours in town and come back with an item of clothing that might actually be worn by hundreds of lads within a few weeks. One decent piece of gear could spark off a craze.

We copied the haircut off the older lads and it was obvious that
there was something sophisticated and stylish about it. There
would be a certain barber, or hairdresser, where someone had
copped for a spot-on cut, and from then on everyone would go
there, knowing the stylist knew what they were doing. The
barbers and hairdressers were tickled pink, watching all these
handy lads come in and ask for a girl's haircut. I had a decent
one myself, but my hair was a bit wavy. I always felt sorry for
those poor cunts that had thick, wavy or curly hair, as they
looked right idiots trying to flick a fringe that might as well
have been made of cardboard. They were the ones who had
crew-cuts, if they had any sense.

'The funny thing was, there were never large-scale discus-
sions of clothes, and especially hair. It was all kept between best
mates, or with girls. As a result, the whole thing took on an even
more mysterious and exciting air. Actions spoke louder than
words. If you knew a shop that sold the right stuff, you kept it
between you and your best mate, and your lips were sealed. If
you knew a place you could rob daft and get away with it, you
said fuck all to the rest of the lads for as long as possible, or until
they slapped it out of you. But it was murder, every Thursday
night, walking in wearing your latest tackle. More and more lads
were turning up, sometimes from other areas, wearing stuff you
hadn't seen before. They always got a rough reception, as those
fashions meant you were there to have it with the natives, and it
was common to see a couple of unknown lads get leathered by
some of our lot after underestimating the situation. I wasn't too
much into fighting other lads for the sake of it, it seemed stupid.
It was more enjoyable giving it to the mods, cos they were
idiots. You would be fairly confident of having bought a decent
pair of jeans or shoes or sweater, but it wasn't until the older lads
gave their approval that you were able to breathe. Once it was
given the thumbs-up by the older boys, it was, "right, next case,"
off to town for something else. The same thing was happening
all over Manchester.'

A Jurassic ethnic cleansing occurred in the streets of north-
west Blighty. The Boys committed a cultural genocide on the

mods, the divvies and anyone else that got in the way. If you were caught wearing Jekyll (as in Jekyll and Snide) gear, you were a target for extinction. Just as *Homo sapiens* had destroyed the Neanderthal tens of thousands of years ago, did the Perry Boys wipe out their fellow hominids in 1979, in Manchester. But it was for their own good, in the long run. Steve-K-, a schoolmate, was a victim of the cruel-to-be-kind wave of intra-Mancunian violence of the time, and was surprised by the organisation of it all.

'One Saturday afternoon in early 1980, on the bus on the way to town, an older lad, Dave-M-, gets on at Sedgley Park and starts talking to these girls about how the "divvy mods" were gonna get a slapping in town that day by the "real mods", or something like that. I knew him only by sight then, but got to know him well in later years. That day he was wearing a blue Adidas st2 jacket (with the red lining), a pair of Pod Boaters, no socks and Lois jeans. I was with Sid, who was famous for wearing mod gear even though he knew it was a big no-no, and sure enough that day he was turned out in embarrassing clobber. I was still into the Fred Perry and pegs myself, to be honest. Anyway, later we were in this joke shop called Aladdin's Cave when a load of boys came streaming in and starting giving a few people a bit of a dig, ourselves included, as they swept through the Arndale on a real mod mission. Everywhere you went in town that day you got legged and slapped by lads wearing top gear. They'd organised it during the week, the Town Boys, the main Perries. I was never a fighter, really, and it was pretty frightening, cos they were everywhere, and you couldn't believe they'd managed to arrange it all like that.'

Conflict between different factions of youths who followed different trends has been common throughout history. But conflict between youths who followed a superior version of the *same* trend was a new and fascinating twist. My hypothesis is that maybe these lads were calling themselves mods in the absence of something else to call themselves at that time, as they clearly hated mods or anyone who even vaguely resembled one, or anyone who was trying to be a 'boy' by wearing their Jekyll gear from the Pakistanis in the underground market because their parents were skint (like mine) and couldn't afford to kit out their kids in cotton or lambswool, so it was acrylic instead. It was adapt or die, and adapt we did, one way or the other. Dave-D- was one of the boys who were regularly travelling to Europe in the summer.

'A good few of us liked to go through France, Belgium, Holland and Germany in summer. Belgium was sound. I really liked Belgium. We used to get back to Manchester with bags full of trainers and lambswool jumpers, tracky tops and polo T-shirts. You'd sell some, but keep a few for yourself, to let people know you were onto it. I remember seeing Scousers over there, doing the same thing, and little crews would form of robbers and blaggers. One minute you were swimming in the Med and the next you were on the Metro in Munich with a bagful of tackle, then you were in some little French town getting pissed on the local brew, wearing hundreds of pounds' worth of designer gear, then it was on the ferry to knock it out back home. It felt like we were completely in charge of our lives. No one was telling us what to do, not the papers or the telly or anyone. The knowledge that it was totally our own invention seemed to put you on a high all the time.'

The membrane was extremely selective, admitting only that which could benefit the evolving body, the skein of stylised self-awareness permeated by this new world. The divvy skin was shed like the dying scales of a gigantic snake wending its way through the arcades and boulevards of continental splendour, acquiring a spangled, studded, piped, corduroy, leather, suede, cashmere, cotton, nylon, striped body of *prima facie* evidence, as it established a strong French connection but remained firmly rooted in the top-quality atmospherics of Manchester's one-off boutiques, sports and outdoors shops. The numbers grew, and they emerged in droves, in crews, on the forecourts of stadia and stations alike, posturing and dancing about with the excitement of Something Genuinely New. It was truly the Nameless Thing, because nobody but us knew it even *was* a thing. But it was more than a thing; there was an enemy out there, one which dared to goad and challenge the scaly beast from the heart of Mancland – the Scouser.

The Scouser was the only animal outside Manchester capable of knowing whether we were wearing the right gear or not. The Scouser was an adventurous creature, fond of roaming far and wide, and helping itself to whatever was going. In fact the Scouser had a more intimate relationship with himself than the Manc did, as a result of his home being smaller, and subsequently he conspired to almost convince the world (and the poor Manc) that in fact *he* was the genuine article, that in fact the Manc was still just a divvy, and what's more he talked funny (the Manc, that is, not the Scouser, if you can believe it).

Another Perry Boy, Goody, was not in the habit of attending the Longfield disco very often. He was a diehard Man United fan and had been known as a bad lad in the neighbourhood since I was a kid, when he once threatened to hit me so hard my 'head would spin' after I stole some tools off him and his mates. In later years I got to know him and found he was an intelligent lad, always seeing around the curve and predicting where we were going. Goody made the odd appearance, bouncing about like a grinning Jack Russell terrier, always wearing the very latest gear, looking like he'd been in it for months. He was a born storyteller, and through him we discovered that another world for all this thing existed, the world of the football terraces. He was always very specific about standards though.

'We'd go to away matches all over England, and always be on the lookout for divvies trying to get in with the main lads,' said Goody. 'You had to be wearing the right gear or you got a twatting. We couldn't afford to run into the Scousers in London, or wherever, and have a load of utter dickheads in Dunlop Green Flash and Harringtons. The Jekyll gear had to be stopped, so you policed the divvies and gave a slap where one was due. If you want an Adidas cagoule then get a fucking *Adidas* cagoule, not a five-stripe job from the underground market. Have some decorum. Manchester is a bigger city than Liverpool, with markets everywhere, and in a way Scousers were lucky they didn't have the Pakistani forgeries to contend with to the same extent. Being a smaller place helped them to spread the word and get mobbed up as a tighter unit in the beginning.

'A lot of the lads were graduating from the 70s mobs and taking to the new styles like ducks to water, as well as all the younger crews we were enlisting, who were the new genera-tion. I loved telling stories to the younger lads, the ones who were wearing all the right gear but hadn't yet worked out that it was part of football and not just a dancehall craze. Us older lads had all been to Europe and slept on the beaches by the late 70s, and we knew that the Europeans saw us as peasants. There were shops over there that had all the latest gear, millions of places full of stuff the lads in England would've killed for. We introduced the younger set into this world, and it was an eye-opener to them. When they realised how easy it was to rob the stuff, they went on the rampage, and that was good because it built our firm up to proper standards. It was easier for the Scousers to get the numbers because they were all together in Europe for the football and were in on it in larger numbers. We just took it as we found it on our little summer trips, and there were plenty of shops in Manchester selling quality stuff anyway. It felt like it was slow off the ground at our end, not like in Liverpool with the Euro trips, but we sorted it, no problem.'

Goody was one of the few who were old enough to drive, along with Big Col. Col was walking around in the latest garb and was fond of a trip up the East Lancs Road for a laugh on a boring Tuesday night. Anytime the Liverpudlians were in town, he was up for a day out. He loved Scousers.

He said, 'It was a new thing; we all had flicks, Peter Werth's, burgundy cords and Stan Smiths. If we weren't the first to wear clothes of a certain type, then our mates were. Even if you saw someone wearing completely different stuff than anything you'd seen before, you instantly recognised that it was the same style, part of the same thing. We were at the forefront, and lads were coming back from France with ideas, and Manchester was fucking amazing at importing stuff within the day. The gear was easy to find, or nick, and it was like a suit of armour when you had on the full issue. Going to the match became a buzz that wasn't the same as it used to be. Now it was about wearing the clothes, and, as always, getting stuck into any bastards who turned up from wherever. Most weeks it was boring because the opposing support was clueless and couldn't appreciate what we were up to. Sometimes you'd be done up in your latest clobber, and your heart felt like a fucking jellyfish when you saw a mob of Leeds cavemen, but it was like the clothes would protect you, they were like a shield. You knew they'd sort of noticed it, and it mesmerised them just enough to give you that extra split second. And then there was the Mickeys. They were wearing the same gear as us, and it was a pleasure when it went off with them. It felt fucking great to meet them off the train at Oxford Road, a massive crew. There was nothing better than bruising your knuckles on some Scouse cunt's head and giving him a good Stan up the arse that he won't forget. The Mickeys were mesmerised in a different way, because they thought they were the only ones in the know.'

Those summers between 1977 and 1979 saw large-scale flocking across the Channel by young lads from my neighbour-hood. My Uncle Geoff went with his mates at least two years earlier, and they stayed for several months in the South of France and neighbouring countries, fending for themselves by hook or by crook. Geoff had a pair of Adidas Bali, the excellent blue suede trainers, very early on in the game. He used to leave them out on his porch, and it was only a matter of time before they were mine, even though they were two sizes too big. As a child, I absorbed his sparkling stories of pillage and mayhem with the thirst of someone lost in a desert. It was no mirage, it was true, and I took it to the marrow, along with all the stories from the lads who piled over there the following years. Every spring, they were off. The Continent drew them to it, and they were all accomplished robbers and blaggers. These little groups returned throughout the summer to Manchester, with their precious booty, and much of it was branded sportswear and other designer gear. These lads weren't travelling to watch football matches, so there weren't thousands of them when they went abroad, but they were there at the beginning, *before* the beginning, a vital presence like the enzymes in the tepid rock pools of the early planet.

Dave Leckie remembered one enterprising young man from that period: 'In the Oasis market above the entrance to the underground market, there was this lad who had a stall. He used to go to Germany and get all the latest Adidas trainers, and he had them set out on shelves, on show. I remember a lot of stuff in there that the shops didn't have in the beginning, and he'd brought it all back himself. His was one of the few places to go at the time that were ahead of Stolen From Ivor or Gansgear and the rest. By the middle of 1980 all the shops knew the score and they swamped the city with stuff, though. This lad never budged, and he kept selling his gear right through that period. A lot of his stuff was rare trainers, Adidas red suede 'uns with brown soles and all that. Some of the shoes cost fifty quid a pair, which back then was a lot.'

★ ★ ★

Liverpool and Manchester are separated by a mere thirty-five miles, but some have suggested it might as well be a light-year; such are the differences between the natives of the two cities. But opposites attract, they say, and herein lies the mystery. If the two are so very different, why are they not friends? People from other parts of Britain sometimes experience difficulty distinguishing between a Scouse and a Manc accent, which disgusts the respective Scouse or Manc involved. It's quite a pickle. Liverpool sits on a sliver of land at the head of the Mersey Estuary, occupying a minuscule piece of the earth's crust, teetering on the brink of the ocean. It has been the receptacle for large inflows of immigrants for many years, further colouring the precarious sliver of a city. A closer inspection of the Liverpool accent yields similarities with Irish and Welsh accents, with those two wrapped tightly around a third point of reference, which is the sliver itself. The fact is, there is no regional English accent there, nor is there any English responsibility. The place is a kind of encampment, a port of receipt, inhabited by a species of person quite different from virtually anywhere else in Britain. They are right on the edge, on the outside, looking in.

Manchester is located 35 miles to the east, further in from the coast. A closer look at the Manchester accent reveals similarities with Irish, Welsh, Scottish and regional English. That 35-mile difference places Manchester directly between Glasgow and London as the crow flies, and puts it within the realm of a regional English accent. Construction of the Manchester Ship Canal not only stole trade from Liverpool, it also stole that incoming foreign colour. These factors contribute to a slight difference between the cities. The land corridor between Manchester and Liverpool is inhabited by a polarised population: those speaking in close analogues of one or the other city's accent, and those speaking in pure regional English peculiar to their own particular town. Places like Runcorn compose the 'Scouse' population and the 'woolly-back' population. Places like Warrington compose the 'Manc' population and the 'sheepshagger' population. The increased pull on the world affected by Manchester's geographic location is reflected in that city's larger role in the Industrial Revolution, its accent and its national role as Britain's 'second city', despite the claims of Brum.

And what an accent. Only those hailing from a very short distance outside Manchester city centre can truly hold claim to having a Manchester accent. The rest of the population of that swarming county come in a huge variety of shades, from Northenden, to Bury, to Ashton, to Altrincham, to Oldham, to Wigan, to Stockport to Irlam. The Scousers know this and delight in imitating the further flung accents of Greater Manchester County, knowing it irritates those from within the Manc accent zone, who speak completely differently from their satellite brethren. Manchester has no response to this, as the Scouse accent is uniform across their smaller city, and instead has settled on boasting of the affluence of Manchester, compared to the economic downturn in Liverpool. The fact that these two old cities have sat side-by-side on the north-west English land-scape for so long suggests that there must have been much human traffic between the two, much merging of DNA. If the Scottish connection and the more anglicised nature of the Manchester accent is the only difference between them, then underneath the war-like exterior, we have two almost identical populations, divided by a small piece of land. Scholars have noted that when we have two such groups, the potential for a more intense rivalry can exist; very slight differences are more noticeable and so appear more blasphemous relative to the more similar remainder. The hatred between Sunni and Shiite Muslims is said to arise from the fact that, apart from some argu-ment about the line of succession of the early caliphs, everything else is equal. The same might be said of the disagreement over predestination and good works between Catholics and Protestants in certain areas.

There are two major differences in the character of these two, though: no Scouser will ever enter a debate with Mancs about who started this Nameless Thing; they just know they did. And no Manc will ever have to enter a debate with *anyone* about whether United and City really hate each other; they just do. There is no brotherly love between Manchester's two biggest clubs, as there seems to be in Liverpool between Liverpool and Everton. Consequently, we think they're lying Scouse shithouses who mob up with each other cos they haven't got a decent crew between 'em, and they think we're a lot of donkey jacket, monkey boot-wearing 'wools', or so they claim. No Scouser would ever admit to being similar to a Manc, and vice versa, as the repulsion between these estranged brothers simmers on an eternal backburner. But when that backburner is brought to the fore and the heat is turned up, then we really do have quite a casserole. And in 1980, dinner was served, big time.

3

MEANWHILE UP THE ROAD

Much of this chapter was written by Dave Hewitson, but fuck him,
the Scouse bastard, I'm gonna take the credit for it.

—Me

WHILE THINGS WERE simmering in the transgenic quantum froth of the Mancunian maelstrom, the denizens of that city by the sea, Liverpool, enjoyed a glittering spell of footballing magic, courtesy of Bob Paisley's clan of athletic over-achievers. Winning the English First Division meant qualification for bigger things, and young lads from Liverpool began to make forays into continental Europe to watch their heroes progress into the big leagues. Liverpool FC took it in their stride, grabbing several pieces of silver to take back to their home city, where the 'other Red Army' roared loud enough to shake the clouds.

Silverware was not the only thing that was grabbed, however. Europe's designer sports shops were an unknown gem as far as most English lads were concerned. While the citizens of this once-proud nation strutted about in their 70s gear, major continental sportswear designers were drawing a firm line along the English Channel to delineate the haves and the have nots. As far as companies like Adidas were concerned, Adidas Kick was about the limit for the British consumer. We were the barbarians, living beyond the glossy possibilities enjoyed by the French, Germans and Italians. It was an economic Hadrian's Wall, and companies such as Lacoste barely bothered to flick their lowest morsels over to the ignorant cave-dwellers shivering in northern rain in the terraced wilderness.

Liverpool's fanatic support composed an unstoppable red tide, one that washed over that wall like it wasn't even there. Being skint didn't prevent the Scousers from travelling to watch their beloved Reds march on Europe, and a closed door was something to be opened, be it by cracking the combination or simply kicking it down; the famed Transalpino 'rub-out' was born in the hands of a few renowned forgers, or else ferries were jibbed in do-or-die fashion. The Transalpino was a cheap student (under-26) rail ticket that covered continental Europe. The destination of the ticket was hand-written instead of printed, and Scousers quickly realised that this could be simply rubbed out and another, more desirable, destination written in its place. The sticky-fingered hordes quickly stumbled onto the possibilities inherent in continental sports shops. They turned the swish boulevards and city squares into a riotous jumble sale, only nothing was being sold – it was being robbed daft. Over there, the various tracksuits and training shoes looked great, but once back in Liverpool they seemed to shine with an unearthly light against the grey backdrop; everything is relative, after all. It was the cultural equivalent of an alien species being introduced into an environment never before exposed to it. It was roses in February. It was beautiful. And it was contagious.

These Scousers were 'absolute beginners', according to Dave Hewitson, author of *The Liverpool Boys are in Town*, the very naked raw products of a brand new genetic recombination. Writes Hewitson:

The day that it dawned, for me, was the thirteenth of August, 1977. We were playing Manchester United in the Charity Shield. A visit to Wembley for a hundred thousand, but this year something other than the football was catching the eye. Sitting on the steps close to the Liverpool turnstiles were twenty or so Scousers, young lads, fifteen to seventeen years old. A good few of the Liverpool crowd were glancing over at them, unsure as to where they were from. None of them wore scarves, and some had a strange, effeminate haircut. They were wearing straight jeans or cords and they had one definite thing in common: an attitude, a confidence about themselves. It was a personal pride in the way they were dressed. Even though they were an infinitesimal fraction of the total Liverpool support, and were surrounded by loads of flare boys and scarfers, they wore steel-eyed cynical expressions, cocky smiles and a way of physically carrying themselves that was a complete contrast to the gait of the lads wearing the colours. They seemed to sway as they moved, like little sharks moving among a school of turtles, and everything about them was bursting with the light of a new creation.

This was a defining moment, if ever there was one. Times were changing. Going to the match would never be the same again. It wasn't just about the football and having a bit of a scrap, it was now also about the clothes and the attitude. A whole new youth culture was about to emerge and a few were there at the beginning. Flares were dead, as far as this new wave of fashionable youth was concerned. Those great pictures of Liverpool's first European Cup triumph in Rome were to be the last time we would see flag waving, scarf wearing, and flared jeans, all in the same place and upon the same person. Developments over the next six months were hasty, but by 1978 it was noticeable that this wasn't just a passing fad.

Back in those days, there were no men's fashion magazines to give you an idea of what to wear, as Hewitson explained:

The closest thing to these magazines at the time would be the *NME*'s pages of stylish bands, and the latest adverts in the back pages from the London clothes shops. Monthly magazines were for women only. So, armed with our Euro booty, Liverpool developed its own perception on style and what to wear. We invented it.

This was to be a watershed year. It was the year every

Scouse kid, boy and girl, in every school and on every street corner wanted a strange girly haircut. The Wedge was synonymous with The Look; a haircut that would set Liverpool apart from every other city. *A style that stood out.* It meant travelling to an away game with the mob, just to avoid being singled out by opposing fans. Travelling by car was definitely *not recommended.* The look was totally Scouse; a wedge, a pair of Lois jeans, and Adidas Samba on the feet. Scousers stood out, but that was the point; we were dressing better than everyone else, being different, far superior to everyone else — which is why it took off so avidly every-where else — plus we had the best team in Europe. Also, the Liverpool music scene was about to take off. *Eric's* was one of the top clubs in the country at the time, and it had a group of members who were aspiring musicians who would become future Top Twenty-selling artists. It was the Madchester of the late 70s, a decade before the fact. There wasn't a better place to live for teenagers at the time, and this was reflected in what came to be.

Herbert was the owner of the hairdresser's 'Herbert's' on Church Street. He had established himself in the city with numerous hair and beauty salons, a restaurant and boutiques. He even owned a nightclub, The Hollywood, on Duke Street. It was in these salons, and later, the clubs, where the hairstyle was pioneered. Herbert explains in his own inim-itable way, 'Although the wedge was a woman's cut it could be done in a masculine way. I sensed the time was right, and made my move. I was the first person to highlight my hair in the late 60s and I also introduced the perm to the Liverpool footballers. This was back when blokes used to wash their hair with soap and after-shave adverts were a novelty. We became the first hairdressers to introduce a wash, cut and blow, and this led to men using shampoo, colognes and deodorants. Men were now looking to their feminine side, and the wedge tied in very nicely with the times. Our wedge appeared in all the top magazines of the time. A fiver plus tip was the going rate.'

Herbert was a character in himself, and most people knew him because of his businesses, and because he drove around in a pink car and owned a pink house. He always said many men would eventually wear pink, and he wasn't wrong. People going into the salons would be informed that the wedge was the 'in' cut of the moment, and were encouraged to have one themselves, even if they didn't know what it looked like. Standing on the terraces at Anfield and Goodison, it soon became apparent that something was in the air, no pun intended.

As a result of their travelling on the continent and locating alien forms of fashion, the Scouse army began to formulate an evolutionary consciousness, a sliding scale based on the rarity of an item of clothing or footwear. They brought back their conti-nental masterpieces like ancient men did with the tusks and pelts of unfamiliar beasts from unusually long and adventurous hunting trips. The Scouse appetite for doing something new had been seriously whetted and peculiar social strata were slowly self-organising in the midst of the scally brainwave. Dave Hewitson explains that trainers were classified according to a hierarchy of style and availability.

Trainers had become the staple footwear to be seen in. They replaced baseball boots and AirWair as the new fashion item. It wasn't just any pair, though. Adidas were the masters of sportswear in 1978. They had been endorsing high profile sportsmen during the 70s and the firm had over 700 patents for footwear and equipment by the time of founder Adi Dassler's death that year. Now they would come into their own on Merseyside. They had a range of trainers out that would suit all pockets. The all-black range were football trainers; Bamba, Mamba, and Samba. Bamba were the cheapest, made of all plastic, and Samba were the most expensive, being all-leather. The price difference was some-thing like Bamba being a tenner and Samba being £19.99. This became a status symbol. Obviously the more expensive

Samba had the status — *and a status symbol such as an expensive pair of trainers that weren't available to all because of price defines a youth culture.* Investing in expensive luxury would ensure exclusivity. Nobody realised this at the time but it was to become the one main objective of this lifestyle for years to come, as the world of trainers hadn't even been remotely experienced yet.

After the 70s trend towards ever-larger collars, the winter of 1978-79 saw the small-collared, usually check, shirt become a staple item of dress. It became *de rigueur* to wear the shirt with the top button fastened, without a coat, tucked into your skin-tight Lois jeans. This habit of going without a coat in the British weather almost had dire consequences; against Bolton at Burnden Park on May 1, 1979, we had a burst of rain and snow that hammered the Liverpool fans in the uncovered Railway Embankment End, and several lads needed hospital treatment for exposure, believe it or not!

The canny Scousers knew that such incidents simply weren't cricket, and a solution was rapidly arrived at: the cagoule. The cagoule allowed one to run about, climb over fences, fight and sing and dance, either wearing the cagoule or with it balled-up in your hand or your pocket. It was an extremely portable item, but like everything else the Scousers were wearing, the cagoule had to be manufactured by a reputable designer, and who better than Adidas? The sight of lads walking about north-west England in these navy blue jackets, with the three white stripes down the arm, became extremely common, especially in Liverpool, who in 1979 were still ahead of Manchester. That summer saw the Pod shoe come into the limelight, eclipsing the loafers of yesteryear, and paving the way for non-sporting footwear, such as Kickers, which later took their world by storm. But in between, another shoe walked into town, and for reasons too complex and frightening to cover in this book, they triggered an expansion of the Scouse style, at which point it became almost a difference in kind rather than degree. It became a Thing.

Hewitson described the escalating situation in Liverpool in late autumn, 1979:

> Stan Smith was an all-white classic from Adidas. Instead of the usual stripes, it had three rows of perforations down the side, and was the first ever all-leather trainer. Stan Smith endorsed it after winning the U.S. Open in 1971, and his face was printed on the tongue.
>
> The average price of a pair of trainers at this time was around £14.99, but the Stan Smith was perched up at the top end of the price-scale, at £19.99. Top Man in Liverpool started selling about six pairs a week, which soon went up to twenty, then fifty, and so on. In the run-up to Christmas 1979, a phenomenal two thousand pairs were sold. They were the trainer of the year for 1979, and were worn with pride on match day by the growing army of scallies jumping aboard this mystery train of ours.

In the alleys and walkways of Scotland Road, the pandemic raged like smallpox in the Cherokee. The scallies of Everton Football Club took up the gauntlet, and appeared at times to be even more numerous in their commitment to the style than their red neighbours. There was no known defence against its virulent assault on the minds and hearts of that population, and in a phenomenally short time a sizeable fraction of the Scouse DNA had been affected by this alien insertion. There is no describing the fever that gripped those who fell to it. The closest comparable sensation is to imagine passing your driving test, getting your first shag, winning the Lottery, and being crowned King *all at the same time*; by the time you've won the Lottery (or even had your first shag), you're already maxed out, and the festival at the palace (read: Anfield) has become a numb and cosmic event. You simply drift through the crowd, feeling like the Boss, brimful of this elixir, this mysterious new sense of being. The whole thing distilled out to the football terraces on a Saturday afternoon or Wednesday night, often arrived at by British Rail service trains (known as 'the Ordinary'), to avoid police escorts on the football specials. Hewitson again:

During this period on Merseyside, it seemed like your dad
was always on strike. There was a three-day week, which
affected everyone with power-cuts, everyone sitting in the
dark with candles, plus numerous other strikes. It was no
wonder that the teenagers grew up wanting that bit more.
Those lucky enough to leave school and find an apprentice-
ship could happily spend their cash on the latest fashions and
a pint at the weekend. Being Liverpool, those who didn't
work still wanted the same things, and so quite a bit of skulduggery took place.

In 1979, Liverpool and Everton fans started making the
pages of all the daily papers. Those taking the Ordinary to
away games often found themselves with a bit of free time to
wander around city centres, with predictable results. Within a
few months, several high profile incidents occurred, and they
all made the pages of the *Liverpool Echo*. There was a lot of
talk about violence and hooliganism, but while many of the
other clubs were trying to outfight each other, those from
Merseyside often had an ulterior motive for causing chaos.

The whole culture centred on the match. The latest styles
could be checked out and the ground became a meeting
place. To be involved in this scene you had to attend the
match. It was a bit like the mods going to the seaside every
Bank Holiday, only this was happening every week. While a
lot of the boys were battling, a sizeable number were using
the distraction to go on the rob. It is impossible to mention
the culture and the clothes without bringing the match into
the equation.

By 1975, Manchester United had earned a reputation as
an unruly crowd, intent on causing problems wherever they
played. At Anfield, it was decided to keep the Manchester fans
segregated from the Liverpool fans in the Anfield Road End.
Two five feet high walls of tubular steel were erected down
the centre of the terrace, with a three foot gap for Inspector
Blackbeard and his officers to patrol. The wall became a
permanent fixture, but was only used for the penning-in of
the United supporters. A few years later, the Road End was

divided again, this time into quarters. All away fans now had an away section.

In 1977, perimeter fencing was erected at grounds to prevent pitch invasions. The trouble inside the grounds was now sorted. What happened was that the trouble moved outside the grounds, into the surrounding streets close to the stadiums. The hooligan of the time was now preparing to do battle outside the grounds, and Anfield and Goodison certainly saw their share of that, as we moved towards the 80s. For the boys in the clobber, it was a plus on several levels.

The pubs downtown became a definite focus. Home match days saw many mobs converge in the pubs around lunchtime, in anticipation of away supporters leaving Lime Street Station. The Sportsman, later to be called Quinn's, with its real racing car hanging from the ceiling, was next to the Royal Court and The Star and Garter, quickly accessible via a subway to the station opposite. Lads would be boozing all over that area until late in the night, and sometimes a drunken nutter would try and climb up into the racing car on the ceiling of The Sportsman, for a laugh. This jumble of close-by pubs and the way they were secretly connected to the station meant nightmares for visiting fans arriving without a police escort.

This Thing had gripped Liverpool, while, 35 miles down the East Lancs Road, it was doing a number on Manchester, too, albeit from a slightly different angle and to a smaller extent. The foreign travel and the sports shops provided the nutrients, and the two cities festered like Petri dishes loaded with some bizarre unknown microbe for several more months, as numbers proliferated. The Scousers were well ahead, and had reached maturity in numbers well in advance of the Mancs, but the process was organic and alive and inevitably subject to many possible twists and turns, as well as hybridisation. The Manchester masses were coming together more slowly, a sleeping leviathan of unknown quantity, and a distant storm was surely brewing.

4

TONKA TOY OR PERRY BOY?

No-one hands you cups on a plate.
                                    —Terry McDermott

DEEP IN THE ooze that flows unseen and unknown at the bottom of the Mersey Estuary, bubbling, fluorescing and belching as it receives untold volumes of hydrocarbons in the back-up from Ellesmere Port oil refinery, there once lived the germ of a terrible idea, an idea that shook the globe and dispersed capitalistic spores all across the air masses, from New York to a little yellow island north of Kathmandu, to Australia, to Narnia even. Not too far away, a similarly peculiar dark force lurked in the slurry that undulated, flocculated and coagulated beneath the deepest sediments of the River Irwell and the Manchester Ship Canal, colonies of the hardiest, vilest little fragments of electrochemically active biological material. The genesis of a powerful and immovable notion began to locomote, just as the trains on the world's first passenger railway had between Manchester and Liverpool all those years before. The winds blew hard that ancient year and the germ was distributed all across the north-west kingdom.

There have been debates for a while now, about who started what and when, between Manchester and Liverpool. These debates are the mad swirlings of animals chasing their tails. How can anyone possibly narrow the whole thing down to a single point mutation in the head of a single scally that resulted in him entering a shop and treating himself to something nice? Perry

Boys lived nextdoor to football lads, and both types had taken
to looking snappy, thanks to Bowie and the *Quadrophenia* hangover. Some styles crossed over, and that was that. Yeah, right.
Obviously, the mutation occurred in several heads at once (or
almost at once), and from there it spread to several more, and on
and on it went for a good while, like a virus reproducing in the
cells of an infected host, until finally it reached a critical mass
whereby any cunt with eyes in his head could just look and say,
'Ello, ello, ello, what's going on here, then?' This is really the
point that people are talking about when they discuss the
beginning of this phenomenon. The critical mass, that is, the
macro-level of intensity where the herd animals are suddenly
able to get a clue and become part of it, because by then it's just
everywhere (relative to being 'nowhere', even though it was
already there in a more dilute form, like the virus the day *before*
you 'caught' your cold).

Paul-S- described the mood of panoramic effect: 'We all
knew, those of us who were wearing the proper gear which
was spreading like fuck, that a lot of people still hadn't even
seen it for what it was yet in Manchester. In Liverpool,
everyone stands a good chance of knowing a friend of a friend,
kind of like in Salford, but across Manchester there were areas
that some of us had never even heard of, let alone been to.
Many were only in their mid-teens, and we were everywhere,
scattered around the different neighbourhoods, seeing each
other in town on a Saturday afternoon. Everyone wanted to be
a so-called Town Boy, and it was there in town that a lot of
little battles took place between Perry Boys from various parts
of Manchester. The clothes set the standard, and if you looked
the part, there was always a good chance of being able to front
people up and frighten them off. If you had a decent Manc
accent then you stood an even better chance. That said, we
didn't mind getting stuck into any cunts who wanted it in
town on a Saturday, and we had plenty of good-style run-ins
with other crews from all over Manchester. The ultimate goal
was to become one of the Town Boys, the top boys, the ones
who got to hang round the city centre unchallenged. The

Town Boys gradually took on a life of their own, and they were lads from all over the city. You knew who we were when you saw us, and you kept out of our way.

'At the same time, everyone shared the same feelings towards divvies – everyone despised them as an embarrassment to our thing. There was a definite scale of awareness, with some people just knowing what to wear, and others incapable of thinking for themselves and turning up in shite and getting a slap just for the stupidity of it. A lot of it was obvious: if a certain type of sweat-shirt was red hot, then anything in that same style would probably be the same. When you went rooting around the shops in town, your heart missed a beat if you found an unknown brand of sweatshirt, of a certain unmistakable cut and material; you knew you'd found a pearl, if all the other factors checked out. You were gonna be a trendsetter. Certain details were well important. For sweaters, the raglan sleeve became the only way, and anything with a different seam was thrown out, unless it was a Peter Werth, which had its own unusual seam anyway, low down on the arm. Even the acrylic Slazengers had a raglan sleeve, so they were accepted, despite the material. But still you got arseholes turning up in a fucking big-collar jumper that just happened to have the same exact print-pattern and colour as something that was well top, but the style and quality of it was wank. A print pattern was a transfer, not a knitted-in feature, it was Jekyll material. Those cunts always got a smack. People had to realise that it was about the style, the seam work and mate-rial, the hardware like buttons and zips, and not the superficial colours and patterns. That's where a lot of the wannabes were held back in other cities. They had no idea, then or ever. In Manchester we didn't rely on designer labels to guide us. It's always been a textile city, and it's in the blood with us. The sign of a true lad was someone walking about in a corduroy jacket with a patterned lining and a sorted bunched waistband, with a few tassels and hood and nice pockets, but no label in sight. Probably got the fucking thing from C&A, but it wasn't the point. It was a quality thing.'

In 1979, while the weird lights of Ellesmere Port oil refinery glowed like an alien city, and the waters of the Albert and Salford Docks sat in the shadow of looming behemoth cranes and storage depots, a young man had his hair cut, scratched his bollocks and swaggered into the brightly lit thoroughfare. On his feet were… what?

When Manchester United played Liverpool at Old Trafford in the 1979–1980 season, I was still young and small enough to claim a place on the ledge, against the front of the railings that ran about half-way up, right across the Stretford End, from the main tunnel, out to the corners. I was with Sid, and he was doing his best that day without knowing why: hush puppies, chunky-knit burgundy fisherman's jumper, white Fred Perry and probably a pair of pegs, which were divvy by then. I was likely wearing some kind of expensive small-collared cotton shirt (French Connection No. 2, Top Man), plus some straight jeans and maybe a pair of Clarke's Polyveldt shoes. We were in the ground nice and early to claim our kids' place up on the railings, and from there we could enjoy the sight of the ground filling up, especially the Scoreboard End, where the away fans were put. Visiting support at Old Trafford had always been inadequate, the human equivalent of trying to fight with a six-shooter against a fully automated magazine, and it was something we were used to. Consequently, Greater Manchester Police had long mastered the art of segregating opposing sets of football supporters. We could see, from which gates were open and which were closed, how many Scousers were expected that day. In the standing section, below the grey wall above which were the red seats of K Stand, there were about eight sections (some large, some small) formed by red metal segregation fences, each running down the terrace from the wall at the top down to the red 'cage' railings that kept supporters away from the pitch at the bottom. The larger sections were bounded by a double row of fences and the smaller sections were bounded by a single row. When it was totally hammered, the coppers would let us stand inside the double rows of fences to relieve the crush. At the top of each fence was a gate, enabling people to walk right across the top of the Scoreboard End terracing unimpeded if all the gates were open. A closed gate indicated where the membrane, the selectively permeable segregation, would be. This type of information could be transmitted to people on the outside verbally through the turnstiles. The lads would rapidly make a determination of the expected numbers daring to make the trip to Old Trafford, and the cohesive pack would divide, position and conquer, out there on that sinister forecourt.

In 1979-1980, I was aware of all this, but believed it had died a death with the 70s dinosaurs. The energy from those old dinosaurs keeps coming back to haunt us, doesn't it? Like petro-chemicals. Liverpool had about three of the larger sections allocated that day, which in 1979-1980 was a lot. We watched from our perch as they trickled in, small groups of merry Mickeys, and occasionally a large group of even merrier Mickeys.

As time passed, a pattern emerged. As they appeared from the tunnel and walked through the gates across the top of the terrace, filling the more distant of their allocated sections, it became apparent that they were all dressed similarly. Even from the opposite end of the ground, we noticed nine out of ten Scousers wearing burgundy long-sleeved polo shirts with thin white hoops, shit-stopper straight-legged jeans and white training shoes that had a little green patch somewhere at the heel. Added to that was the fact that they all sported mature, advanced flick, or wedge, hairstyles, many of which were auburn rinsed and tossed like Beatlemania about their moppy Scouse heads as they danced and boogied across the Scoreboard End. From the tunnel came dribs and drabs, then a full crew, then dribs again, then another big team, slowly filling their allocation. Eventually, the coppers had to open another gate, and they spilled in a roiling mass across the fence towards United Road Paddock at the corner. There was still a small corner section separating the two sets of supporters and it was full of men in blue, objective, funny-hatted sentinels of the oh-so taut membrane between Mancs and Scousers, always professional, never biased in favour of their own, unlike the Scouse coppers. I was fascinated, excited even, and tried to talk to Sid about it.

'Have you noticed they've all got the same clothes on?'

Sid's daft mug smiled at me like I was an idiot.

'Seriously, what the fuck are they wearing? Don't you think it's dead like what we're wearing?'

'You can't tell, it's too far away,' he said, the silly cunt. I knew this was a big moment, which represented something totally new, and we were in on it.

The Stretford was slowly filling, too, and spontaneous chants were breaking out around the entire stadium. From nowhere, a couple of young lads made a beeline for me and Sid, but seemed unsure what to say to us once within speaking distance. They were small and skinny, but bigger than we were, probably around sixteen years old. Their hair was *very* Perry. They had burgundy hair and polo shirts with hoops around them, sleeves stretched down over their hands for gloves, and straight jeans. I could now see that the little green patch on their heels contained a white Adidas logo, with the words 'Stan Smith' written under it. Evidently they thought we were from Liverpool, like them. They had misjudged the situation, and it wasn't hard to see why; the Stretford was chock-full of older beer-monsters, with perhaps only one in ten lads wearing anything even vaguely resembling what Sid and I were wearing. I realise now this was because United's lads were up against the segregation in United Road Paddock and United's section of the Scoreboard End, but I was fourteen, still being pushed back and forth by those strange aimless currents of the time. I caught the eye of one of the skinny scallies, but he was mesmerized, cautious and inaccessible, moving slowly with his mate, taking it all in. He knew I'd keep shtum. The two appeared to be shivering, with their makeshift gloves and scruffy auburn wedges. The shaking was surely a symptom of the molecule called adrenalin. Fair play to 'em. They lingered a while on the walkway next to us before drifting off, probably still thinking we were Mickey Mousers.

The match was unbelievable; they were chanting their hearts out in the United Road Paddock all the way down to the Stretford End. Nearly 58,000 people contributed to the most electric atmosphere I'd ever experienced. Even the seats were singing, raising the cantilevered roof of the giant cauldron. It

looked like all of Salford was there. The sound was non-stop for
the entire game, all the different sections singing independently,
with frequent thunderous renditions suddenly coalescing in the
same song, creating that sensation of madness at the whole-
stadium noise level. I remember Kenny Dalglish retrieving the
ball from the hoardings and what must have been the lads in
United Road exploding in a frenzy of spit and language and
hate-filled gestures behind that red cage. Then Dalglish standing
to take the throw-in, as several bangers went off around his feet,
simultaneously. King Kenny didn't even flinch, the Scouse bastard.

That was the first day I'd seen a large crew and *known* I'd seen
something. A question loomed in my fevered mind: how could
it be possible that, instead of eight Perries walking in two
columns of four down Deansgate, or even sixty Boys all well
turned out at the Longfield Disco, here were 2,000 of the
fuckers, identically dressed, going berserk in the Scoreboard
End, and what's more they supported the hated Liverpool!
Some genotypes are more susceptible to the virus than others,
and the Scousers in their Scotty Road warrens had apparently
gotten themselves into a serious case of the Nameless Thing.

It was by no means the first match I'd ever been to at Old
Trafford, but somehow it was a milestone, a gnarled marker,
protruding from what would be the foothills of a whole new
way of life. Manchester was undoubtedly well represented that
day, but we were still tying up our hiking boots, while the
Scousers were planting their fucking flag. Fortunately for us,
they were planting their flag at Base Camp One, not at the
summit, as they might have imagined at the time. There was
unfinished business here. Business called Evolution. We were
about to go up the mountain, and there were no stone tablets
up there telling us what not to do. There was just this boundless
sense of exhilaration and a bit of fear, which kept us all pushing
on, on, into the unknown.

That night, hanging about outside the various rows of shops
in the neighbourhood, the older lads were making the rounds,
further informing us of developments. Goody, as ever, was
present, and positively overflowing with information.

'Yer seen 'em, today, right, the Mickeys? Did yer see 'em in all the gear, the shirts, and the Lois and the Stan Smiths?'

He nodded toward his feet as he said that name, and, looking down, I was alarmed to see that he, too, sported the electrifying shoe. I sheepishly tried to examine one, but he brushed me off. I daren't look too much; something about them bespoke sacredness. They were so different and unexpected, yet so fitting. I was filled with an intense anticipation. Things were happening and I was right in the middle of it. Goody continued.

'This is what it's all been coming to for a while now. It's us and the Scousers, we wear these clothes and have this haircut, and no other cunt in the world knows what's going on! Everyone else is walking about in fucking shite gear, like cavemen!' It was obvious he was referring to the rest of Britain.

'We were in London last week, and the coppers had formed a barrier outside the Tube station. They were stopping all the scarfers, and the boys just steamed through them like they weren't there. They didn't even have us down as football lads, cos the cockneys are still going to matches in fucking scarves and bovver boots!'

How we laughed.

'Are my clothes alright, or what?' I asked him, feeling the hairs on my neck standing up. It was like I'd been invited into a secret society.

'Well… not bad, but yer need to get some decent trainers and for fuck's sake, get yer hair cut, if it's only a fucking skinhead. But, no, you lads are alright. You're gonna have to start coming to the match with us.'

Us lads made firm plans to hit town hard very soon, to equip ourselves with the necessary materials, by hook or by crook. Goody gave us a long, rambling account of what had transpired that day in the streets of the city centre, a non-stop series of confrontations between these special creatures, the Perries and the scallies. It dawned on me that a completely developed culture had been wrought, beyond the blind periscope of the so-called 'underground press'. Likkle monkeys were going at it all day long; they ran us, we ran them, and heroes were made.

Goody was like a public relations officer for United's Boys. He single-handedly recruited all the young lads in the neighbourhood into the life, mainly as a result of his gift of the gab. He defined the moment perfectly.

It would be a lie to omit the importance here of that weird resonance between the two cities. While Manchester's football teams did not enjoy the European success of their Merseyside rivals, firms of Mancunians travelled the continent in summer, simply enacting the right of passage of young, light-fingered Englishmen, as generations had gone before. It is impossible to believe that they had failed to have made the acquaintance of Liverpudlians during these trips. Collyhurst cowboy Colin Blaney, in his book *Grafters*, cites numerous examples from the 70s of mixed Manc-Scouse outings on the Continent, suggesting that lads from the two cities were at it together a long time before this new fashion exploded onto the scene. In fact, these mixed groups were directly responsible for many of the novel styles that seemed to emerge from nowhere. Tony O' Neill also relates several Euro-rob-and-rampage tales in his book *Red Army General*, from way back when he was a mere Private. General O' Neill relates several fascinating accounts of his continental football travels in the mid 70s, including a trip to the Kristiana free-love commune in Denmark, where he became a friend of Herb, not to mention the English tendency to help oneself to other people's money as you went to replenish dwindling funds. O' Neill's description of his attempt to cross the frozen Alps on foot is nothing short of heroic, the Wythenshawe lad being only the second man to even consider such a mission; the only other known instance of such an undertaking being that of the notorious French visionary poet Arthur Rimbaud 100 years earlier (as some of the more sophisticated London readers may recall). Blaney, O' Neill and company were truly the prototypes of the Perry and scally genesis, overriding the traditional limitations of the price tag and succumbing instead to adrenalin-fuelled free-for-alls in which only the best would do. And why not? While it is ridiculous to imagine General O' Neill making nice with that particular enemy, as the north-west shaped up back home, some other strange alliances were where at least part of the Nameless Thing was hybridised and polished.

The end of the 70s had indeed witnessed an end of scarves at the match. Sensibilities had changed, and it was common for young lads to buy football kits and tracksuits (especially track-suits, as this seemed less blasphemous) of clubs they didn't even support. When the youths of north-west England embarked on their summer trips, it was inevitable that the superior sports-wear would catch their eye. Thieving their way around France and Germany, those on the Manc roadshow were often to be found back home wearing unidentifiable Adidas trainers, creating a market in England for those who wanted the same. What began as a football accessory evolved into a football fashion statement, and became another one of the kaleido-scopic fragments of socially-credible objects and behaviours with which inner-city Manchester was saturated. The shops quickest to cotton on to the new look were obviously manned by vigilant sentinels of style, and the growing Adidas range was wisely positioned in the window beside the emerging 'mod' fashions such as the Fred Perry T-shirt, and, as autumn 1979 turned to winter, the long-sleeved polo shirt by Peter Werth. Roxy Music's fluid product became inextricably synonymous with the expensive small-collared shirts and narrow jeans on show under the fancy lighting in Manchester's boutiques and markets, and as the fringes grew longer (and turned a suspi-cious shade of auburn), those controlling the knuckle around town took on the electrifying, unexpected appearance of the Perry Boy.

Manchester approached the issue from a label-independent perspective, instead focusing on simple, well-made gear, indif-ferent to whether it came via Adidas or Marks & Spencer. These clothes were more muted and camouflaged than those sported by the jolly Mickeys – not quite as much turquoise and yellow and white – but overall they looked just the ticket. The next time the two teams met, Base Camp One copped for a nasty shock. The Manchester lads had generated the numbers, apparently having been working on a serious case of the Nameless Thing themselves, and from the Collyhursts, Pendletons and Wythenshawes, the Eccles, Prestwiches and Failsworths, the Newton Heaths, Broughtons and Kersals, there erupted a most virulent response (see Figure 1). As England became accustomed to the notion that the 70s skinner menace had subsided, Man United re-emerged as a powerful terrace force in the 1979–80 season, and this force, initially a tiny minority of its more active support, had succeeded in rendering all other factions extinct, almost, but not quite.

The Scoreboard Paddock was a drunken gigantic triangular terraced slab of violent large men who refused to be cowed, mainly because they were hard as fuck and not to be trifled with. They were *not* the Stretford End, which became a joke. The Old School beer monsters from this legendary segment of the Old Trafford crust never lost respect, and they always offered the Perries the option for an old fashioned intra-club ruck whenever the Perries fancied it, which wasn't often.

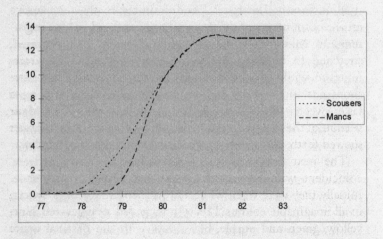

Figure 1: Proliferation patterns for the Nameless Thing exhibited by young men in Manchester and Liverpool from 1977 to 1983. Note the exponential curve for Manchester between 1979 and 1980. This is how we come back on 'em and done the fuckers, good style.

While the Scousers followed Liverpool's continental triumphs, collecting their labels like Penny Blacks, the Manchester crew underwent a number of critical factional and cultural mutations, resulting in a huge army of Boys. The Scouse onslaught on Europe was carried out by hundreds, if not thousands, of scallies at a time, who brought home their booty by the vanload to that peculiar city by the sea. This guaranteed an exposure to the new styles by anyone with eyes and who was literate enough to read a designer label in Liverpool at the time. Mancs ignored labels and focussed on quality. They were a more remote set of units, tight-knit bands of trendsetters, tea-leafs and blaggers, separated by the larger precincts of their sprawling city, and the coalescence of the Manc monster was slower, but all things come to he who waits.

In Liverpool, the novelty was quickly drowned by the ubiquity of the gear, and it led to a desensitised army of scallies, all done up in the best clobber, but somehow unappreciative, ignorant of what they were doing. Only the main Scouse faces, the connoisseurs, remained appropriately transfixed by the amazing style explosion. The rest followed numbly, in their impressive crews, outnumbering the Mancs head for head in the beginning. In Manchester, the novelty was drawn out, sustained, stretched to breaking point, as those little mobs of pirates returned with the stuff, and Manchester's superior city centre shops got some in with gusto. Anything which is prolonged tastes sweeter in the end, and this was no exception. The Manc version of the explosion erupted like a volcano, and the monster spewed forth, extinguishing all else within a substantial radius.

The next few months saw the inter-city rivalry increase, coincident with the zenith of the Stan Smith tennis shoe. Initially, they were worn white, but were soon subject to dyeing, in all imaginable colours. I recall orange, red, orangey-red, blue, yellow, green and purple, but always with the original white version lurking in the background. Another shoe, Kio Riders, exploded onto the scene later in 1980, initially available only in white but later in various colours. The two shoes were almost identical, aside from the Adidas logo on the heel of Stan Smiths

and the red rectangle in the side-sole of Kios. They were made
of leather, with three lines of perforations marking stripes down
their sides, from the laces to the soles, which were a thick white
rubber. Kios were available as shoes or boots, and rivalled Stan
Smiths in popularity by the spring of 1980. The Technicolor
explosion made the waters thick with plasma, the predators
moving in on the coral reef, bristling with the tread, the laces,
and the red rectangular insert in the side sole that challenged
Adidas's grip on the situation. The fact is, the double seam
running out from under the 'Stan Smith' Adidas logo down to
the top of the sole at the heel bespoke superiority over Kio's
single seam. It's the little details that make life what it is. One
unfortunate alternative were the 'padded' Kios, ones with silly
criss-cross sewing on the sides, resembling leather cushions in
the court of the divvy kings. I saw a Scouser at Everton, though,
sporting a red pair of padded boots, and he was pulling it off
quite convincingly, mainly because they were so dirty and
neglected. These merchants were the heart and soul of the
movement, they were the backbone, stood on the forecourt at
OT, Goodison, Anfield or Maine Road, wearing trainers that
had come out *days* earlier, cost a fortune, but these lads were just
sloughing around in them, all scuffed and filthy, like they'd been
hedge-hopping in them for years. Living embodiments of the
Who's *Quadrophenia* track 'I'm One'. At the opposite end of the
spectrum were what we called the Tonka Toys – lads who didn't
even like football, never mind go to the match who kept right
up-to-date with all the fashions, but wore them with a view to
never seeing them even slightly defaced. The rough-and-tumble
was not for them. Tonka Toys featured in the United song, 'City
boys make no noise, when they play with Tonka Toys' but this
may have been a coincidence.

The growing awareness that it was just ourselves and the
Scousers wearing these fashions, and exhibiting the slang words
and attitudes, only succeeded in ramping up the pressure
between us and them. Everyone wanted to be in on the
onslaught whenever we played them, be it at Old Trafford,
Goodison Park or Anfield. Paul-L-, a Manchester City boy, was

involved in a particularly violent day out at Goodison Park in 1980:

'We were massed in Victoria Station that morning, excited as fuck, knowing we were on a mission into enemy territory, a place where what you wore said something about where you were from. I'd had a flick haircut for months by then, and as I was considered a hard-case, never mentioned the hair side of it. It was as if a lot of the lads didn't want to discuss certain aspects of it all. For instance, a lot of us had auburn rinses or blond streaks, and it was obviously something that caught on, but whenever anyone turned up with their new hairdo, they would get the piss took out of them by them who already had the colour in their hair. It was kind of a way to take the piss out of someone jumping on the bandwagon, while having a dig at the hairstyle itself at the same time. We knew exactly what we were doing, and we knew how different it was. It was dead funny, cos there was nothing at all on the radio, or in the music of the time. We knew the Scousers were into it but had no proper idea City had boys at this point. We had a fair sized crew of boys and went on the service train. We were met by a mob of Everton that was massive, and we were on our toes the entire day. I can have a fight, and am not used to being smacked that many times. There was one point when a few of us were in a bus-stop, getting the shit kicked out of us by a massive crew of scallies, well outnumbered, but I know they were surprised that we even turned up. They were basically pissed off that Manchester lads had the same idea. But they did give us a pasting that day. This was before United went there that season, and to our credit we gave a decent showing. The lot of us were back in school on the Monday, all with big shiners and cuts on our faces, amazed at what a rough reception we'd got off the Everton scallies. The look on their Scouse faces when they saw us was worth a black eye alone. It was a fucking great day out, though. I'm ashamed to say it, but I was looking forward to United going there that season, as they were our best hope.'

I remember noting at some point in the spring of 1980, that not a single day had gone by since Christmas Day, 1979, when

I hadn't been completely kitted out in gear that was the latest
fashion. Fred Perry in its many colours was overlapping with
Lonsdale sweatshirts and Adidas cagoules, and everybody was in
the same boat, relishing being part of a new thing. There was still
not a word from the media about it, and there was a constant
sense of disbelief at how out of touch they truly were. Kenny
remembers an article in the *Manchester Evening News* around this
time, which he cherished. 'Apparently some punks or whatever
had been twatted in town one Saturday night, and got a right
pasting,' he said. 'They were interviewed by the paper and gave
a description of their attackers. The reporter for the *Evening
News* described the lads involved as "self-styled trendies". It had
me pissing myself and a bit surprised at the same time. That was
the only time I saw anything about it, ever, back then.'

Lads became inseparable from their Stanley (or 'mickey')
jackets, a black, thigh-length canvas coat with an elasticated,
pinched waist and a sleeve pocket. For the more discerning
there were padded mickey jackets (from British Home Stores, of
all places), similar to Stanleys but made from a high grade
anorak-type material, thigh length, with the slightest hint of a
pinched elasticated waist. At the time, nobody knew where to
find these padded Mickeys. They were extremely rare, but Kezz
had one. From early 1980 into 1981, there were Lois, Inega and
Lee jeans; Adidas Jogger, Adidas Gazelle, Adidas Samba and
Adidas ATP, Nastasé, SL80, Grand Prix; jockey jackets; French
football tops from le Coq Sportif; bike tops, and all the old
chestnuts from places like M&S, Burton, C&A, Kendals,
Debenhams, Lewis's, Austin Reed, Hurleys, Ellis Brigham,
Stolen From Ivor, Oasis, Clarke's and myriad other sources and
brands providing a wealth of well-made, expensive and
extremely good-looking clobber.

One of the earliest times I saw a full crew of boys wasn't at
a football match, but at the seaside. It was the day the SAS
stormed the Iranian embassy, in May 1980, a Bank Holiday
Monday. Myself and my mum and dad were going to
Southport for the day. Sid was coming with us. I was sat in our
house, all decked out in my Jekyll burgundy fisherman's jumper

and whatever jeans, waiting for Sid. He turns up in a pair of grey pegs and a white Fred Perry and a *tie*. I mean, the fucking tie with a gorgeous two-tone suit would have been bad enough, or even a Fred Perry on its own by that point in the game, but a *Fred fucking Perry with a tie?* There was something seriously wrong with that kid. I barely spoke to him the whole way there, just staring out of the window in a smouldering fourteen-year-old rage, and had to really make the effort once we got to Southport. Mum and Dad went their way and we went ours. We went into the funfair, and stood by the waltzers, like you do when you're fourteen. I instantly sussed several small groups of Scousers plotting to give us a kicking and grimly informed Sid, who responded by laughing out loud in such a way as to make me want to fill the cunt in myself there and then. Within seconds, these groups were manoeuvring, and I had to drag shit-for-brains with me, as about fifteen of the fuckers had us on the run. They never caught us, and I recall panting behind a hot dog stand and side-show, wondering what the fuck we were going to do next.

A little while later, keeping away from the funfair, we approached a large expanse of green, a huge field thickly dotted with people. In the centre of the field was a particularly large, mottled mass of humanity. Suddenly, from the funfair, there emerged a similarly sized mob, all lads in straight jeans and the rest, flicking heads a-plenty. This group (I would estimate at least 100, probably more) moved over to the other group, who all jumped to their feet in unison, quite a sight in itself, before merging with each other like a vast many-faceted organism. This merging complete, the entire crew, numbering about 300, slowly moved off towards the beach. I discovered later that the Scouse Boys and the mods were going to have it that day, and silly Sid had gone and dropped us right in the eye of the storm. (This was typical of the situation the mods found themselves in in early 1980. They were probably praying for the rockers of old to make a comeback, as the Boys were slaughtering them.)

One night a few weeks later, when Prestwich were having it with Kersal back in Manchester, a load of us turned up at the

top of this hill near the flats, and awaited the Kersal Boys, and
Sid turned up for the action in a Coq Sportif green silk T-shirt
with red white and blue elasticated neck and cuffs, minus Fuzzy
Felt advert on the front – a poor man's St Etienne shirt, which
was fair enough – *and a pair of two-tone pants, white socks and
loafers! In 1980!!* How he didn't get twatted for that one I'll
never know. This is a chemist not a joke shop, Sid.

This was a fast-paced era, and it is a blur to most. Andy-H-,
a true hardcore red and something of an intellectual, saw it all,
among the smudges and the war-paint. 'I was there at the outset,
and am not ashamed to say that the Scousers had the numbers
for about four months,' said Andy. 'Manchester caught up pretty
fast, though, and the whole era became a true, battling, terrace-
based phenomenon. Young working-class lads in the north of
England turned out to have a proper eye for quality and this
Perry thing just brought it to the surface. The mod craze melted
like plastic in a fire, and the punks got twatted twice too often
to stick around. The look was secured at either end of the East
Lancs Road by mid-1979, by the hardcore on the cutting edge.
The wearing of tracksuits can't be ascribed to the 'boys' when it
overlaps with a basic fascination with football, especially
European football, which Liverpool played a lot of back in the
early days. The true genesis of the 'boy' came when lads were
conscious of style, of looking different and associating that look
with being somewhat 'naughty', as well as chinning any mods or
punks that dared attend youth clubs and discos in their territory.
It was as much about jeans and cashmere sweaters as it was about
training shoes and tracksuits. For Scousers to claim absolute
jurisdiction over the phenomenon I find some room for doubt
– the European success happened to them, they didn't invent it
themselves. No, we have to look to the domestic front and to
the self-awareness inherent in the movement, in order to locate
the true epicentre. The Scousers had the numbers for a while,
but Man U responded in good style and by the beginning of
1980, we were up there with Man City, Liverpool and Everton,
the only four true firms of Boys in existence in the world.'

Many of us in Liverpool and Manchester could claim we

were hot on the scent of the new styles some time around 1978-ish, maybe even earlier. We must guard against being overly prophetic when it comes to the murky years of 1977-79, because there really were no standards at that point, at least in the north-west, and many, many of us were getting into the look without even knowing it. As kids we'd been wearing replica kits and associated training wear by Adidas, so the new stuff was just a more adult, expensive version of that. Manchester and Liverpool are massive football cities, and the number of replica kits and tracksuits sold there provided the foundation for what was to come. This is an important factor in the history of the entire story.

Andy-H- continued, 'The sometimes misrepresentation of this era makes me sick, when people draw the timeline towards themselves and distort it for everyone else, for instance trying to pretend that Mancs and cockneys got into it simultaneously in 1981, and that Scousers were walking about in top trainers in 1976. I think generally the Scousers were caught napping in 1979-1980, through no fault of their own. We just exploded onto the scene, from a small group that was already fully formed, and it was the start of the great wars.'

Those wars, between the Manchester Perries and the scallies of Merseyside, raged for years before anyone else got a sniff of what was going on.

Scientists will tell you that it takes *three* points to make a line, as two points are just two points, and the line between them is meaningless. You need that extra data point, to confirm the existence of an emerging pattern. But they will also tell you that it takes *two* points to generate relativity. It's no good having just one point; a bunch of vainglorious folk mutually applying perpetual pats on the backs of their brethren, isolated from the world, all happy and gay. No, you must have relativity. When the Scousers realised Manchester was with the programme, they choked on their conny milk sarnies, but like the men they were, they got stuck into it. The relativity created a new dynamism in north-west England, one that galvanised young people in a way not seen before, in those camouflaged and sensible clothes.

Mancs and Scousers, Scousers and Mancs, it was a new relativity
that even Einstein would've been hard put to solve. I say to the
Scousers, you amazed me when you turned up with that mob
all those years ago, and it is a sight I shall never forget, but don't
pretend you didn't recognise the importance of the fixture
yourselves, lads. Just tell it like it was, and bask in your Scouse
glory, but remember that many 'Scousers' you encountered in
1979 were not Scouse at all, and you escaped with your hides
intact purely because we were just as mesmerised as you were
by the sight of a foreign animal bearing the same pelt.

   There is a take-home lesson for this entire book, and that is
this: we are the same today as we have been for 100,000 years,
genetically, physiologically, emotionally and psychologically.
Plants and animals survive by recycling vital nutrients via
molecular pumps and pulleys, and are consequently harvested by
Mr Fila and Mr Adidas once they reach a certain desirable level
of maturity; they lived and died so that young lads and lasses
could look good, and as a result you are now worshipping those
plants and animals through the nostalgia of this book. The
indigenous peoples of today are modern analogues of the
cavemen, and their 'primitive' totems are identical in nature to
yours, as your totems are identical to those of the cavemen. Any
new phase in the life story of a species triggers growth and
excitement, be it the end of the Ice Age or a new hairstyle. The
excitement described here is not just the excitement of a football lad caught up in a craze, or the synthetic enthusiasm of a
Saturday night robotic raver – it's the incomparable feeling of
actually being at the head of the wave, of surfing high on the
advancing crest of a new lifestyle and, moreover, being able to
witness its effect on those in the process of becoming enlight-
ened as to its existence and engulfed by its trajectory. The
molecule called adrenalin is secreted liberally by animals under
these circumstances, and it is addictive. We were the Buddhas of
style, bringing verve and a new species of swagger to the barbarians, with knuckles, knees, boots up the arse, and a sense of
humour to die for. I'll shut up now, as I'm starting to sound like
a Scouser, or worse, a cockney.

A distinguishing factor between the two cities was the use of unique slang words and expressions. Some of these were imported from London, and many were associated with the underworld. Some were Yiddish, some were cockney, but when we blended them all together they became definitely Manc. It was a combination of old slang and some new words, emerging from the situation with the clothes and the attitudes. Dave-D-was an expert purveyor:

'All sorts of words and sayings came in at the same time. Some rhymed, some were just words, and some were borrowed from the Anglo-Celtic criminal dictionary. Beadage was money. A funt was a quid. Sky rocket was your pocket and a skydiver was a fiver. Radio rental meant mental. Dolly Dimple was simple, as in stupid. Hanging meant ugly or putrid. Ice cream was a bloke, rhyming with ice cream freezer – geezer. Radar was someone dead thick but funny without knowing it. Top was a piece of clothing or a lad who wore the best gear all the time. There were others like *mechuganna*, meaning mental, and marzipan, which meant brilliant or great. The hat-rack meant the back. A drink was a shicker and being drunk was shickered. If someone was staring you called it piping or blimping. A woman was a kife, to rhyme with wife. Breasts were obviously thre'penny bits. So if you were in company, and there was a bird there with a nice set of bladders on her, you could say to your mate, 'Pipe the kife's thre'pennies,' and he could cop a look for himself and no-one's any the wiser. Town halls were balls. A nervous wreck was a cheque. The weirdest one was the word for a big bloke, haemo, named after haemoglobin, the part of the blood that carried oxygen. It was short for he-man. If he was really massive, then you'd call him an oxy-haemo, which is the name for the same thing but with oxygen in it, so it has more energy. The mythical Leeds and Geordie cavemen, and any other large males, were referred to as grizzlies. Other big things, including people, were called jockers or dockers, and you'd say "it was docking" or "he was jocking" to describe something or someone massive. We had some totally weird slang, but it served us well in the future.'

Mancs are famous for speaking nonsense continuously, as well
as incorporating strange terminology into their discourse. They
also speak in different accents all the time, as if unable to remain
focussed on who they are. This led to a massive curiosity about
what the rest of the country thought of us. Manchester was a
neglected city until relatively recently, and back then was an
also-ran in the league of cool, behind London, Liverpool and
Glasgow, whose native speakers had locked up the media.
Apparently, a cockney, Scouser or weedgie represented the
'authentic' face of cool, criminal Britain, especially the accents.
The truth is that Mancs weren't into joining the local drama
club and trying to be actors – there were no drama clubs in
inner-city Manchester and Salford. With the exception of the
legendary Salford Players, the drama clubs in our county tended
to be out among the satellite towns, and this gave rise to the
incorrect diagnosis that we spoke like sheepshaggers. Famous
Salfordians graduating from the Salford Players include Ben
Kingsley, Ian McShane, Robert Powell and Albert Finney,
gentlemen not exactly known for sounding like typical thick
northerners. The Salford accent was simply too correct to jibe
productively with the garbage stereotypes perpetrated by the
British media of the time, and had to be pigeonholed somewhere higher in the social structure. We got on with our thing
and left the pantomime to those who enjoyed it, although that
didn't stop us moaning about the lack of Mancunian visibility in
the media. The only time you heard a full-blown working class
Manc accent, the actor would be cast as a Scouser! You've gorra
love the British media. Those years out in the credibility cold,
taught us much about how robotic most of the country was,
especially the south, where people appeared incapable of
thinking for themselves in any kind of creative or critical
manner. Mancs sat out the fantasy, living the fact, and all the
while we knew the world was gonna get a shock when they
finally worked us out.

5

MUSIC AND MAYHEM

There's a snap about Liverpool that just isn't there [I've changed this
from something else]

—Ron Atkinson

MUSIC IS LIFE. It fuels the major transitions and provides
solace and inspiration to us like a faithful hound. Music
has always accompanied the great discoveries, such as the
sprouting of pubic hair and the fumbling with unseen tits
beneath the orange halo of drizzly streetlights. The sound of
Chrissie Hynde telling me in 1979 she was gonna use her arms,
legs and imagination, while I shagged my pillow, will haunt me
for the rest of my life. But was there really a musical accompaniment to what transpired in 1979-81, aside from Bowie, Roxy
Music and the death-rejuvenated Beatles. John Lennon's murder
helped galvanise Scousers and Mancs both into a new respect
for their musical heritage, for the bands that were played in the
legendary coffee shops in the two cities in the late 50s and early
60s, like Billy J Kramer (Scouse) and the Dakotas (Mancs), The
Searchers, Herman's Hermits, Wayne Fontana and the
Mindbenders, The Big Three, Scaffold, Freddie and the
Dreamers, and Gerry and the Pacemakers. Many of the bands
from that era were influenced by the American rock 'n' roll and
rhythm and blues brought back from the States by sailors who
docked at the two ports, and young people in the north-west
enjoyed a lot of these sounds, while their counterparts in other
regions toiled oblivious to the music of their parents' genera-

tion. The Beatles were simply the best of that crop, but you could hear all that music in working men's clubs and pubs, a fond reminder of how our region kick-started the British music explosion of the mid-60s, the most famous example of which is when Lennon and McCartney wrote the Rolling Stones' first single for them, 'I Wanna Be Your Man'.

Lennon being gunned down in New York City in December 1980 brought it all up to the surface for a new generation, and every night on *Granada Reports*, we watched an army of scallies mourn and sing together in Liverpool city centre, for at least a week. Members of both tribes succumbed to the lure of the man's music. Despite years of enduring Munich 1958 chants, the lads from Manchester revelled in the music of the Beatles, and enjoyed a brief, big-city moment of neutrality. The frothing Scousers shopped all around, hiding their accents and beating it back to Merseyside with their Manchester-bought prizes. The teams met on Boxing Day, 1980, and despite the goalless draw and the weather, the tropical coral reef terraces were alive with myriad ski coats, hats, corduroy trousers, ski jumpers and training shoes, roaring their frenzied blood-hatred between the exclusive disciples of the Nameless Thing. The Boys in United Road Paddock sang, 'All we are saying, is Lennon is dead!' to the tune of 'Give Peace a Chance', and 'You'll Never Walk Alone' ('You'll never get a job… sign on, sign on'), holding up ten and twenty pound notes, instead of scarves. The era of fun, games and slashings had well and truly begun.

John Lennon's murder affected the youth mind of the north-west like a mechanical rotor-tiller, churning up the good old trippy stuff like the Beatles, along with all the London greats – the Stones, the Kinks, the Yardbirds, the Small Faces, the Pretty Things, the Dave Clark Five, and British and American psyche-delica from the late 60s. The beginnings of a fertile furrow had been dug, though the harvest we would not gather for at least another seven years. The great man was no more, but somehow his energy contributed to events in the future, as we shall see.

The pop charts were quite a different story. Most of the music was considered garbage at the time, but the memory writes rosily

with time. OMD's 'Enola Gay' conjures cold autumnal/winter
nights in 1980, necking with the girls, in Kio Riders shoes; lads
in bubble coats, cardigans and ski coats; French Connection
sweatshirts and jumpers with Christmassy images of snowflakes
and skiers and pine trees and the cardigans with the big silhouette of a deer against a full moon on the back. To brave the
winter nights, people outfitted themselves with mittens from
Ellis Brigham's outdoors store. The Specials performed on *TOTP*
in ski jumpers around that time, and it appeared that Terry Hall
was bringing back the word to Coventry from his trips to watch
United. But let's not forget the New Romantics: Teardrop
Explodes' 'Treason (It's Just A Story)' and 'Reward', or The
Associates' 'Party Fears Two', or Blondie, or Yazoo, or Soft Cell
and Haircut 100, Simple Minds' 'Promise You a Miracle' and the
Human League. The fact was, we hated, or pretended to hate, that
music with a passion, but though we gave most of our ear to the
60s' giants, Antmusic remained the music of the time.

Adidas released K. Abdul Jabbar basketball boots from the
USA, and the shop Jean Machine in the Arndale in Manchester
sent people mad with FUs jeans and cords. FUs were unique to
the city, and the two-storeyed superstore was staffed by top boys
and mobbed at all times by the Perries. There were Lacoste,
Munsingwear and Slazenger cheesy, stretchy V-necks. Second
Image coats, half-salmon, half-black, and the whole suede Adidas
trainer selection, everywhere. Thigh length leather jackets with
elasticated waists, shorter leather flying jackets, sheepskin and
pigskin all over the show. If you were skint you could nick a
French Connection T-shirt from Debenhams, the ones with the
dots and stripes across them. For chuckles, you could bleach a
pair of bright yellow or blue Wrangler cords, and cut the
bottoms off. You'd be left with an alarming white or sky blue
pair of cords with furry bottoms like you wouldn't believe.
Clarke's Polyveldt Oberon, AKA 'pasties', tan-yellowish or
brown in colour, were always the business, and they made a
comeback. Sovereign and krugerrand rings were quite big for a
time, and other assorted jewellery items, originating from the
smash 'n' grabs but often paid for.

I had a pair of ice-blue Lee cords, and some jade Razzy that got all ripped one night after the entire contents of the Lithuanian Club in north Manchester came out to fight four of us. Kezz had dragged us there, looking for his ex-girlfriend, who he suspected of being there with one of their lads. If anyone could have taken on the entire Lithuanian Club, it probably was Kezz, but the odds were always against the crazed animal. Myself and Tez-H- managed to launch ourselves over some railings into a back garden, right as they steamed in. What happened to Kezz and Cousin Trev was far worse than what happened to my ripped cords. Kezz was always turned out immaculately, and he had the first pair of Adidas Jogger I ever saw. But he was a machine back then, cat-like and vicious, always ready to have it with you, with a fantastic sense of humour often used as a tool with which to persuade you into some mad session. Once, Dave-D- asked him was he ever going to settle down, and he spat, 'Yeah, I'm gonna marry Fag-ash Lil, an' live *there*!' pointing to a spot on the pavement in front of him. He was serious. On another night, we were stood talking in a den of iniquity in the centre of Prestwich, and Kezz announced he was having an early night. He poured the remainder of his pint of Snakebite into his mouth, before stepping forward and spewing it vigorously into the face of a mate of mine, Sean (AKA Bonehead, AKA *Boxcall giganticus*), and athletically volleying him right in the town halls. *Boxcall* crumpled like a sack of shit, as Kezz strode out of the door without turning back, like a Zen Master. Adam-G- and Dave-D-, who were also present, were most alarmed, and helped *Boxcall* to his feet. To my shame, I found myself laughing my thre'pennies off; it had been such a surprise. While researching this book, I asked Kezz if he ever owned a pair of Adidas shoes. He replied, 'Yeah, I had a pair of slip-on brown ones. The first time I ever wore 'em I spread someone's nose across his face with 'em, and ended up with a fucking blood stain that never went away.' It was always a pleasure to go out on the piss, and especially to the match, with Kezz. You were guaranteed an epic of some form.

In June 1980, I went on holiday with my mam and dad to Prestatyn. I'd spent the previous week with Steve-K- and his folks in Towyn and gone for a nightmare day out to see some girls we'd met, in Runcorn New Town, getting legged round a jungle of multi-coloured flats with round windows in our Coq Sportif football tops by mobs of Scousers. We were conspicuous, being unfamiliar faces in those expensive shirts, and the Mickeys sussed us and called out the guards. The entire town was looking for us, but we still went into a housing estate to see the girls, who were more than a little surprised that we'd turned up. All over Towyn, Rhyl and Prestatyn was the enemy. The younger members of the species actually sported more developed wedges than the older Mickeys, a lot of whom wore 'taches and Lonsdale sweatshirts, with the telltale tightly-cut hair across the top of the ear. The younger Mickeys had started it off, and their moustachioed compadres were trying to get with the programme, in serious numbers. After Steve's mum and dad handed me over to my folks, and we retired to our chalet, I realised there were hordes of Scousers staying on the same site (Presthaven Sands), and that was the first time I ever saw Ritzy or Razzy jeans, but literally every one of these Scousers had them on. Steve went home and I spent the following week in the arcades, surrounded by Scousers, in my Inega's, turquoise Jogger, le Coq Sportif, and Adidas T-shirts, fighting aliens, myself a silent alien among the enemy. The day I got back from Wales I went to the underground market, as it was a denims goldmine; I was confronted by the sight of a million pairs of Ritzy/Razzy before my very eyes! Those Pakistanis were right on the ball. Probably been talking to their brothers in Liverpool, who were saying, 'These Mickey Mousers are wearing such a thing this week, you'd better get some in Rashmad, cos those Manc twats of yours will all be wanting them before too long…'

I plumped for a pair with blue ticks in the pocket corners, as opposed to red (I forget whether they were Razzy or Ritzy). I do not recall seeing any numbers of blue-ticked pairs of those jeans, ever, which is typical of me since I always seemed to manage to land something a bit different (like the turquoise Jogger I got from Salford Precinct prior to the Towyn trip, even though the bloke serving me was virtually insisting I took the

Gazelle instead because they were down to fourteen quid from twenty-two). Certain 'real mods' at the time took the piss out of my jeans but I held my head proud, having spent a week with the boys from the Mersey, and sure enough those same real mods were wearing Razzy themselves within a month, a long time in those days.

Arcades were integral to being Perry, as integral as going in Wimpy, where the black Town Boys hung out in the window overlooking Piccadilly Gardens, City Kats on the look-out for divvies and Tonka Toys to tax. From the original 'tennis' TV games of old, a new generation of cosmic adventure was born. It was a starry ride: there was Space Invaders, Galaxians, System One, Cosmic Guerrilla, Space Firebirds, Phoenix, Asteroids and Moon Crest, and, of course, the matchless Defender, with its split screen and smart bombs. Asteroids was interesting but difficult to control the 'thrust' function of the little triangular fucker, which always made it whiz off the screen uncontrollably. System One was a version of Space Invaders but it wasn't in colour and the noises were different, a pulsing succession of weird gulpy sounds. They had one in Oasis in Manchester city centre, a Man City hang-out. Then of course there's the whole debate about sticks versus buttons on the Invaders... which did you prefer? I'm inclined to say buttons, even though it seems counter-intuitive, as the response from the machine was more rapid with buttons. There was also a more-colourful version of Invaders, Space Invaders Mk II or something, or *deluxe*. The beauty of those arcade games was that they were free; some lads would obtain a length of the nylon cord off a Strimmer (hedge trimmer), place it in boiling water for a moment, and then bend it into a hook, which when set up (hardened in cold water) could be inserted into the machines for ninety-nine credits a pop. After a minute of that, bright sparks like Mike-B- (Prestwich's white version of Mike Tyson, and a proper rum 'un) also realised that they could use them on the change machines, thereby taking money as well. Eventually, a lot of kids were banned from every decent arcade in town, but they always managed to sneak back in. The arcades near the train station on

Oxford Road, or Hazels in the old Shambles Square, opposite Sussex Armoury, were among the favourites. There was another game, usually a table job, which me and *Boxcall giganticus* called 'Nuts 'n' Bolts', featuring a load of weirdly shaped/coloured bits and pieces moving slowly about the screen, *a la* Space Invaders, while emitting a very muted little emm, emm, emm, eek, ook, arrg, eerrm sound. We never did find out what it was actually called. It was right in Piccadilly, next to Wimpy. *Boxcall giganticus* was one of the first people I knew who owned a computer, which he'd had for a while, even back in 1980. One day he phoned me to tell me he'd installed Defender on it. Needless to say, a lot of time was spent in his house, playing that excellent game.

Around this time, people acquired the habit of signing their names on walls with their first name, followed by the initial of their surname with dashes either side of it, such as 'Dave-B-'. Everyone was doing it in Prestwich, and I believe several of us had latched onto the habit simultaneously. The first time I saw it was in Rhyl, in the form of 'Ray-B-, EFC scallies', on a wall in magic marker. The walls of my school, Heys Road, soon to become Prestwich High, were covered in names bearing this scally hallmark. The girls also used this marker, and it was common to see 'Mandi-B-, Anita-G-, Julie-J-, or Joanne-H- scrawled across desktops and walls, usually in places where we hung out to pose and act the goat. Another affectation was to stand with your cuffs stretched down over your hands, as a substitute for mittens, which were often worn with your hands behind your back, while you shivered in the rain in a hundred quid ribbed multi-colour ski jumper hoisted from Ellis Brigham's.

There was a place we were obligated to go, every weekday, for years, and we didn't mind at all, as it was a blast. That place was school, and ours was a total riot. The school was an old place, an all-boys job that had recently been massively refurbished and added to, in preparation for the merging with a local girls' school, Hope Park. The schools had always been divided into four houses – Stanley, Langley, Wilton and Edgerton – and there was plenty of inter-house rivalry. The merger happened at the beginning of my third year, and it caused no end of disrup-

tion to the lives of all concerned. The sudden appearance of girls
in the same classroom, at age fourteen, is not something you can
ignore. Those of us who considered ourselves the dog's bollocks
were to engage in a ridiculous barrage of peacockery, aimed at
impressing the girls, who themselves were wearing all the latest
gear of the time, and a profusion of multi-coloured footwear of
the Stan Smiths and Kio variety shone out from the bottom of
our otherwise black or navy blue uniforms. Half the kids in my
school sported wedge haircuts by mid-1980.

The trendy gear was frowned on by the authority figures at
school. Attempts were made to alert parents to this slide in standards. Everybody would be given notes from the headmaster to
take home, as the policy was black shoes only. We would sigh, and
in our best Salford poverty accents, inform the teachers that our
parents could only afford one pair of shoes and this was it. There
was nothing they could say after that, even though we probably
had a decent pair of Royals, Brogues or Gibson's at home, gathering dust. One of the few things besides shoes you could wear
that said something, in a school where uniforms were required,
was a coat. People went to town and bought the most expensive
and elaborate ski-coats imaginable, in the most alarming colours
available, for the fashion parade at school. These coats varied from
the common blue and white issue from British Home Stores to
items more suited to assaults on K2 or Kilimanjaro, obtained
from more obscure shops in places like Derbyshire, where
rambling was popular. People started to wear anything they
wanted, using the poverty excuse, saying their parents couldn't
afford the uniform at today's prices, even though the clothes we
actually wore were worth orders of magnitude more than the
uniform (especially acrylic snides from markets everywhere),
which was officially available at the local Co-op.

The uniform was gradually corrupted by tracksuits and
Lacoste sweaters, Adidas Jogger, bike tops and Kios. Break time
became a mini version of Old Trafford, as we played 'champs',
the football game with one goal in which teams of two
competed in a series of knockout rounds until only two teams
were left in the final. We used two of the posts of the bike shed

roof as goals, and as each team was successively eliminated, they would take their place behind the goals, under the roof of the bike shed, chanting the names of whoever they wanted to win. As more were eliminated, two sets of supporters would develop – separated by a couple of bikes perpendicular to the by-line in the racks, in a mini version of the Scoreboard End at Old Trafford – chanting at each other across the segregation, occasionally breaking through to engage in some slaps and kicks up the arse. Once, we caught the teachers, standing far back in one of the woodwork rooms across the yard, observing it all. We all instantly began to chant obscenities at them, and they beat a hasty retreat back to the staffroom.

Lunchtimes meant a stroll into the centre of Prestwich for some chips. There were many chippies, but only two decent options: 'The Doss-house', a chippy with a few eat-in tables, often occupied by mental patients and winos from the nearby Prestwich Mental Hospital, and 'Greasy Joe's', a chip and chicken barbecue place run by a Greek guy with a fantastically long, voluminous head, his thick, black hair styled in a flamboyant quiff with a comb that had apparently been immersed in the chip fat.

Schooldays back in 1980 were barbaric compared to today. Most of us received the cane, the slipper, the steel rule and the cricket bat as a matter of course. 'The teachers at my school, I have concluded, were mostly emotionally stunted bullies, who delighted in hitting small children with trainers and pieces of wood and steel,' said Sean Whittaker. 'They never offered any guidance to those of us who were under-performing in class, instead choosing to take solace from the fact that we were all destined to turn out losers. That would be punishment enough for the way we giggled and pissed about at the back (or front) of class every day. Even those of us they knew could really produce something, if we were the least bit afflicted with the wrong kind of accent, and fucked around in class all the time, then we were gladly sent to the poorhouse for the rest of our lives by these arseholes. It must have been nice taking advantage of kids like that, not to mention getting to batter children on a regular basis to relieve frustration generally. Funnily enough, most of us turned out alright, professionals in many fields.

The one exception was the headmaster we had for the first three years, Mister Bracewell, a Salfordian and a season ticket holder at Old Trafford. He always had a kind word and a few minutes to chat about life, and the match. And funnily enough, his cane hurt far worse than the rest of them put together! It was long and thin and splintered, held together by bits of Sellotape at the end. But when he brought that bastard down on the palm of your hand, you knew about it.'

Indeed. Mr Bracewell's cane was merely a tool through which intense pain was injected most effectively into the neural system of an average-sized mammal, namely us lads. Other teachers administered canings but their sticks were either too thick, too short or a combination of both. Bracewell's technique, combined with the frayed and flexible nature of the delivery system itself, optimised all parameters, and the result was an impulsive dancing from foot to foot, as the good man delivered a five-minute lecture, while the physical character sought unsuccessfully to neutralise the pain and release the energy recently introduced to the shocked system via the palms. It was like the difference between good and bad Ecstasy; the instant you received that jolt, you knew that *this* was what they were talking about.

The fights and the primate posturing at school were all just practice for what went on at the football, the crews of lads roaming the streets looking for the enemy. Instead of away fans, it was other schools. Our school had a reputation in the borough for being a tough one, a reputation earned from our many trips to do battle with our unfortunate neighbours, adventures which rarely resulted in much actual fighting. We were the Manchester United of our borough, that is to say we had the biggest, gamest crew and were not shy about travelling. One lunchtime seventy of us, all decked out in the gear, descended upon another local school, Parrenthorn, and steamed across their field to have it with them. They were well organised; we could see teachers holding doors open, while long

streams of kids disappeared into them from the rapidly emptying
yard. It was as though they actually had a contingency plan for
just such an event. Maybe they did. Two lads, Phil-D- and Lee-
M-, stood there in a green and white jockey jacket and grey
leather flying jacket respectively, wanting to have it with us, but
they knew they were heavily outnumbered by the Heys Road
boys. When a load of teachers came up the field to confront us,
they were pelted with pebbles from an adjacent track, and as the
police arrived, we scattered in all directions, hiding in gardens
and vaulting hedges. I know there were about seventy of us
because we were all summoned to Bracewell's office simultaneously, based on a list of names that was found, and we all
crammed into the little office for a lark, as the headmaster wasn't
there when we arrived. The list had been made by Mike-G-,
who'd been instrumental in organising the battle, and contained
fifty-eight names. An additional eight to ten fifth-years had also
turned up for it (we were fourth years at the time), including
Kezz of Lithuanian Club fame; in fact he chinned one of our
own lads on the walk back to school for calling him a 'sono-
fabitch', after he accidentally stumbled on him. Mike-G- was a
character. Once, when two of the hardest lads in our year were
going to have a fight (Paul 'Big Boy' Buxton and Dave 'Eddy'
Edwards), he turned up on his mountain bike, taking bets, with
a huge, smouldering cigar in his mouth, wearing a Fred Perry.
He was fifteen years old at the time.

Another time, some young lads ran into the yard, saying Saint
Joseph's, another local school, were at the end of Heys Road in
a mob. Within seconds, a crew of about 200 lads in all the latest
fashions was at the end of the road, to the horror of two kids in
Joeys uniforms, who looked shocked and white as ghosts as they
emerged from a corner shop bearing ice-pops. They couldn't
believe the two of them had caused that big a reaction.
Ironically, St Joseph's had a perfectly good mob of its own,
containing some original Town Boys, but not that day. We were
always on high alert and ready to have a riot. There were innumerable ambushes, chases and confrontations in which public
property and vehicles were smashed and wrecked, but few actual

injuries. This was not a situation unique to Manchester. Every region of Britain engaged in the age-old tradition of moving in a mob and rampaging against one's neighbours. We were all little Romans, Saxons, Vikings and Celts at heart. We couldn't help it. It was the nature of the molecule called British DNA.

Aside from battling with the other schools in the area, we would also engage in feuds with other neighbourhoods, specifically Kersal and Whitefield and Bury, which all abutted Prestwich. One Thursday night in spring 1980, around thirty lads, done up like dog's dinners, gathered on a hillside near Kersal and began having a go at some of the locals. We were strutting about like kings, having legged them a few times, when a single column of lads, in Slazengers, gold and burgundy cords, Stan Smiths and wedgeheads, came strolling, casual as fuck, from the bushes, down the hill opposite, towards us. Prestwich had thought up till then that Kersal were all soap-dodging donkey-jacket merchants, and people started whimpering about 'town boys' as we quickly removed ourselves from the situation (i.e. were legged for about a quarter mile). It was a funny transformation, a cacophony of uncertain voices.

'Hold on, who, who the fuck's that coming down the hill?'
'Wha- it, it's a crew of *boys*, innit?'
''E' y'are, who is that? They've got wedges an' everythin'!'
'Is that a Fila tracksuit?'
'Hang on, it's fuckin' *town*. It's *town!* Run!'
'It's the town boys! Fucking run!'

It was Kersal's lads. The next night was a face-off, with the police breaking it up. Being from Salford originally, I was secretly relieved and proud of the fuckers (as Kersal is 'over the border' in Salford), but I was also from Prestwich, which is considered Manchester, and proud of that too. That Saturday, droves of Prestwich lads roamed around town, and a load of us went on the 92 bus back to the borderland to face them again. The bus took a route through the high-rise flats in Kersal, and if we'd been seen up on the top deck, there'd have been a mob assailing the vehicle for sure. It was a titillating ride through the heart of enemy territory. Once back at the border, a couple of us younger ones were used as bait to attract their mob up the hill, and as they reached us, two large groups steamed in in a pincer movement from both sides. They legged it and we went after them, over the road, up their hill, and there we were, over-looking the Kersal Estate, a mass of high-rise flats and maisonettes, a hive of nutters. We couldn't believe we'd had the balls to go this far. People were nervously discussing calling it a night, as there were probably hundreds of heads down in the hive coalescing right then.

Eventually, one man, a 70s' giant called Jonah (he was as big as a whale) came up from The Castle, a notorious pub on the estate. He stood alone and faced about fifty of us. Then, with a roar, he steamed into the heart of our crew. The scene that followed resembled a man being attacked by a swarm of enraged hornets: the giant Jonah, batting people with his immense fists, while the frenzied, skinny scallies got the better of him. He went down and was mercilessly battered, kicked and generally twatted all over the place. But he went down in legend. He was one of United's Old School, and would sometimes pass us on the fore-court with an evil glint in his eye, on his way to the Scoreboard Paddock. He knew who we were. Kersal flats were among the first to actually be wiped off the map, as they apparently were bad even by the jaded standards of Salford. A few years after our little battle, eight high-rise blocks were simultaneously demol-ished by controlled explosion on Kersal Estate, the biggest simultaneous demolition of its time.

At night, after school, we would hang around outside various rows of shops here and there, migrating from one site to the next like the 70s' dinosaurs of old, leaving our new-style graffiti instead of the old 'MUFC' stuff. The mighty Kezz migrated to the red side of the Manc spectrum at this point, and began attending matches with vigour, as the gaggle swelled. The numbers of young people simply hanging out in the street was vast. The girls would be there, too, and of course there would be some slap and tickle here and there. This was when groups like Visage, Ultravox, Human League and Soft Cell were hitting the charts. The pleas-ures of alcohol were a novelty to us, and we quickly incorporated

it into our other habitual patterns. We would go to an off licence
and ask older blokes to go in for us and get us a few bottles of
cider. Kenny was my drinking partner at the time, as well as Dave-
B-, who described those memorable evenings:

'We'd drink the cider in about five minutes flat, and spend the
rest of the night making total pillocks of ourselves, falling about
and singing, showing off to the girls. People would be out in
deerstalkers, with joss sticks in their mouths, massive wedges and
Fila Borg tracksuits hanging down over their shoulders to reveal
the labels on the chest. Someone might produce a knife and
someone else would take it off him and slash at him with it, then
someone else would pull one out and start stabbing at someone
else, while the word 'Scouser' was spat in whispers. We were all
playing the waiting game, waiting to meet up with the enemy
again someday soon. Some of the lads would actually travel to
Liverpool in a car, stuffed to the gills, and park up somewhere off
Scotland Road. Goody and Big Col were regulars at this game.'

Goody described a typical visit to our neighbouring city.
'We'd park the car somewhere well naughty, right in the flats on
Scotland Road. About eight of us would be packed in that
fucking car. We'd go into a shop and start talking in loud and
obvious Manchester accents. Within seconds there would be
some kind of confrontation. The Scousers would be in uproar,
with a lot of alarms being sounded across the courtyards and
over the balconies, and the fun and games would follow. Many
a time the Scousers chased us back to the car and we just
managed to escape. Once, Big Col took a snooker cue. A
Scouser was walking across Scotland Road and he stopped in
the middle to let us pass. Col leaned right out of the window, as
he drove towards him. I can still see him, getting knocked out
cold in the middle of the road by this fucking big pole as we
drove past into the night.'

If we weren't just hanging around, we were playing football.
The late 70s and early 80s saw many heroic figures appear on
the scene, figures we liked to imagine we resembled while
running down the wing, or rising to meet a volley or header
coming into the box. Between 1977 and 1983, every European

Cup-winning side was English, a fact we tend to forget today, but which surely infused us all with its pulsating truth, providing momentum for our own little epic matches in the park. There were the boys wearing Aston Villa's claret and blue, Tony Morley, Gary Shaw and Peter Withe, regularly gracing our TV screens and stadiums with their unstoppable streaks into the penalty area and explosive shots at goal. There were the blue and red Adidas-silken players of Ipswich Town and Nottingham Forest, bearing their team numbers in the three stripes on their backs: Eric Gates, John Wark and Paul Mariner for Ipswich, Tony Woodcock, John Robertson, Trevor Francis and Kenny Burns for Forest. Villa and Forest won three European Cups between them during that time, and Ipswich beat Arsenal in the 1978 FA Cup Final as well, being something of a force in the league. Tottenham featured the striking pair Garth Crooks and Steve Archibald, who helped Spurs to their share of the domestic and European silver, and individuals such as Norwich's Justin Fashanu amazed us with their sensational goals. Plenty of other sides, such as Ron Atkinson's West Bromwich Albion, with Bryan Robson, Cyril Regis and Laurie Cunningham, tantalised us with outrageous strikes every week on *Match of the Day* or *Kick Off*. It was a glorious era for football, one in which reaching the FA Cup Final was a huge thing. Football was life itself, and the park was always swarming with lads looking for a kickabout. For some though, a kickabout in the park was as far as it went. They weren't interested in playing for the school team, as the schools played on Saturdays, and Saturdays were reserved for something else. Saturday morning was a time of great anticipation, when youngsters travelled into the city to go in the clothes shops, amusement arcades, fast food outlets, and onward to the match. We lived and breathed football during this time in north-west England, and so it is all the more amazing how what we wore came to be at least as important as what happened on the park. Fashion and football coalesced into an entire way of being. This exhilarating combination is what makes people look back down the decades and still feel the thrill of being there during this special time.

The culture of thieving and blagging was also rife in quite a few cities, and in Manchester it was a way of life. Working class kids had no money to buy things with, so they unashamedly stole everything, and there were many targets and many dangers. Some of the lads would go to Blackpool, for a spot of handbag snatching. Mostly it was a piece of cake, they said, but sometimes you'd get a bloke who was quite athletic, and that could be a problem. They had a term for the heroes who would chase them for miles; they called them 'Sebs', or 'Sebastians', after Sebastian Coe, the famous runner of the time. 'Have-a-go Seb Coes' would be the curse of the handbag lads; they'd leg you for miles without letting up, and it meant handbag snatching could be quite a dodgy way to cop for a few quid.

For those entranced by the dubious allure of secondhand clothing, there was the art of washing lining. That is, hitting the posh neighbourhoods and relieving their washing lines of lambswool Adidas sweaters, Fila tracky tops and bottoms, cashmere no-label jumpers from Austin Reeds and Kendals. We were all seasoned 'hedge-hoppers', hedge-hopping being something of a local pastime; basically running through an entire street's worth of back gardens by vaulting the privets and fences as you came to them, until some have-a-go Seb Coe came steaming out to chase you down and kill you. Washing lining was an extension of that, once the shops up town were shut and you were back in the neighbourhoods at night. And ragging? That was piling into a shop and, rather than exhibiting an Oliver Twist-like deftness of hand, simply grabbing everything that wasn't nailed down and making off with it. In my capacity as Anthropological Gazetteer, I scientifically observed many naughty boys at the match having a blast, going into local sport shops (in places like Shitford and Crapchester, where the locals hadn't a clue yet) and leaving the shelves empty of product and the owner on the blower to the insurance company. It's a cruel world, but the cruellest blow of all comes in 1980, when you're poncing about in a pork pie hat and two-tone pants and tie, while a full crew of Mancs or Scousers is hammering the bejesus out of your local Hurley's on a Saturday morning ragging spree.

'Once in a while, in some shithouse town, or in London, we'd see a sports shop and they'd have decent gear inside,' remembered Goody. 'A few of us would go in and start fucking about with the stuff, trying out cricket bats and boxing gloves, while the rest filled their jackets and pants with as much as they could. Sometimes it was just easier to smash the window and grab whatever was available. This was a guaranteed attention getter, so it had to be clever sensible little firms that did it, and it was. You tended to concentrate on something worth the risk, so that's when jewellers started getting it. It was hilarious to be walking toward some football ground, surrounded by lads with these funny haircuts, all wearing tons of expensive continental designer gear and gold chains and sovereign rings.

'We got a bit of a shock at Stoke that year, though. A little crew of our boys got steamed near Stoke train station, down under the bridge. There was a proper team of them and they laid into us and honestly battered fuck out of everyone. I've never seen so many of the lads in such a state. Stoke did us totally, and they showed no mercy. Everyone was fucked up — black eyes, broken noses, the monty. But that's what it was all about, wannit?'

We may not have been seen dead wearing the ska fashions, but we lived its reality. One night, a mixed Prestwich–Kersal crew went prowling around, and upon spying a couple naked through the window of a posh luxury flat, the lads brought the lyrics of The Specials' song 'Stupid Marriage' to life when they launched a chunk of concrete through the window, probably terrifying the occupants, and themselves. It appears from the point of view of history that the rest of the country were still mods or ska boys at this juncture, and never managed to undo their top buttons till it was too late. By then the party was over, and the lads were sitting in the pub with their feet up, reading the paper, waiting for Rave, waiting for Techno, waiting for the next phase of this most peculiar journey... we'll get there, yet.

6

SLASHERS' DELIGHT

History could pass for a scarlet text, its jot and title graven red in human blood.

—Eldridge Cleaver

MOVING FROM THE train stations in town to the vast Old Trafford forecourt, waiting for the police escorts and rare independent mobs to arrive, became the human equivalent of the crocodiles and the wildebeest. They'd be poised at the top of Warwick Road, localised and potentially lethal, like a virus on a spike, haphazardly protruding into the bloody escorts as they washed by. The fixtures involving Liverpool and Everton, and to a lesser extent Manchester City, were the high points of the season during those years. After an eternity facing up to Dolly Dimpletons clomping down Warwick Road in their scarves and Doc Martens, the disciples of the Nameless Thing would clash once more. Thousands of lads from both cities would be drawn to the site of action like track-suited leopards to a life-giving waterhole. From the train station to the stadium, a bizarre combination of fashion show and bloodbath would unfold. Herds of zebra would scatter in the face of organised lions, vans full of truncheon-wielding wild boar exploding from nowhere, while the baboons and hyenas dissolved into the alleyways. The same thing in reverse happened after the match. It soon became obvious that only audacity and sheer weight of numbers could win out. It was wildlife. Sweet and tasty.

Then there was the size of the mobs. 'Back then, it was

common, *common*, to come up against crews of Scousers over four hundred strong,' said Kenny Lewis. 'We regularly turned out in crews of between two and five hundred lads, every week. When you read the reviews, on Amazon.com, from lads who jumped on the bandwagon years later, they call Scouse and Manc hoolie writers liars, because they have no clue what it was like back then. They came in when it was fifty against fifty. We were in at the beginning, when it was two thousand lads on Chester or Scotland Road, going at it, when it was total carnage and mayhem. The funny thing was, you didn't hear of too many people getting that badly hurt back then, unless some Scouse cunt used a blade. There were too many bodies around, and it was too psychological for anything too personal. It was just hundreds and hundreds of boys running at each other.'

In May 1981, while Liverpool were in Paris for the European Cup Final, I went on a school trip to the South of France. Sean, AKA *Boxcall giganticus*, came along too. We were excited to be in France, and amazed at the wealth of decent clobber on hand. In St Tropez one sunny day, among the potted palms and the pastel-painted buildings, we found a shop selling a shoe called Adidas Easy. Easy was the first strap-over trainer I'd ever seen, an off-white, unfinished leather, with Stan Smith-like perforated 'stripes', consisting of several variously-sized holes configured in a repeating pattern down the side. There were two straps. The soles were extremely thick, soft white rubber, with the familiar blue tennis bottom. They were the boss bastard Christ almighty of trainers, and I had them. *Boxcall giganticus* had a pair as well. Kezz gravely informed me that he would personally rip the head off anyone who tried to soil or steal them, which was reassuring, but even Kezz couldn't have prevented the following.

Later that year, we went to Anfield without tickets. On the train we ran into some Scoreboard Paddock dinosaurs, who told us to stick with them, but they looked like shit so we went our own way. A mixed gaggle of us arrived at Stanley Park, after an eventful journey involving bangers a-plenty, as it was near Bonfire Night. A small crew of hefty Mickeys in Patrick cagoules came through Stanley Park and around the houses and led a

charge of malnourished scallies against us, bricks raining down
like you wouldn't believe. They were blocking our way to the
away end, and the dibble was nowhere, it seemed. The spell was
broken when an older bloke grabbed me by the throat, roaring,
'Stand yer ground! Stand yer ground! No fuckin' surrender!' as
everyone went back and forth. Nobody budged and soon
enough we had them backing off, still throwing bricks. The little
street was crammed with lads, trying for some toe-to-toe, as the
bricks came down and we moved towards our goal.

We took it to them all the way to our turnstile at the Annie
Road End, making slow progress in that narrow shithouse
street. At the turnstiles, things were more heavily policed.
Everyone was in line, as the dibble moved along, checking
tickets. Hundreds of Scouse vultures sat close by on the railings,
salivating, while this horrible copper dragged us into no-man's
land and gave us a loud dressing-down about travelling to
Liverpool without tickets. Three of us stood in the middle of
that narrow street, and were soon joined by another two. The
coppers told us to 'fuck off back to Lime Street'. We were dead.
Then I had an idea: speak in Scouse accents and pay into the
Scouse section of the Anfield Road, fuck it, it'll be alright. I was
a dab hand at the Scouse, but the same unfortunately could not
be said of Kenny and Dave-B-. When I looked round, as we
entered the home fans' turnstile, a queue about 100-strong had
materialised behind us, and they were rubbing their hands in
anticipation. Not one of my better ideas. These brick-lobbing
bastards were in for the kill. We steamed through the back area,
through the tunnel and down to the front, before walking
rapidly across to the corner at the far right, well away from our
own fans, unfortunately. I looked around and witnessed a
bowel-curdling sight; the shout had gone up, and there were
hundreds of them pouring down at us from all sides. It was a
total shit-up like no other.

'They cornered us, and the punches and kicks went in, but
they were hitting each other, out of control, there were so many
of them,' remembered Kenny. 'We were fifteen years old, apart
from Dave-B-, who was sixteen that day. He was wearing his

birthday presents: a pair of red Kicker boots, brown Levi's needle cords and a khaki knitted Levi's jumper. I can still see his blond-streaked wedge disappearing over the top of the steps in the corner. He made a run for it, and spent the day getting chased round Stanley Park by gangs of hyenas on the lookout for Mancs caught alone. A rare Scouse steward took pity on us, and told us to hang onto the railings at the corner and not let go. We were arsing it hell for leather at this point. They were lining up for a crack. He spent most of the match helping us fight them off.'

I was wearing my Adidas Easy, a pair of bleached FUs, a light blue Jaeger cashmere round-necked jumper and a tan suede jacket with small collars from Burtons, that I'd actually nicked off my dad. Kenny was wearing some array of dazzling gear as well, probably Diadora trainers and bleached, frayed jeans with a unique lambswool sweater of some kind. Both myself and Kenny sported long, Argentine-style perms. I'm not sure what happened to the other two who came in with us. I think they successfully merged into the crowd as they came out of the tunnel. Every few seconds, another cunt would emerge like a weasel from the crowd and try to land a punch, and two or three would give it the sly kicks. They probably thought we were giving as good as we got, but we were really flapping and just trying to protect ourselves, managing the odd back-hander and knee into some twat who tried to land more than one at a time. Eventually, things calmed down, and they stood all around, staring, panting, and lusting for Manc blood. They started looking us over, up and down, up and down.

And then they saw the Easy.

A couple actually asked, 'Hey Manc, where d'yer get yer trainees from?' *a la* Dave Hewitson in *The Liverpool Boys are in Town,* trying to hide their curiosity under the scorn in their eyes. The reply, 'Saint Tropez,' proved too much for them, and several went absolutely ballistic, dropping and scrambling to pull them off my feet, clawing wildly at me like rabid animals, while the steward fought valiantly to save the prized Adidas Easies.

After a little while, United scored, and things reached an

advanced state of grimness. Liverpool equalised, and fights were breaking out in other parts of the Annie Road, as Mancs were outed here and there. Some horrendous blade merchant in a black leather jacket appeared towards the end, dripping wet with the rain, hovering about with his little crew of vultures, barely coherent through his hatred at the beauty of our perms and clothes. This lad had undoubtedly entered the ground at 'three-quarter time', an Everton scally bladed up and prepared to use it, if possible. He talked for ages about what utter twats Mancs were, and how we'd nicked the whole idea off the Scousers.

'Look at yeh! Look at yeh, yer Manc bastards! Where d'yer get yer fuckin' ideas from, eh? Yer fuckin' nicked 'em off our lot, didn't yeh? God, I fuckin' 'ate Mancs, d'yer know 'ow much I fuckin' 'ate Manc twats like yous, eh?'

Looking as top as we did that day, it was easy to understand how he felt. We stood there and took the scolding, like good little boys, wondering if he was going to calm down at some point, but he was a bottomless fount of pure hatred. He was angling to stripe me for what felt like an eternity, as his adoring entourage salivated all around. We were too numb from the adrenalin overdose by this point to be shitting ourselves. The glands had pumped themselves dry and we were spent shells. With minutes to go, mindful of this horrible cunt, they let us stand in some little enclosure in the corner, and as we slinked into it, United scored again. By now we couldn't contain our joy, and we jumped up and down, arms aloft in victory. They couldn't get at us as we danced gleefully. At the final whistle we were walked across the back of the goal to United's section. As we jumped in we got a few looks, which turned to smiles as we celebrated wildly with the rest of them, relieved to be home and dry. Walking outside the ground later, a bus went past, and the same sad cunt was still going off his head on the top deck, shouting threats out of the window at us. When Dave finally dragged his sorry arse into the crew somewhere on Scotland Road in the dark later that night, he was saturated and totally bollocksed, his new clothes covered in mud and shite. He told us many horror stories of Mancs caught alone he'd seen battered severely by the mickeys. Brave bastards. But how we laughed, as we got on with some fun and games all the way back to Lime Street.

One season, probably 1980-81, we were corralled and put on buses at Lime Street and transported *en masse* in a convoy to Goodison Park. Unfortunately, the majority of people on our bus decided to wreck it, and windows, seats, ceilings and even stainless steel poles were thoroughly brutalised in an orgy of gleeful destruction. Fragments of foam stuffing from the uphol- stery whirled about in a kind of frenetic, crazed Brownian motion, while lads lobbed pieces through the windows or just booted the windows out and then lobbed entire seats through them. I personally didn't take part in this disgraceful show; I was laughing too hard at the antics to participate even if I'd wanted to. Not that I was enjoying myself, mind. I was there purely as an Anthropological Gazetteer. I wasn't there for the fun of it.

When we arrived at the designated parking spot, about a mile from Goodison, the driver grimly informed the dibble of devel- opments (not that he needed to; the fucking bus looked like al-Qaeda had paid it a visit), and this big Scouse copper climbed aboard and screamed at us with a purple face, 'Right! Yer Manchester scumbags. For this yer'll be held on this bus till all the rest of yis are at the ground then yer'll have to make yer own way there.' This happened, but instead of letting us off together, which might not have been too bad – most of us were lunatics, and were gagging for a battle with the Mickeys anyway – they made us get off in twos and threes and made a big performance of letting everyone in earshot know who we were, as we alighted in the overcast streets of Hostility Central. Me and Kenny, of Annie Road fame, must have been brain dead that day, but it probably saved us, as we strolled leisurely to the ground, oblivious, for some reason. About fifty feet from the gate to the outside pen for the away fans, we pushed past some lads, and one sharp-eyed fucker sussed us. He made several grabs for my back, growling about someone getting a blade out, and only utter terror (and decent trainers) propelled me from his grasp and into the holding pen. The possibility of being slashed at Everton always ensured a plentiful supply of adrenalin. They should

bottle the stuff and sell it on the train. Crank it up as you roll
into Lime Street. I remember seeing a Scouser with a long
gangly perm like my own that day, a pair of navy blue Adidas
tracky bottoms and Adidas ATP trainers, looking cool as fuck. I
went looking for some tracky bottoms the same, but ended up
with black ones instead. You can't win 'em all.

The author doesn't often discuss events which occurred in
1982, '83 and '84, mainly because he considers these years to be
outside the jurisdiction of his breed (1979–81), and the ultimate
territory of the true 'Casual' rather than the Boy; the scally or
the Perry. But there were many great adventures from the
summers of 1981 to 1983. One was a Tuesday night game at
Anfield, in April 1981, when the United contingent were kept
from the Scousers by no more than a piece of tape stretched
down through the crush barriers, while the Annie Road Enders
were penned in by actual railings. It was a balmy evening, at the
very end of the season, and there wasn't much to play for. We
scored a goal and won 1–0 in the strange dusk light of spring,
there in that evil place. United hadn't even filled their usual half
of the Anfield Road End. It was a low turnout, or so it appeared.
However, with a little more than fifteen minutes remaining on
the watch, an enormous crew of Mancs began streaming out
down the front tunnel, such a large mob that it was reduced to
a snake so it could pass between the stewards, and it flowed for
ten minutes. During this time, three mates and I discussed the
possibility of getting down there and getting out into the
Liverpool streets for the usual fun and games. God only knows
where and when this lot got organised, but they just began
flowing out. Eventually two of us went down and flowed with
them. The most hilarious part of this is that from up where we
were initially stood, we could see the Scousers going ballistic,
trying to get through the coppers and the stewards that fought
to hold them back. United's massive mob was splendidly turned
out, and the Scousers were more pissed off than I've ever seen
them (and I've seen them pissed off, believe me) at what they
believed to be pretenders to the crown getting away with
getting away, so to speak. They were literally fighting the

coppers and stewards, who did a valiant job of containing what was a frothing ocean of steaming lads all hell-bent on slashing some Manc arse for having the cheek to turn up at their place.

Outside, another mob of coppers were now fighting to keep us from getting out into the street. The Scouse coppers had misread the situation, opening the exit gates believing there'd be no issues with this low United turnout. There was a massive to-ing and fro-ing, with coppers, vans, dogs and horses all going at it (this was the night Cockney Sam punched a police horse, I saw it with my own eyes, sorry, the author saw it with his own eyes), as they tried to push us back into the Annie Road. A good few of the boys managed to squeeze through in the mayhem but a lot of us were stuck inside. We ran back up the steps to watch the end of the game, and noticed loads of young scallies sat around in alcoves up the stairway, obviously Scousers. They had probably come up the back steps when the dibble opened the gates, then we'd all come steaming through the bottom tunnel and now they were caught in the middle of it all, trying to look unflustered. They were doing a pretty good job, to be fair. Back inside, the lad standing next to me against the tape received a huge nut and bolt on the napper and went down like a sack of shit, and then a Scouser with a Stanley knife managed to sidle right up next to me before being decked by a couple of coppers and dragged off. The strangest thing is I don't remember feeling even vaguely worried by it all; it was what we were there for.

The walk back to Lime Street was mainly them coming down the grass verges by the Scotty Road flats, and United legging them back into the flats, all the way to town. Sometimes they came into us, and sometimes we went after them into the evil ginnels, a mass of shouting, bouncing, gesticulating, but little prolonged fighting. What began as two massive crews ended up as a diffuse riot of expensively-clothed smithereens as we ran them and they ran us, and pincer movements from both sides mutually broke down the organisation, ramping up the adren-alin to very satisfying levels. Smaller splinter groups would become momentarily confused, both Mancs and Scouse, zigzag-ging back into formation, eyeing each other up, trying to hear the accent, as the clothes and hair were all the same. This was the true chaotic peak of the whole Boy phenomenon, and at times like this the big danger was everybody becoming so broken up and fragmented that we all simply became individuals, merged in a bizarre geometric dance of danger beyond the group consciousness, loaded with energy and excitement. Holding the thread of organisation together in small goggle-eyed gaggles, the disciples of the Nameless Thing rode high on adrenalin all the way to Lime Street. At one point, about fifteen of us came into a courtyard in the flats, a patchwork of wedges, Fila Borgs, Coq Sportifs, burgundy and gold cords, and Adidas Grand Slam and ATPs, and about ten Scousers, convinced we were friendly, were shaking their heads at how identical we looked to them at such close quarters. They couldn't believe, didn't want to believe, we were Mancs, and they listened hard for a clue as we jogged and gestured toward them. Oh aye, we spoke Scouse alright, but it was a strange, new kind of Scouse – Scouse minus the skidmarks and the smudges, AKA pure Salford. They nearly jumped out of their skins and scattered into the further entryways, eyes popping from heads, as they clawed past each other.

We left Base Camp One in complete tatters that night. It was top. The coppers left us alone, due to the performance earlier, probably hoping we got a twatting. I can assure you we didn't. I swear I still have nightmares to this day of being stuck somewhere in Liverpool trying to get back to Lime Street with my scalp intact. I wake up sweating in the night for a piss and a drink of water to calm my nerves, wondering, *where have all the good times gone?*

Another amusing incident occurred in the late summer of 1983. It was Man U v Liverpool at OT, the very beginning of the season, and again we won 1–0. All the lads were there in their newly acquired togs, ragged from the Europe-wide free-for-all of summer or the shops down town. At the end of the game, everyone poured out of the ground and a sardine-crammed mob of literally 3,000 lads walked right up Warwick Road to the Old Trafford station, next to the cricket ground. Myself and Salty just missed a train, and the copper pulled the sliding gate shut, and told us we were shit outta luck. Looking back down Warwick Road towards the ground, all you could see was a sea of tightly packed heads, literally thousands of lads. Hundreds had just got on a couple of trains, so this was a contender for the biggest mob of boys I'd ever seen.

Anyway, the train arrives, and we jump aboard, bound for Oxford Road or Piccadilly, the usual fun and games. After a moment on the trundling train, it suddenly hit me that every lad crammed next to, in front of and on top of me, was yammering away in a Scouse accent. Oops. I stole a sly glance at Salty, who was sat opposite me, and we exchanged a grave message of secret doom. At least it explained the size of that crew back there; it was both crews together, and we'd been severed from ours into this nightmare. The dibble had pulled a blinder, not counting me and Mr Salt. When the train started to slow down at Deansgate, Salty, a Red Army veteran, made a brave move and dragged me with him. There were Scousers jumping off and dancing about on the platform, just to get away from the cramped conditions for a moment, and more than a few gave us curious looks as we smiled, swaggering casually along the platform and up the steps. Once on Deansgate, post-traumatic shock set in. Salty was disgusted when I told him I was going home, but home I went. That Post-Traumatic Shock will get you every time, if you get crammed on a train with those bastards. I must have missed a night of epic proportions in Manchester, because there were thousands of individuals at large in the city, while I was at home in Salford with my Horlicks and Mr Kipling's.

In 1981, a night match at OT against Everton, we almost pulled a clever little trick. I was split off from my mates, and found myself in an unidentified United mob. After roaming down Chester Road in a crew of about 300, we saw another crew of about 200 coming at us through the stilts of the Chester Road flyover. We engaged in the usual bouncing and shouting, as we homed in on our individual targets, on a collision course for satisfaction in this shithouse of a world. In the nick of time, we identified certain heads as United, and the two mobs joined as one. This mob then continued to search for Everton, as we knew they were out there somewhere, but were suddenly surrounded by coppers, on horses, in vans, with dogs, the monty. We were being chaperoned towards Deansgate when the main copper on the horse, asked loudly, 'What train station are you trying to get to?' We exchanged puzzled glances for a split second, before lads started shouting, 'Oxford Road', 'Victoria' and 'Piccadilly' in Scouse accents. Amazingly, the coppers started taking us to Victoria Station to put us on the platform. We planned to wait for our quarry there and give 'em a right surprise, but then the coppers worked it out, and it was chaos. Radio contact had finally established that a serious irregularity was occurring here. Apparently, a huge mob of Everton had been intercepted and was being escorted to Victoria by some other coppers and they were due any minute. The Scousers were detained elsewhere, and the coppers started trying to nick anybody who was daft enough to stand there and take it. We pissed off home, after a brief sniff around the general area. The next day at school, I found out that my mates had been in another United crew, about 100 of them, and they'd been repeatedly legged by this Everton firm.

Kenny said, 'I swear to fuck, there was this decent little crew of United, walking down Chester Road, looking for the rest of the lads and the Scousers. All of a sudden, we hear this big roar from behind us, and we turn to see a fucking massive crew of Scousers coming right at us. *Massive*. We got legged for what felt like miles, and thought we'd lost them. A few minutes later, they reappeared, and it happened again, that horrible roar and hundreds of Scousers chasing us, right down Chester Road. Where the fuck was you lot?'

I told him we were in a crew of nearly 500 lads, so many of us that the coppers thought we must be the away support walking *en masse* back to the station. I was glad I didn't splinter off into that other crew, that's for sure. Back in those days you sometimes had to walk home with the Boys just to be safe. If that crafty plan had worked there'd have been widespread disorder at Victoria.

Some time into the 80s, a mate of ours, Dave Nixon, got slashed to ribbons by the Scousers at Anfield, just walking to his car with a couple of mates. He wasn't a trouble causer. He had dozens of stitches in several cuts across his face. Mike-B- had nicknamed him Captain Pugwash due to his resemblance to the animated pirate off the telly, and after the Scouse bastards had seen to him he looked like he'd had a bad run-in with Cut-Throat Jake. It served as an illustration of the importance of being mobbed-up, because the police can't be everywhere and this was a dangerous era.

The return to Stoke was quite memorable for a couple of reasons. One, I found a gold chain with a trinket on it in Piccadilly station before we set off, and two, the walk from Stoke train station to the ground. A good few hundred lads had turned out, and after a short free-for-all right outside the station, when thirty Stoke were recipients of Manc discipline, the Viking raiding party went walkabout. The sound of windows smashing and alarms going off was all around as every shop along the way got done, and even houses. The crew was moving rapidly, and you had to make sure you kept up the pace. I was absolutely dying for a piss and the whole thing turned into a big nightmare, as you can't exactly ask 300 lads to hold on while you have a slash. Fortunately I didn't piss my pants, but fun and games meant nothing, as I couldn't wait to get into the ground and to a shithouse. Nobody was going to believe that I *found* that gold chain after that performance, though.

The vast number of shops available to Mancunians wishing to pursue the new fashions was something we took for granted. Manchester is an inordinately fashion-conscious city, and innumerable outlets for these clothes suddenly sprouted up everywhere, in contrast to Liverpool, where it seems just a couple of shops stocked the desired goods. At the peak of this unnamed phenomenon, there were tens of places we could go and buy the very, very latest fashions. Those who worked in the shops were incredibly well clued-up and they'd have the dead bang-on next style on offer in the window each day. That's right, each *day*. Some of those lads were purported to be *the* top boys; they could order the latest gear *and* nick it, too. Sometimes, you would go to town on a Tuesday night to look in the shops, simply because you might actually miss something between midweek and Saturday. Gansgear, Jean Machine, Stolen from Ivor, Oasis, Jeanery, Ellis Brigham, Austin Reeds, Hurley's, Kendals, MC Sports, Jean Jeanie, Top Man and many others began to sell only lad gear and nothing else, and the whole movement swarmed across the city in a gleeful, extraordinary quest.

In the Arndale Centre, large groups of black kids from south Manchester would often cluster around the benches, overlooking the lower level. Their gait and general demeanour was slightly different from that of the white lads. Sounds such as Kool and the Gang's 'Get Down On It', and Lipps, Inc.'s 'Funkytown' were being played in the boutiques, interspersed with tunes by bands like Odyssey and KC and The Sunshine Band. The black kids favoured the American sounds and apparel, notably basketball and baseball gear, and they seemed to foster a New York atmosphere on the city centre, deliberately or not, it was difficult to tell. They were known for grouping around outside Gansgear, and it wasn't uncommon for lads to be taxed of their new gear before they even had a chance to get home and try it on. One day they taxed the wrong lads, and Salford went on the warpath.

'The following Saturday, a fifty-strong crew of 'skinheads' went sweeping through the Arndale, twatting any blacks they saw hanging around the benches,' said Dave-D-. 'They weren't skinheads, they were the Salford Lads, who always went for crewcuts over flicks, it seemed. It put an end to the sight of black lads in the Arndale in large groups. I was surprised the blacks didn't come back at Salford the next week, but they had a lot of other places to go, and Salford didn't really hang around town that much anyway. This was a long time ago, before the two groups had a serious bone to fight over.'

Where white Liverpool lacked meaningful interaction with its black population, Manchester enjoyed a whole other aspect to their thing, courtesy of the blacks in their city. Lads of Afro-Caribbean descent were an intrinsic component of the

Nameless Thing in Manchester in 1980 and 1981. Some of the black or mixed-race lads in Prestwich, like Bri and Jimmy-S-, Kurtis, Geno, and the late, great Goodwill, were ever-presents in town and in Heaton Park, trying their 'black magic' on the girls in summer. Geno and John Clucas used to take off for the city centre during lunchtime at school, and they often returned bearing cashmere and cotton prizes. Whether it was the reggae sounds, or Joan Armatrading's 'Me, Myself, I' or Odyssey's 'Use It Up, Wear It Out' blasting out of speakers in Oasis, above the underground market, or the distinctly African vibes in the Oasis café, where Manchester City's Kats hung out, smoking pot, serving food and playing Space Invaders, the entire core of the city centre was consumed by the black take on the phenomenon. The black population in Manchester was extremely active during this whole era. They wore the same clothes as the whites, with the added tendency to sport silk teabag shirts with numbers on. Baseball bats were synonymous with the black lads, as well as the rest of the town boys, many of whom were Kool Kats. Stolen From Ivor had obtained a stock of miniature baseball bats, which were exhibited in their window next to the silk teabags and the American football jackets with the leather sleeves. It became a Perry pose all of its own to walk along in your American football jacket, vertically twirling a miniature or full-sized baseball bat in one hand. Some people even bought baseballs to go with them, but that was kind of missing the point. In many ways, it could be said that City *were* the town boys, while United sat back and did their own thing, confident that they were the true lions of Manchester. This aural blend – black American disco music, electronic New Romanticism and 60s bands – would in time spawn a second phenomenon in the city, as we shall see.

When the riots of June 1981 erupted, many stories of looting and chaos filtered out from Moss Side, and some whites even made the trek in the hope of securing a television or stereo. Every little village and centre around Manchester staged their own copycat riot of the real one on the Frontline. In Prestwich, one lad lobbed a petrol bomb at a police van, which bounced

off and set his mate's pants on fire. The whites were affecting a
rebellious stance without a cause ('rebel without a brain', as
Manny-B- called it), little understanding the decades of friction
that had led to the situation in The Moss. My Uncle Bill was the
Fire Chief of Moss Side Station at the time, and he had some
proper tales to tell. One Saturday afternoon during the riots, a
crew of hundreds of largely white Boys came together in
Piccadilly. The thing had been relatively unplanned, but the vast
numbers of young men hunting sartorial prizes in the city
centre were rapidly directed by spontaneous word of mouth to
Piccadilly Gardens for a strange get-together. There was an eerie
silence as the massive mob, both red and blue, quickly grew and
took over Piccadilly, while several coppers looked on in puzzle-
ment. The mystery was solved when a convoy of police vans was
bombarded with missiles as it made its way to Moss Side.
Obviously, certain parties had planned this, and no doubt they
were satisfied with the results. The police in Manchester easily
dispersed the mob, but it was an interesting exercise in rapid
response by the Perry Boys without any tangible enemy to fight.

There were so many shops we didn't even know the name of
that sold myriad Adidas trainers, Fila trackies, Coq Sportif soccer
shirts, cashmere sweaters, sovereign rings, etc, that a visit to town
was like a voyage down a fascinatingly dendritic labyrinth,
loaded with relevant and credible materials at every turn. We
took it for granted from then on, and why not? Little did we
know then that the fabulous choice of stores crammed with the
now well-established styles, was unique to Manchester, and it
was all thanks to the top lads who worked in them, most of
whom could be seen gracing Maine Road or Old Trafford on
match days.

7

THE NAMELESS THING
VERSUS THE CASUAL

Go and make your mistakes in the first team. You'll learn more in a
month with the first team than you will in two years with the reserves.

—Sir Alex Ferguson

AFTER MANY YEARS of ferocious battles and bloodshed between the ancient beasts of Liverchester, they turned upon and infected the rest of Ignorant Blighty with their toxic fangs – and the nationwide divvy was born (read: Casual). These later creatures were more the afterbirth than the real thing, and their comical attempts at affecting a decent walk, or accent, or determining what to wear without having to tune into *Match of the Day* with a giant magnifying glass whenever Man U or Liverpool were on, were observed with resigned mirth by the Boys. I digress, and I am cruel. But there's much I have missed out from this ridiculous genesis. Let us examine it some more.

United played a couple of alternate Saturdays at OT in the 1980–81 time segment, against Liverpool and Sunderland. Both games drew over 57,000, and the turnout from the visitors filled the Scoreboard terrace. The turnout for United, in United Road Paddock, was equally amazing, and we were on the crest of the wave, watching all these Mackem cavemen chanting and showing their colours so proud. Sunderland wore the red, white and black for us on a grey damp day, and the intensity and number of Manchester lads present at that game was beyond quantification. On the terraces, down the tunnels,

outside the ground, everywhere they swarmed. Adidas ATP,
Nastasé's, Grand Prix, Fila Borg tracksuit tops, unidentifiable
quality coats from Christ-only-knows-where, heavy flicks
framing the faces of the cherub urchins from Mamucium.
Many had chopped off their fringes and adopted the 'step' or
'mushroom' cut, which was a difficult one to pull off with style.
Some had turned to crewcuts, a Salford look. Out of the corner
of your eye, as you watched the match, was the constant
twitching. Thousands of spinal cords, variously jerking their
pelts back across the right ear, a most peculiar phenomenon. I
can still see Swifty and Goody, immaculate in their Adidas ATP
and Grand Prix: Swifty leaning back against the tunnel, flicking
his hair, one foot up against the concrete wall of the mighty
theatre; Goody, lunging about in the crowd, laughing, flicking,
shouting, the life of the party, as ever.

The previous three seasons had seen a migration from the
Stretford End. First, rumour went around that the Scoreboard
End wasn't a bad place to go; there were a lot of nutters and there
was more singing than the Stretford, as you were directly adjacent to the visiting supporters, with just that little segregation
between you. But then, some time in 1980, United Road
Paddock became the place to be, on the other side of the away
fans, across a little corner segregation. United Road ran along the
touchline (as opposed to the by-line) and as such held higher
status. Instead of paying the 80p to get in the ends, we were now
paying £1.20, assuming you were one of the lads who actually
paid. That day against Sunderland, we breathed the air and braced
ourselves against the truth; we had finally somehow managed to
outdo the Scousers, in quality as well as numbers. We were
number one, surely. This crew was outrageous. But even as we
closed in on the summit, with memories of Base Camp One
fading, we beheld a strange sight, another, distant peak, even
higher than this, shimmering and bathed in a purple haze. We
knew it was where we were heading, but that's for later.

The following season, United played Leeds on a Wednesday
night at OT, and four of us young 'uns went to Victoria Station
to see what was going on. As we rounded the corner at the top

of Chapel Street, Jimmy, a lad of mixed race, was in front and turned round to us, shouting, 'Leeds, Leeds, run!' This was a par for the course wind-up in these situations so we laughed, but as we came around the corner we were confronted by a growling mob of fat Union Jack-sporting skinheads, obviously aggravated by the sight of a small 'black' male, among other things, cosmopolitan buggers as they are, like. We all legged it. My mates went back towards Salford, but I cut round by the Cathedral, and as luck would have it, saw a crew of about thirty lads outside the old Saturdays club, formerly Pips (or was it Fridays? I forget; the brain cells are reeling, the membranes melting). I ran to them and let them know that Leeds had just arrived, and *smack!* took a belt right in the eye off one of them and a few kicks up the arse as they gravely informed me they, too, were sheep-shaggers and up for it with a sixteen-year-old Manc like myself, the game bastards. I legged it again, and met up with my mates somewhere around the corner. They couldn't believe it when I told them Leeds had boys now. Flicks, wedges, trainers, straight legs, the lot. An hour or so later, on the OT forecourt, word came in that a crew of 100 or so Leeds boys were at White City, down at Chester Road. A small platoon was despatched that way. I oversaw the proceedings as Anthropological Gazetteer, and can assure the reader I had no fun there. The Leeds crew was met at White City and disposed of like a bag of dogshit, but it was a milestone for us, to realise that now a third city definitely were having a go. It was hilarious and fascinating. I can still see Big Len dropping a sheepshagger with a blade, an awesome drop-kick in the flowing traffic on Chester Road.

On the same theme, I watched *Kick Off* one Sunday after-noon, and Villa were playing at home against someone, I forget who. At just one single point in the match, I actually saw a lad in a Villa section flick his hair. I patiently waited and then saw him again, flicking his hair and wearing something burgundy (a fisherman's jumper under an Adidas cagoule). I couldn't believe it. He was totally alone; there were no others with him, but he was there, in Birmingham, flicking his hair at Villa Park. But

does one flower a meadow make? When I met my mate Kenny
later for some skulduggery, after we'd performed our usual ritual
of running towards each other, throwing our coats off our
shoulders to reveal the labels on our shirt breasts and pounding
our fists back against our chests and outward in a manner befit-
ting a gorilla or a football fantasist, he said excitedly, and by my
expression he knew I knew:

  'Fucking hell, did you see that *lad* at Villa?!'

  I told him I had indeed.

  And then there were four. Cities, that is. For all I knew,
Sheffield may have been on it at the time. Phil Oakey of the
Human League certainly had a fringe. It was a very interesting
development. The 'three points make a line' rule was rapidly
turning into a multi-species proliferation pattern (Figure 2).

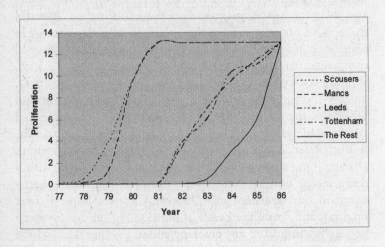

Figure 2: Proliferation patterns for the Nameless Thing and the Casual
Movement in England through the mid-1980s. Only Leeds United
and Tottenham Hotspur mounted any kind of substantial response to
the north-west in what may be considered 'real time', i.e. 1982. Leeds
exhibit proliferation across three separate exponential spurts, and
Tottenham exhibit a novel convex curve. For convenience, the author
has included an estimated curve representing the rest of the country,
which was apparently in a coma during much of this period.

As already stated at the beginning of this book, there are strange and savage parallels between the development of this whole phenomenon and the globe-shaking events at the end of the Ice Age and the transition from hunting and gathering to agriculture over 10,000 years ago. The Casual liked to give it the big arms and the flick, as he swanned along the road, but his attire was likely paid for, and was of a ubiquitous nature – every fucker had the same gear on, most of it wooden-looking pastel golf V-necks over pastel polo T-shirts. The jeans were actually the correct length, and weren't scrunched up around the Adidas at the ankle. The wedge was nicely trimmed, and not chaotic and wild as had been the lads' of yesteryear. Something was missing from the ensemble. It was called creativity, nature, spontaneity and wildness. Let's try to merge the parallels. 1980/20,000 BC: When the English Channel was nonexistent, the hunter-gatherer roamed across the plentiful savannah, plucking the colourful fruits of his endeavour from the abundant trees all around. He rejoiced in his wealth, migrating happily across the uncharted continental landscape, from clutch to clutch and herd to herd. Windows were smashed, jewels and clothing were grabbed, much poncing and posing was had, at venues the length and breadth of the pagan landscape. The merchandise was pursued and secured for the good of the emerging tribe: Lacoste, Fila, Adidas, Peter Werth, le Coq Sportif, Ellesse, Kios, Tacchini, Diadora. One strange day, however, the tribe was faced with a new concept: how about we simply plant the plants of our gathering on our doorstep (read: Decent Clothes Shops all over England) and corral the beasts of our hunting on our doorstep (see above), instead of just plucking and murdering them where they dwell, out there in the continental wilderness? The tribe began to do just that – the plants were sewn by the cavern door, and the beast was caught and held, alive, in specially-designed pens, next to the grain, the cotton, etc.

At this, the tribe realised that they had chanced upon a weird and inexplicable truth, which had implications for the history of all mankind. Their choice was clear: remain in the insular world of Scouse-Manc/Ice Age hunter private rivalry, riding the wild

frontier of a new idea/glacier, or else export this important new
reality to the rest of humankind (cockneys, Brummies,
sheepshaggers, Geordies, wurzels, woollybacks, etc). But could
these proto-scallies give up the adventure, the frolics in the
garden of opportunity, for the sake of an organised form of what
had been up to now a purely natural and free expression of their
humanity? Could they bear to be cast into a world of nine-to-
five Asian sweatshop bullshit, without the possibility of
obtaining a quality wild and original tracksuit by wits and
cunning alone, made in Europe? Just as humankind was able to
move from a hunting-gathering lifestyle to an agricultural one
10,000 years ago with the end of the Ice Age, the Boys of
1982–83 were plunged into a changing world, a world where
lads from places like Birmingham and Bristol, London and
Leicester, were able to pretend they were indulging in natural
exploitations of their environments. When the Man took the
apple from the snake, when the farmer slew the herder, when
brother slew brother and watered the fields with his blood, the
story began to be told by those who had not given it Life. This
is when Adidas and Friends saw a chance, and moved, lock stock
and barrel, to the Far East. This is the Fall from Paradise. This is
the moment when the decline in standards began: 1982–83.

I've seen it writ by another, namely Andy Nicholls in his
book *Scally*, that Tottenham brought the first cockney teams up
in the early Casual days, and I agree 100 per cent. Tottenham
came to OT in green windjammers, Doc Martens and skinheads
in late October 1981, in the League Cup, and then we played
them again in mid-April 1982, in the league, and there they all
were, in Ellesse and Tacchini trackies, black guys sporting gold
and top training shoes. It was a wondrous fucking transformation, bizarre to behold, but they'd managed it. It was a convex
growth curve and no mistake, increasing numbers that were
increasing at an ever-slower pace, due to their being surrounded
by other cockneys who represented unresponsive, stony ground.
Leeds and Tottenham were properly the first lads to formulate a
semblance of style outside the north-west, but the rest blun-
dered along soon enough. They would saunter down Warwick

Road in diamond Pringles like they'd invented fire, staring at us from the safety of their escort, until some bright spark simply lunged at the escort, roaring unintelligibly, for a nobble, and they'd jump out of their skins and fill their panties with poo-poo. Happy days. I should probably leave the remaining pages of this book blank, in protest at those young men from other regions spoiling my private little dreamland, in protest at the Asian sweatshops where third-rate clobber is being churned out for fat Yanks, fat Brits, and other athletes the world over. But I won't. Instead, I will tell you some more stories, true stories, about things that went down back in the day that not a lot of people know about. Enjoy.

PART 2

THE FALL

8

WHO CUT BOWIE'S HAIR?

I have always had a repulsive need to be something more than human.

—David Bowie

THE POVERTY-STRICKEN youngsters of Liverpool and Manchester had created a new style, one that was to catch on and be aped by others across the country, and, in time, the globe. It was incredible, but true. But how did it start? Was it really just a confluence of ideologies, the timely clashing of working class nuances, wherein Perry Boy encountered Adidas-wearing football lad, and hey presto! Or was it something more?

Who cut David Bowie's hair in 1977? What genetic lineage commanded the smooth and melodious vibrations issuing from Bryan Ferry's throat back then? Why did The Who decide to re-release the album and film *Quadrophenia* in 1979? When the bondage trousers and safety pins merged with New Wave mohair, shitstoppers and sandals, leaving a giant pause and a question mark hanging heavily over the end of the 70s, it was a moment unvarnished and Now. Just as the Buddhists instruct us to take deep breaths and to concentrate upon the moment of transition between exhalation and inhalation, working class culture in England found itself suspended, *en masse*, in this very state. It was a culture gap, a space between worlds, and those who dared lunge forward with the most plausible form of living were rewarded with the fruition of their Idea. As ever, those doing the lunging were located in the north-west of England, that mine of originality, while the rest toiled oblivious. When people are young, the things they see, especially things pertaining to fashion, are of enormous gravity, and most of the participants were exceptionally young, probably little more than eighteen years of age, if that. Many were still at school. Those children pursued their Thing with alarming fidelity, never failing in their quest for improvement on style. Outsiders fail utterly to recognise exactly what occurred during the years 1979-81. This is because they were themselves involved in previous, more indulgent and obvious forms of 'rebellion', usually lacking in social impact apart from shocking upper crust Sunday tabloid readers. Teddy boys wrecked cinemas, but their music, their focus, has been accepted as a valid and precious art form by society. Hippies ingested chemicals that distorted the mind beyond anything previously observed, but even that era has been exonerated, thanks to media figures of a certain age, their music and a prevailing tendency for admiring shamanistic practices. Punk rockers were, in time, exposed as a group dedicated to a non-violent form of peacockery, which hid behind a façade of spit and swear words, but which itself was largely impotent and subject to the plot twists of its ludicrous pop stars. It is possible for anybody to enjoy punk rock music, as it is possible for anybody to enjoy classical music, today. Both are thoroughly understood and catalogued, members of the cultural establishment.

But try to describe the Nameless Thing to anybody who wasn't there, and you will receive a base reaction to the raw violence and inexplicable lack of representation in the British media, a reaction that still insists the Nameless Thing was nothing more than the actions of criminals. In this lies its beauty. In this lies the truth that all other movements were the blind followings of sheep, of meek, pretentious, and unconscious flocks of woollybacks. Our thing was the first youth movement shaped and dictated by its participants. There was zero media awareness and therefore no famous figurehead. There was no Free Trade Hall milestone, nor were there censorship issues; in 1979, rock 'n' roll was something your parents danced to at weddings, and spitting on people was a way to precipitate a major violent assault, not a form of pretentious, wannabe

naughty boy decoration. We laughed at those harmless
dinosaurs, even as we ourselves rocked and pogo'd to their
wacky sounds. This is important. It constitutes an evolutionary
endpoint. Everything that came before was deemed irrelevant,
because it was, relative to the Nameless Thing.

I grew up in a poor family. My parents probably wouldn't
like to see it described as such, but it was. We were from Salford,
and anyone who comes from the Manchester area knows what
that means. But simply coming from Salford wasn't enough for
my old man, when it came to declaring your poorness, and
above all, your fitness for Salfordian citizenship. You had to
come from a specific quarter, a place avoided and feared by
anyone not directly connected to it. Even people hailing from
other parts of Salford, like my mate Kenny, of Annie Road
fame, failed to qualify as true Salfordians in my dad's eyes. To be
proper Salford you had to be totally dirt poor, and hail from the
network of streets that surrounded the docks and adjacent area.
This was Ordsall, Weaste, Pendleton, and the Langworthy
section of Seedley. Nowadays it is largely rebuilt, or replaced by
vast industrial and business parks, but back then it was a maze
of two-up, two-down terraced streets cloaked in a carbonised
haze that flowed in tendrils from the rows of innumerable
chimney pots. My dad and Auntie Jacqui would often regale us
with soot-stained tales from their Weaste childhood. Their
mother, my nana, who apparently had a great fondness for
money (other people's), ran endless scams on unsuspecting
suckers in their street, along with her cronies. My dad and his
sister regularly had to deliver mysteriously bulging envelopes to
equally mysterious people, sometimes even taking two buses
into the wilds of Cheshire to do so. Much money and much
mafia were afoot, and the inhabitants of this ruddy ecosystem
either ate or were eaten.

Nana opened a 'catalogue club' once, and spent several months
taking money and orders from all and sundry. No items were
forthcoming, and the dosh went straight under the lino on the
kitchen floor. When I was born, she went to Masters, a large store
in town, and had a load of stuff delivered to our house, including

a huge teddy bear, to the delight of my parents ('She's finally changed her ways'). A week or so later, my mum and dad got the bill, as she'd bought it all in their name. My dad used to have to take his baby brother's pram down to the gasworks to nick coal when they couldn't afford to buy any, which was more often than not, as my granddad was a gambling and drinking man. Everything got pawned and re-pawned and sold to different people simultaneously. When I was born, that world hadn't changed much. It looked the same as it had decades earlier. If you have any doubt whether I really had it rough as a kid, let me tell you something: *one year we went to Liverpool for our holidays.* That's right. My mother was born of a Salfordian mother and Liverpudlian father, whose family were scattered far and wide across England, but the bulk of her Scouse side still resided on Merseyside. They were from Walton and Bootle originally, but lived all over Liverpool. They were mostly Evertonian. Normally, we went for a one-week holiday, to Blackpool or Rhyl, but this occasion was special; we went for two weeks. To Liverpool.

The first week, we went to stop with her cousins in Wallasey. Each morning, I got up early and ran to get the paper with my mum's cousin's son, David, across several blue metal bridges, across docks where large boats were skulking. We always ran, for some reason. Their house was situated on a quiet road near a small field. We spent that week trolling around some local park that had a large pond and some crumbling shithole that sold ice cream. There was a swimming baths at New Brighton, that for some fucked-up Scouse reason was filled with salt water, some shops and a flea market, from where I obtained an amazing *Fantastic Four* book, softcover but as thick as any hardcover annual. We would return to my mum's cousin's house each evening and report our discoveries of the day. Christ only knows what they thought of us. I vaguely recall my old man having to return to work in Manchester, but that wasn't until the second week of our foreign tour. At the end of the Birkenhead leg of the trip, we found ourselves waiting for a bus to Liverpool on one of those overblown grand avenues on Merseyside, among a substantial margin of grass, at the edge of some massive road, along which it was difficult to imagine any bus ever travelled, houses resembling posh Manchester council jobs and lots of fast-moving traffic, while my old feller watched over the flock and my mother looked forward to the Liverpool leg of the voyage. It was a Sunday. We waited all fucking day by the side of that road, and eventually a bus came. There were a myriad of examples of this sort of thing, growing up as I did.

Anyway, we ended up in Liverpool, and it seemed the holiday had truly begun in earnest. Imagine that, arriving in Liverpool and actually believing you were on vacation. Anyway, my old man eventually pissed off back to Manchester to work. He drove emergency ambulances in Salford at the time, often in the evenings, and his tales of carnage were long and vivid. Me, my sister Jane and adoring half-Scouse mother, were left. Truth be told, my mum's cousins in West Derby (it was actually the notorious Cantril Farm Estate, but West Derby, supposedly a classier neighbourhood, was just a block away, so they claimed to be from there instead) were quite the hosts, and they provided me with a selection of cultural and social devices during that week that had eluded me in Manchester thus far, such as pen-pals. As a result, I acquired pen-pals years later in Australia and America, and vowed to travel when I was older. That week in Liverpool I thoroughly enjoyed myself, but actually came very close to being converted to a wrong and alien religion.

Apparently, Liverpool had won the UEFA cup that week, and were due to return some time very soon. Return they did and I accompanied my Uncle Joe to the event in Liverpool city centre. Uncle Joe was a rare red in my Evertonian Scouse side of the family. Taking advantage of my father's absence, he decked me out in many red and white rosettes, badges and scarves, and maybe even painted my face for all I know; I was seven at the time. We found ourselves in the heart of a vast and vociferous crowd, as the Liverpool team addressed their army, and Uncle Joe sat me on his shoulders, where I could survey the proceedings. Some distant signal, some psychic lighthouse of the spirit, held me firm that night, preventing me from being corrupted by the Scouse agenda, instead guiding me back safely to the rocky coves of Salford, and United. Uncle Joe's evil plan was thwarted by true love, thank ye fates.

The next few years saw me sink from being a normal kid growing up in poverty, to being an expert shoplifter (chiefly books, having read everything the children's section at the local library had to offer, and which, having read, I often returned), to being quite determined to live as I saw fit, regardless of lack of money. In Liverpool, my Uncle Joe had given me an assortment of books to take home, recognising an inquisitive mind that went unnoticed in Salford. I cannot put a number on the books I lifted over the years. Let's say it was around one million. Ditto booze. A mind is a terrible thing to waste, is it not?

My parents made a mistake common to most working class parents of the day; they compared what my sister and I had with what *they* had when they were kids – fuck all. This made what we had seem better. Kids these days live in a computer-generated wonderland, but our childhoods were a distinctly charcoal-coloured affair. For a weekly treat, Jane and I were allowed a single yoghurt or mousse each, from the fridges of Kwik Save, and that was that. It was something to look forward to. My mum worked on school meals, and used to bring home food in steel trays, croquettes crammed next to jam sponge. The croquette took on the flavour of the dessert, and vice versa. It was a standing joke in our house that it looked like the first course but tasted like the bleedin' second. I'm surprised we didn't turn into croquettes, we ate that many of the bastards. We were regaled every Christmas Day with the same grim account of the 'apple and orange and last year's *Beano*' that the adults had received as kids each Christmas, as we gazed forlornly at our own prezzies: secondhand bikes. And compendiums of games. And tape recorders, and table football, and TV games, and selection boxes, and board games, and records and clothes. And. And. *Who am I kidding?! We had it great as kids!* There's no substitute for being loved by a big, close family, and all the money in the world won't change that.

The first time I had sense enough to receive clothes that weren't replica United kits as presents, aged thirteen, I got expensive shirts from Top Man: a thick French Connection No.2 of herringbone brown/purple cotton, and a top button-down collar job made from interwoven orange and green cotton that almost had a two-tone effect. I also got a Fred Perry, all black, no stripes. The old man was aghast at the price tags, but he knew the score. I was wearing one of those shirts when the Scousers approached us on the Stretford End in early 1980, and its quality had doubtless called to them like a beacon. Back in the late 50s, Dad had been a top teddy boy, and often would describe to me the difference between what the 'real' Teds wore and what the 'other' Teds wore: subtle aspects of the seams, the shape of the pockets, the length of the jackets. All those years later, he still spoke scornfully of those who didn't wear the proper tackle. Life is a cartoon, and we are genetically identical to cavemen, destined to repeat the ageless patterns of the species. It's true.

Salford is where I originate, and I'm proud of it. I come from an area known as Langworthy, where all the streets were named after different trees — a metaphorical jungle. Laburnum Street, off Langworthy Road, is an area so fucked that by 2000 it was described by HM Government as having Third World health and poverty levels, so beneath and beyond that it didn't even count as part of the mythologised Hanky Park it once rotted next to. My mum comes from Hanky Park. My dad comes from Weaste. I spent years prowling the brickish matrix, among the cobbled entryways and Morris Minors and stray dogs, in the two-up, two-down redbrick labyrinth just outside the city centre. The opening credits on *Coronation Street* actually show the streets I came from, but they in no way do them any kind of justice; the brainless arseholes responsible for those scenes need a swift kick up the shitter. The rows of chimney pots looked down like terracotta sentinels upon all activities in the streets. We adorned the paving stones with coloured chalk, and picked the black pitch out from between the cobbles on the road on the hot summer days, using it to make models with, or to eat. We called liquorice 'Spanish', sherbet 'kay-lie' and carbonated drinks 'mineral'. My cousins lived a couple of doors down the street, and we would regularly sleep over at each other's houses. My Auntie Viv, my mother's sister, was as much a mother as my own; it was that kind of family. Auntie Viv was always larger than life, and remains so to this day. Nothing gets her down, and she lives for her family. More cousins lived behind us, in neighbouring Fir Street, and the same relationship existed; my mother was as much their mother as their own. Growing up, I had no sense of blood ties, even when it came to aunties and uncles on the in-law side, because everyone was so close.

As a kid, I helped my Uncle Dave pluck the feathers off wood pigeons he'd bagged with his shotgun, and sat on my dad's knee as he let me drive his milk float around the streets in the snow. We would walk around Salford Market up the street, eating baked spuds from paper bags, or trek to Ordsall to visit still more cousins. Ordsall was another world back then. The smell of exotic ships from faraway places wafted on the air, and the docks were alive with traffic. Sailors, the world over, knew what it meant to drop anchor at Salford's 'Barbary Coast', with its gigantic dancehalls, rowdy pubs and even rowdier ladies of the night. The grim thunder of systematic demolition was often in evidence, as Manchester's ambitious slum clearance programme picked up steam and entire terraced streets, factories, churches and rows of shops were crushed by the knockout ball. They were driving us out, in order to erect the notorious towers. What had been close-knit community streets were being converted to vertical 'streets in the sky', the actualisation of some idiot socialist vision by middle class 'revolutionary' Leftist cunts. Some of England's most genuine souls were forced into a multi-storeyed, zoo-like existence; the bulldog spirit of D-Day was smashed and sold to the highest bidder, becoming a pile of bricks next to a fire in a dustbin.

We would climb among the grey brickish carnage and cluster around the workmen's fires, the aroma of fresh toast on the air. Each evening, everyone would sit outside, with the kids all lying in their doorways, drinking in the sights and sounds of the street, like little cats at the openings to a network of stony caves. We were all buzzing with the news that The Man had come to destroy our ancient home, like Afghanis in the face of Uncle Sam, and like

those people we had our own heroes who would strike back
against the tide of cheap shit they were trying to lay on us. The
women would gab about the changing vibes in the atmosphere,
and the men would return from the alehouses and set upon each
other viciously, swinging their docker fists and hobnail boots in
an orgy of unbridled violence. The cobbles ran red with the blood
of hapless citizens, there in that herringbone warren where the
heart is, but it was all in the name of honest bloodlust. The donkey
stone was always hard at work, ensuring the front steps were
turned out a treat, and the recycling rag-bone man would come
round every week with his horse and cart, to snap up anything no
longer wanted by the denizens of this beautiful ecosystem. It was
an immaculate life, described with an immaculate accent, by
immaculate people, smack in the middle of Britain. There were,
of course, certain parties who it paid to avoid, people who were
'bad', who would make you disappear if you fucked with them
too much, and everybody knew who they were. But in time they
would become our militia, our last cry against the might of the
British system – and they would rise to power in a way so natural
that we knew it was justice. Salford would not be kept down, and
we cheered them every inch of the way to glory, for they were
our flesh and blood. The society within this world was stratified
and complex, bristling with dynamism and cruelty, fascination
and love. Love, love, love. Oh aye, I'm a Salford lad, to the marrow.
It is the country of the Gifted.

And then, when I was four (and five, and sixteen, and eighteen
– we moved a *lot*), we moved away from there, to a new house.
Housing prices had plummeted dramatically, and my parents saw
their chance to escape the inferno, to a brand new house that
seemed false and plastic. Ironically, Laburnum Street escaped the
projects, and remained as an eyesore for decades. We lived there
for a few months, before moving again, this time to Prestwich, 'the
country' as my mother amusingly put it. After spending my first
several years on the planet surrounded by extremely busy roads,
Prestwich did seem quiet; you could literally lie down in the
middle of the road in the middle of the day and be undisturbed
for a long time. This was a habit I acquired early on, and one

which stayed with me until adulthood, usually when intoxicated. Prestwich offered greenery, fields and trees, and small creatures. When my nana, who by then had been involuntarily catapulted to the eighth floor of a Salford tower block, visited us, and heard my mother comment on a hedgehog in the back garden, she said, 'Oh, a hedgehog. Whose is that?' How we laughed.

Prestwich has since come down in the world, and I sometimes wonder if our moving in there didn't mark the beginning of the end, as it were. When we moved in, the area was occupied by a mix of genteel English and Irish folk, of distinctly middle class persuasion. Without realising it at the time, we tended to hang around with those kids that were also spilling in from the urban core, as they spoke the same as us, and more importantly, thought the same as us. The year before we moved there, Kezz, his brother Brian and family had arrived from Moss Side. Later, my cousin Trev and his family, exiled to a maisonette in Cheetham Hill from Ordsall by the knockout ball, moved into a house a few doors down and the place was never the same again. Cheetham Hill was closer than where Kezz and I had come from, but still a world away. Around the corner, Kenny and Pete Lewis had come up Bury New Road from Higher Broughton, and there were many others in the area. There were also quite a few local lads, like Paul-L-, Dave-D- and Rob Tyrell, who were only too happy to wreak havoc on a daily basis. Prestwich was an unspoken overspill town, being annexed by those with the sense and scraped-together funds to enter the realm of private ownership. But you can't take the Salford out of the people. We were almost an ethnic minority.

When our washing machine broke, I was given the job of humping loads of heavy bags of washing round to a launderette that felt like miles away. Sometimes I'd have to carry the bags in relays, running with one, dropping it, then quickly running back to hump the rest to where it was. It took ages to get to the launderette, and I was such a good little worker that the washer stayed broke for over a year! I don't remember receiving a single penny for my endeavours; it never occurred to me I might deserve one, even though the bags were almost as big as I was.

The gentle people living on the street would twitch their curtains as I lumbered by with my Herculean cargo, probably considering phoning the welfare to report child cruelty. Cousin Trev and I would go round, nicking empty mineral and beer bottles out of peoples' porches and sheds, and take them to the corner shop for the deposits. We'd wait outside the shop's back gate a while, and the shopkeeper would put them outside with the rest. Then we'd climb his back gate and nick them again, before returning to the shop for more deposit money. If we left a respectable number of bottles there for 'flash' purposes, he wouldn't notice, and some nights we'd be in there five or six times, with the same bottles every time.

The two of us, along with Dave Roberts, my stowaway buddy, also used to steal men's magazines. Trev would go in, sneak one off the counter top, pass it to me at the door, I'd pass it to Dave outside, and he'd run off with it. We developed an unwholesome appetite for *Rustler* and *Men Only* at a very tender age, but the thing we went for most was toffees. The newsagent and the cake shop sold loads of these, and along with Kezz and his brother Brian, we regularly steamed in there and blitzed the place. We'd run off up the street and divvy up a gigantic pile of sweets on the pavement, away from our parents' watchful eyes, laughing at how easy it was, while the ever-twitching curtains silently observed.

Our accents resounding in the roads of Prestwich must have come as a shock to the dialect-conscious British judgement merchants already living there. As the years wore on, more and more people from Salford and Manchester moved in, and the suburb rapidly became a memory. As we had played unaware in the woods, the roads were widened, and the population had exploded. The roads were not so quiet any more. We had turned the place into an arm of the city. By the time we were in our early teens, we had left tree climbing, frog catching and skate-boarding behind. Clothes were the passion, and Prestwich was a leader in Manchester.

9

ADIDAS BLACK SHADOW

I have been through some terrible things in my life, some of which actually happened.

—Mark Twain

THROUGHOUT HISTORY, there have existed mythical, semi-mythical and legendary specimens, fragments of a fantastic other-world that were reputed to dwell in this one, often giant beasts, magicians, 'little people', superheroes, or sacred stones. Inane commodities we confront in our daily lives are often named after these fabulous and unlikely beings and objects; people will want to own them, imagining that they possess the qualities inherent in those fabled things. Names such as Pegasus, Cyclops, Wizard and Warrior are attached to products by manufacturers, in the consumer rush to fill the hole inside, that which threatens to engulf us should we neglect to feed it.

Then, of course, there are the non-mythical beings and animals and stones. We have football superstars, who command fortunes and legions of berserk supporters; we have creatures such as the giant squid and the blue bear, living things that populate the extremities of our planet, in deep ocean trenches and glaciated wilderness; we have the Rosetta Stone, which enabled archaeologists to decipher the pictograms of ancient Egypt and solve mysteries long believed unknowable; we have automobiles, powerful and sleek, bearing names like Silver Spirit, Interceptor, Pontiac and Silverado...

And then we have Adidas Black Shadow.

Rumours of the existence of the Black Shadow began circulating through the labyrinthine ginnels and walkways of Liverpool
and Manchester in early 1981. Most were dismissed as myth. In
that whooshing whorl of new discoveries every week, it wasn't
unusual to catch whispers and fragments of non-existent training
shoes, tall tales spun by mischievous scallywags for a bit of sport
with the more serious collectors. The Black Shadow, however,
came to be more than some beerhouse/terrace fancy; it destroyed
young men who foolishly insisted on embarking upon brave
voyages to seek it out. It acquired a sinister power all of its own, a
dark pull which threatened to unhinge the most reasonable of lads.

Sightings of the shoe were rare, but reported faithfully by
those observant or obsessed enough to have apprehended it. The
original story was somewhat difficult to believe, due largely to
the style of clothing allegedly worn by the man in the Black
Shadows. According to popular accounts, a stranger approached
a group of young men on a Liverpool (or Manchester, take your
pick) street corner, wearing a black shirt bearing a black paisley
pattern in relief, matching trousers and a hat (also black).
Descriptions of this hat vary, from a fez to a ten-gallon, and are
generally considered unreliable. During their brief conversation,
during which the unknown gentleman asked for directions to a
local landmark, the young lads noticed that he was wearing a
striking pair of all-black Adidas trainers.

The trainers were apparently of soft, black, unfinished leather,
with black stripes of an almost imperceptibly different shade of
black to the rest of the shoe, also unfinished. A thick rubber sole,
panelled and intricately grooved to differing depths and other
specifications, apparently composing several strata of different
material and colour, was securely sewn and glued to the uppers,
with black stitching around it, in a charcoal-coloured groove at
the very top. The strata were variously (top-down) charcoal,
caramel, cream (thickest layer), black and deep chocolate brown,
and appeared subject to different degrees of compression and
overall flexibility. The arch of the sole exhibited a novel
contoured effect via the sole's colours, as its topography
described a smooth curve into the differentiated depths. A small

rectangular panel completely transected the side-sole, made of an unspecified transparent, prismic rubbery material, not unlike a superball, which apparently contained very small, three-dimensional moulded plastic Adidas logos set in various orientations. A tiny and peculiar array of Adidas logo shadows issued forth from this panel onto the floor immediately adjacent, due to light passing through from the other side of the sole. Witnesses claimed that the panel itself appeared to contain a small light, enabling this effect even during the hours of darkness and apparently powered by photovoltaic compounds embedded in the prismic rectangle. The uppers featured an unassuming toecap, of uniform material to the rest of the shoe. The middle stripe of the three had the words 'Black Shadow' cut out of it, in reverse (mirrored) on the outsides and correctly on the arch side of the shoes, revealing the black leather beneath it. The other stripes contained tiny geometric shapes, also cut out. The edges of the stripes were perfectly straight, and appeared to have been fashioned from considerably thicker (approximately a quarter of an inch) material than usual, most likely a form of high-grade pig or kangaroo skin. On the heel, the Adidas logo appeared on a piece of shiny, black, finished leather, in a dark mustard colour, along with the words 'Black Shadow', again in reverse. The tread resembled the tread of a tennis shoe, with hints of hiking boot about it, in the chocolate brown bottom section of the sole, and in the centre of each sole was a plastic dark mustard Adidas logo, with 'Adidas' under it, in black.

The stranger was purportedly requested to remove a shoe, in order that the lads inspect the interior, and in some cases obliged, with the expected results; the interior of the shoe was as luxurious and complex as the exterior, a highly-organised foam and leather configuration, designed to provide maximum comfort to the wearer, be he playing sports or climbing a strange and vicious mountain.

This description was put forward by several individuals, quite independently, in the late winter/early spring of 1981, spawning a search that broke hearts and minds. Some lads began to miss important fixtures to follow the trail of this legendary shoe to

places like Beirut, Palermo and Marseilles. By far the most
contentious issue in all this was a burning drive to discover what
exactly was printed, or sewn, on the *tongue* of these things, as this
detail had not thus far been reported. On 4 June 1981, three
young men, two from Liverpool and one from Manchester,
wired an urgent telegraph home to the lads, stating that they
were almost upon their quarry, down some filthy entryway in
the heart of Sao Paolo, Brazil, and to expect scores of Black
Shadow in the post soon. They were never seen or heard of
again, according to rumour. A young man named Danny
Holden, a six-foot four Salfordian with hands like bunches of
crowbars, allegedly wrote a letter to his girlfriend declaring the
shoe to be in his possession, somewhere in the desert outside
Cairo, in late June of that fateful year. Two months later, his body
was delivered to Manchester Airport under armed guard.
According to those in the know, the coroner reported no immediately apparent cause of death, other than the remnants of a
charred and melted piece of leather and rubber that had
somehow been rammed up his anus and set alight. No commercial or industrial laboratory in the West was able to successfully
analyse forensic samples from this unidentified object with
certainty. Five Pakistanis were supposedly discovered in a warehouse in the Ancoats district of Manchester, their throats slit,
hanging by their feet and bled like halal turkeys. Close by, a
number of Adidas shoeboxes were piled in a heap, their unusual
black colouring spangled with a curious array of inlaid holo-
graphic Adidas logos, from which issued an unearthly inner
light. No footwear was located in the area.

Grisly stories of discoveries like these were not uncommon
during this dramatic and mysterious period. Reports of Black
Shadow sightings continued to trickle into the network, while
an army of policemen, scallies, private detectives, weirdos and
freelance mercenaries worked around the clock to put the lid on
the affair. They say Adidas refused to comment on the ruckus,
stating that they were in no way obliged to divulge trade secrets,
while le Coq Sportif, Puma, Diadora, Dunlop and even Gola
demanded answers.

Stories of how certain Top Boys owned a pair of this legendary shoe were to be expected. Some reckoned that the infamous Everton pair, John Hopkins and Ray-B-, both owned a pair of Black Shadows. Some Manchester City faces, notably members of the Kool Kats, were also said to have been seen in them, always under difficult-to-prove circumstances, in fleeting scenes that provided no solid evidence. Tony O' Neill is said to have worn a pair of Black Shadow as he led the Men in Black against West Ham on the Night of the Balaclavas – and that account comes from West Ham themselves (typically years after the fact)! All in all, over seventeen young men supposedly perished in a three-month period in 1981, and the mystery was never solved. Who was that shining stranger? Was he ever real? The great search was disbanded in November 1982 after a fruitless quest spanning seven continents, and the phenomenon consigned to the filing cabinet of history. Some of the hardcore original lads often discuss the phenomenon of those Missing in Action, but currently all is quiet on the Western Front. The Adidas Black Shadow: now there was a trainer.

I know; I started that rumour myself, and my cousin in Liverpool helped me.

10

THE RED ARMY SEGMENT

I never lie because I don't fear anyone. You only lie when you're afraid.
— John Gotti

IN THE 1970s, North Manchester became a sprawling, multi-level neighbourhood composing various maisonettes, houses, factories, and high-rise flats. The area had its own character, its own identity, a palpable presence around a section of the city centre circumference. Victoria Station and Red Bank gave way to Oldham and Rochdale Roads, on the very edge of Manchester's inner-core, and finally to the weird, non-commercial dereliction of Stevenson Square, whose unvarnished architecture defied geographic analysis. The Square sat in a clearing surrounded by a variegated network of offices and workhouses, through whose windows one might glimpse women operating bizarre machines, or faceless men in suits making notes in the harsh gleam of industrial lighting. Traffic ran non-stop through the illuminated artery of Great Ancoats Street, circumnavigating central Manchester in a trice, bestowing on the jaded locals a larger than life intimacy with their 'little' city neighbourhood.

The general attitude exhibited by the inhabitants of this ultra-urban slice was a tough-nosed proclivity towards actively attending boxing clubs and engaging in barbaric pub crawls through the sinister, endless tangle of council houses and deserted industrial open spaces directly adjacent to Oldham Street. An unquenchable need for laughter, and to be spattered with the blood of one's neighbours, was tempered by a complete refusal to accept the poverty of their lot. The windows of the Collyhurst high-rises, a five minute stroll from Piccadilly Gardens, cast a white, inhuman beam onto the commercial and residential buildings basking in the Mancunian rain, below an illuminated white sheet of aerosol hanging in the endless traffic like a linear halo. In the pubs there sang vociferous militant units of flat-nosed, lightning-fisted red devils, snug from the lashing cold air behind the tight doors of their strongholds, where it seemed everybody knew everybody else.

Smithfield Market, a hive of colourful industry smack in the middle of the area, operated on its own time schedule and provided fresh meat, fish and produce to its population, as lively as any Neapolitan arcade, where Mancunian Irishmen would tip a measure of port into a pint of Guinness on their lunch break at four in the morning. Glaswegians rubbed shoulders with Dubliners, who in turn might enjoy a drink with the odd Welshman or Geordie. A self-contained, tight-lipped world clenched its teeth like a seasoned fighter on a rock-hard caramel toffee from an old drum of Quality Street. Empty crisp bags took mere seconds to ride in on the gritty winds from Piccadilly, like tiny, crumpled plastic tumbleweeds through an urban cowboy landscape. Its jurisdiction ran from those hard caramel city precincts of Ancoats and Collyhurst, through the rain-drizzled streets of Miles Platting, out through Harpurhey to the dovetailed concrete and grass of Blackley. The Blackley area at the time resembled a pseudo-Mediterranean layout, especially in the summertime, as the new red, white and grey apartment blocks would shimmer next to the vegetation sprouting between shops, flats and parks. The corrugated topography, coupled with its beehive architecture, promoted the liberal 1960s dream of a Britain populated by happily thriving apart-ment-dwellers who, despite the fact they were paid fuck-all for what they did, were deliriously content at all times. The vigorous local squadrons rejected this fairytale, and attended Manchester United games on a weekly basis as a regiment, fending for themselves however they could.

The giant high-rise complex known as Salford Precinct was constructed in the 60s and 70s, a couple of miles from Old Trafford, and populated by thousands of United fans, as well as people simply being shat on by the British Government, minus the redeeming experience of watching the mighty reds. It was the west side version of the north side jungle, only with more concrete, if that were possible. Tower blocks stretched across several acres, some with balconies, some without, looming tellingly beside the Manchester skyline. If Blackley was pseudo-Mediterranean, Salford Precinct was pseudo-Manhattan. The estate and its surroundings bristled with innumerable renowned fighters, capable of giving as good as they got, regardless of the opposition, in the Salford tradition. As in north Manchester, several motley battalions were scattered loosely all across Salford, from the Precinct and Eccles, to the estates and high-rises in Ordsall, Weaste, Langworthy, Broughton, Greengate, Duchy, Walkden, Little Hulton, Kersal, even beyond to the glades of Prestwich and Whitefield. It was a primeval outlaw brotherhood, nurtured by generations of Salfordian-Mancunian poverty, stubbornness, and humour. In the world in which they developed as individuals, it was inevitable they would go to the match and become addicted to the molecule called adrenalin.

Salford was always notorious for its criminal families, and its ominous code of silence was the traditional alternative to urban north Manchester's hard-bitten caramel. The boys who patrolled these two dovetailed segments of inner-city Manchester regularly attended 'Gentlemen's Mornings', when hundreds of roaring Red Army storm-troopers would assemble for drinks and entertainment, provided by ladies and whoever fancied joining them onstage for fun and games, while the laughing legions watched. It was a reward for upholding the values and keeping the mob together, not an easy task. Nobody ever thinks about how these phenomenal groups maintain their intra-personnel adhesion. There is no official building, no retirement plan, and no guarantee of anything; there is just the enticement of the game, and the game is all that matters. The game includes everything from the twenty-two players, to the jib on the train and turnstile, to pacing oneself on the ale as the day progresses.

The two giant-sized urban segments became acquainted partly through attending matches at Old Trafford and beyond, and their respective divisions and corps quickly galvanised into a like-minded force, dedicated to taking on the locals at away games. This became the considerable mob of now well-known Salford-north Manchester allies. Many of these individuals were involved in martial arts and boxing circles around Manchester, and through some unknown agency allegedly became proficient in the Brazilian fighting art, capoeira. Various anonymous claims supporting the fact that these lads had mastered the Latin American slave discipline caused the legend to grow. People started to talk about Brazilian Jiu Jitsu, and inevitably the opportunity for exploiting a psychological advantage was seized. When some of the boys began to assume the distinctive stance of a martial artist during certain face-offs, and you obviously flapped, the joke was on you. These soldiers were truly of the warrior spirit, often attending away matches midweek in tight-knit platoons and engaging in violent confrontations with locals after invading their pubs and taking on large numbers. That they actually returned from a lot of these situations relatively unscathed earned them a fearsome reputation outside Salford and north Manchester, but inside the area was a different story – the harder you're supposed to be, the longer the queue of lads wanting a pop at you, and most of those in the queue were reds. It is surely the case in all truly tough areas of cities. Salford and north Manchester are not completely unique, just a lot bigger than most other cities' *unified* regions. It is mainly from this extensive sprawl around a sizeable chunk of Manchester that United's notorious boys hailed. Other cities, such as Liverpool, Birmingham and London, certainly had the rough areas, but somehow they lacked the numbers and the consequent grit that this crew possessed. When distant, riotous council estates like Wythenshawe and Langley were added to this already monstrous equation, the result needn't be writ here; you know, and you

don't need me to tell you. This crowd were the English analogue
of the Riffs, or even the Gambinos.

As the 70s entered the Perry Boy era, the Red Army's own
Style Commandos changed the uniform, bringing knocked-off
trainers and tracksuits back from Germany and France and
selling them to the hungry infantry back home. The new look
was somehow easier to appreciate and aspire to, and many
youngsters were enlisted overnight, drawn from the various
paddocks and the Stretford End, taking their positions in the
thick of the action. The Red Army veterans, those who'd seen it
all during the 70s, wore the continental fashions almost
begrudgingly; they were there to hold the corps together, not to
fuck about posing in daft clothes, and they were truly wolves in
sheep's clothing, older and stronger than their teenaged
brothers-in-arms. This swollen mob, the hardened Old School
on the front-line, backed by legions of wedge-headed Perries,
waged a holy war on the rest of England, for, as the 70s' slogan
stated, MUFC was a *religion*. Dozens of willing participants,
many of them equal to most other teams' so-called 'top boys',
were to be found at the head of United's mob in 1980. They
rampaged through cities far and wide, dragging their young
lieutenants, captains, sergeants and designer urchins with them,
and the list of charge sheets from police stations around the
country was long indeed.

Members of my battalion included Big Col, the athletically
overweight plasterer who bought a double-decker bus, which
he would pilot to the away matches, often illegally down the
motorways, crammed full of the crew. When United played at
home, this orange and white double-decker would strike fear
into the hearts of wandering visitors when it trundled into view
on a search-and-destroy mission, obviously not following any set
bus schedule. If first glances did not suffice, the sight of the bus
executing a *Starsky and Hutch*-style U-turn upon sighting a crew
of visiting lads left one in no doubt as to the nature of its occupants, who would disgorge onto the street with various and
frightening degrees of athleticism, not least the driver. Col
weighed over twenty stone, but his ability to vault high obsta-

cles, sprint at near-Olympiad speed and play a graceful game of football, was legend.

There was also Danny Barton, AKA Scorpo, who began travelling to Germany, France and Holland in search of designer gear as early as 1977. An old Bowie disciple, Scorpo is credited with being the 'first of the Perry Boys'. While this title is somewhat erroneous, it is a fact that he was sporting a Northern Soul-style 'French wedge', Adidas tracksuit bottoms and training shoes long before anybody else. His ability to con and rob people was legend. He went to a small women's hairdresser on the corner of a terraced street in Kersal, Salford, and requested his hair be cut in a wedge, with an auburn rinse and blond streaks, in late 1977, and the fringe was massive, almost as long as Phil Oakey of the Human League. His effeminate appearance disguised his toughness – he was known for being able to handle himself, but rarely fought. The familiar sight of his bandy legs, often in colourful cords, and the bizarre tone of his rough-arse voice, masked a brilliant mind that never missed a trick. He once removed the plain rubber soles from a pair of casual corduroy shoes, replacing them with those from an unknown pair of Adidas. It is said that the fastener-stitching was immaculate, a combination of scarlet and gold thread, matching the gold corduroy of the uppers and the red piping around the ankle of the shoe with uncanny accuracy. The son of two cobblers, Scorpo actually constructed a sports bag from a particularly supple and fragrant piece of tan Italian leather, using a Stanley knife and his mother's sewing-machine, in 1978. He personally screen-printed a logo of his own design onto the front of the bag. The logo was of a peacock exhibiting several multicoloured scorpion tails, with the words 'Scorpio Detox' underneath it. The leather handles of the bag were sheathed in a knobbly rubber made from the handlebar grips of a tracker bike, multi-coloured to match the tail of the peacock. This bag was the first of several vehicles he used to stash his amazing rarities, but he progressed to bigger things in time. There was a story circulating in the early 80s about how Scorpo and a Scouser bought a little boat, which they used to bring various forms of cargo from the Continent back to England. Allegedly, the Scouser knew how to pilot a boat, having worked on the docks, and the two met in Brussels on a robbing spree. Scorpo had relatives living in some little village in Pembrokeshire, and they would use the private coves there to load vans full of stuff. Quite a few Mancs and Scousers were involved in this little scheme, and a constant turnover of mad-heads was heading for the Continent and returning, while the little boat made its way back and forth across the Channel. Needless to say, the mob was a well-dressed one.

When the crew began sporting polo shirts and Stan Smiths in late 1979, Scorpo was already wearing suede cardigans by unknown Italian and French designers, rare Lacoste corduroy pants, as well as Fiorucci jeans and Kickers. He'd been there, done that, and sold everyone else the T-shirt before most people in Manchester and Liverpool had seen their very first Perry Boy.

There was a certain breed of lad about at this time, known as a 'waffler'. They were people who talked a lot of shit about away games and battling, but who made it all up. Clive-S- and Goody were ever-presents on the bus, and they were not wafflers but great non-fiction storytellers, pure information merchants. The beauty of Goody was that he had done the business, and he delivered his stories like a professional, much better than the tight-lipped battlers, but with greater skill than a waffler. He delighted in informing the younger lads in the neighbourhood, those that hung round the off licences and rows of darkened shops late at night, of the amazing exploits of the crew around the country, but especially on Merseyside. They were responsible for keeping the bus stocked with fresh faces, as the Nameless Thing exerted its massive pull on youngsters in the 1979–81 era. They made it all seem so much fun, because it was, bar the odd unfortunate mishap.

Jason-L- was by far the most troubled of the crew. He was basically a dirty bastard who liked to spit, piss, shit and puke on people. He called shitting on people 'giving a ring sample'. He even wanked all over some Italian fans at Juventus in 1984, long after our era was over. He was never arrested, but probably should have been for several reasons. He was a familiar sight, in piss-stained burgundy jumbo cords three years out of date and a faded blue snide Adidas four-stripe cagoule, worn for a laugh, flicking his considerable blond fringe frantically, eyes darting this way and that. He actually acquired the cagoule from a skip in back Piccadilly, after wearing another Adidas five-stripe for years. His only attribute was a head of fine hair perfect for flicking, but his wardrobe bespoke The Divvy. He didn't give a fuck. But twisted? He'd decided, in early 1980, to be the hero of the divvies, by insisting on wearing their sub-standard gear with impunity. In fact his overall agenda was to create a divvy army who weren't scared to use a blade, but it never happened. Occasionally at matches, the chant, 'Jason's Divvy Army!' would issue, but it was a joke between the lads and never caught on. The truth was, Jason was an interesting head but totally opposed to the paying of exorbitant sums of money for clothes that had been copied quite faithfully and were available at a discount by lesser outfitters. Funnily enough, his brothers ran a couple of sweatshops that manufactured vast quantities of snide gear of every stripe you could possibly imagine. It ran in the family.

Jason carried a blade and was apt to use it if necessary. It was just in his nature, unfortunately. In the midst of the action, it wasn't unusual to see the enemy suddenly scatter, melt into nothing, even when the lads were heavily outnumbered (that's the way they liked it), the words, 'Fuck! They're carrying blades! Run!' resounding down the street. Jason would calmly put it away, usually having wiped it clean on someone's face, hair or clothes, while the crew berated him for playing the shithouse card. When the shit hit the fan at Diamond Lil's in Blackpool in the summer of 1981, however, nobody complained about the badly-dressed weirdo with the carpet hook Stanley knife who sliced Scouse flesh with abandon. Jason became an enigma, even to lads much more capable than he. He disappeared in 1985, supposedly abroad, but some claimed he'd been done in by gangsters on a contract after slashing the wrong face in a brawl.

This author often reflects on all the kids in his neighbourhood from the distant past that were part of the football experience, all of them total Perries in the springtime of their lives. There was nothing evil in it, it was a way of getting yer ya-yas out, and all growing boys need that. Paul-S- worked in all the cutting edge shops, and wore the extreme latest gear spectacularly, setting trends everywhere he went. He was a big lad who did weights (like a lot of them), and nobody wanted to ever get on the end of what he had to offer.

Bowie, a crazed protruding monster at about six foot seven, literally stood out in a crowd. He would drink himself into a frenzy, and be seen everywhere – in town early doors, at the bar in the ground, at the station later on, stumbling and leading all the songs, with his auburn-rinsed flick and a demented gleam in his eye.

The magnificent Kezz made the decision to jump ship sometime in 1980, and sprang, catlike, into the depths of the United experience, leaving the City boys behind and embracing the fun and games with that immaculate athlete's gait. He was another you didn't fuck with, and you prayed you didn't accidentally step on his trainers on the terraces.

Dave-D- maintained his habit of prolonged continental voyages, and his motto was, 'You've got to keep moving.' He certainly kept moving, and was always there when the chips were down, popping out of the woodwork unexpectedly at badly-attended games, before disappearing for years to a faraway island in the sea. There are many more, but words cannot express the bond you develop as the memory matures and peers back with a ruddy eye. They are all grown up now, but they were, and remain, the lads I stood with, drank with, went utterly fucking berserk with on occasion, and I love them all.

The rest of the bunch were a bizarre collection of proven hard-cases, science fiction buffs, drunkards (goes without saying), intellectuals, conmen, drug dealers, thieves, ufologists, tradesmen, New Age hooligans, dossers, musicians, poets, beggars, businessmen, burglars, travellers, boxers and, above all, comedians. If you lacked the ability to make people laugh, you went extinct. That's the single biggest indicator that Mancs and Scousers are originally derived from the same genetic stock, by the way. You Brums and Geordies and what-have-yez can be funny at times, but you're not professionals, let's face it.

By 1983, many of this gang declined to attend football matches as nutters, and turned their attentions elsewhere. Many continued to attend matches, but restricted their movements to a booze and a song and dance. Some inevitably left the country, while others went into legitimate ventures. Others drifted into one or several aspects of the Manchester drug/gang scene, with predictable consequences: bother, and lots of it. The culture in Manchester pushed us all into certain avenues, and many grafted on markets, selling everything from china plates to video recorders at mock auctions in dodgy Moss Side pubs. The concert swag game and the hotdog stands were always possibilities, as were the transportation of machines necessary for manufacturing snide textiles. But whether the boys ended up knocking out timeshares in Tenerife, or taping acid tabs to their inside upper lips in Amsterdam, they were all committed to one very important mission: the worship of Manchester United.

There were other mobs following Man United at this time, but the one described above was among the originals. They were driving to Liverpool on school nights in 1980, in a car crammed with headers, just for the thrill of walking into a Scotty Road newsagents at 8pm and asking for a 'Manchester Mars Bar, please…', for a bit of action with the beloved enemy. A lot of the other United lads knew them but, as ever, at a club as big as United they were just another brick in the wall.

11

COCKNEY KRYPTONITE

*It was severed at the bone by a machine, a machine the likes of which
had never been seen before.*

—Dave-D- referring to a marijuana cigarette in his pocket,
broken during the chaos of a typical Saturday evening

THE FIRST FA Cup Final I remember watching was in 1975:
West Ham v Fulham. We were at my nana and granddad's flat
in Newbank Tower, Salford, up on the eighth floor. My granddad
was a kind of Alf Garnett: he lived in a tower-block, had a bald
head, and was conservative and patriotic, thanks to spending years
as a tail gunner in the RAF's 'Brill Cream Boys' during World War
Two. The only difference was, he was from Salford, which made
him even more Real McCoy than any Alf Garnett in my book.
He'd had a bet on West Ham to win 2-0, with Taylor scoring both
goals. I sat with my dad, granddad and Uncle Geoff and watched
the match, and the men, cheering as the Hammers beat Fulham
2-0. Taylor scored both goals. Whether it was Tommy or Alan
Taylor I forget, as both were playing that day, and my granddad
gleefully realised that he hadn't specified which man he had his
money on, so he was getting two odds for the price of one. I fell
in love with the FA Cup that day. I liked the way West Ham
played. Like United, they seemed reckless at times, and regularly
went on attacking runs into enemy territory without heed for
their own defence. Off the pitch, I had no idea that they were
considered hooligans, like United. To be honest, it didn't matter
to me. The football was what it was all about.

But beyond the football and hooliganism, there was a regional rivalry that I only became aware of as I aged, a rivalry that fired me up outside sport, outside music, outside everything. It was based on a mythical and ridiculous border called 'the north/south divide'. It was invented by morons, for morons. The British media has forever been centred in, and kissing the bottom of, London. It's as if only things that happen in London are of any importance, and anyone wishing to make a living in this field must bend over and take their medicine, regardless of where they're from and whether they believe it. The British media has long been a disgrace and an embarrassment and is only now starting to pull its head from out of its arse and smell the provinces. Though I suppose if the British media had been at all clued-up, it is possible that those exciting underground years in the north-west might never have happened at all, because everyone would've known about the style revolution, so we at least have that to thank them for.

If you were told of a small army of faceless, chinless men in suits, who lived like rats in the tunnels beneath Big Ben's tower, desperately trying to compete with the continental giants like Italy, France and Spain for cultural supremacy by essentially robbing and stealing anything in the UK that was worth a wank and relocating it to the London area, would you believe it? If I were to postulate the existence of a clustered group of shivering mongrels, all preoccupied with getting in with the French while disowning the Hovis hillsides, who sometimes even drank red wine down the boozer to that end, and who inexplicably believe that average temperatures in England vary by as much as ten degrees as you pass the Watford Gap, would you call me insane? If I informed you that there are hominids alive today who firmly believe it is better to live in a rat-infested council hovel within a fifty mile radius of Buckingham Palace than a stately mansion house in deepest Cheshire, would the yellow van be at my door? If you find a Roman sword, bejewelled and splendid in your back garden, keep it to yourselves, and show it only to closest friends, my little devils. Fuck the National Trust, for they are part of the conspiracy.

* * *

In East London, there was once a man named John Smith. He was an Englishman. A fine head of mousy hair, jagged cheekbones, blue eyes and a donkey jacket black as coal bespoke his West Ham pedigree. Smith polished his Doc Martens religiously, like a mountaineer on the eve of an assault on Everest, an assault that was for some reason always postponed. He was quite an expert on the various species of the AirWair boot in that golden decade, 1973–83. There was the cherry-red, with the yellow stitching round the sole, and the black trim around the top, with eight holes, with that sacred yellow and black tag protruding from the top at the back. Or the brown, with the white stitching round the sole, and the dark brown trim around the top, with ten holes, sacred protruding tag included. Or the black, with yellow stitching round the sole, black trim around the top, and black soles. Then, of course, there were the alternatives: Major Domo's, for instance, brown, with the square toe, and most important of all, two rows of stitching describing an arc around the lower heel, as opposed to the single row of stitching on Doc Martens. Then there were Sergeant Pepper's, red, or black, with four rows of stitching arcing back from the bottom of the laces to the sole (as opposed to just three rows on Doc's) midway back, and very pronounced yellow stitching around the thickly ridged soles, slightly higher than Docs, and Colonel Cherries, with their – well, you get the point anyway. He kept his donkey jacket hung behind the kitchen door, always available in case someone was taking liberties and needed their legs slapped.

The divvy analogue for these bovver boots (i.e. the Dunlop Green Flash to the Adidas Stan Smith) was the 'monkey boot'. No cockney lad (not that they used the word 'lad' – they ridiculed it – until around 1998, when it became fashionable) would be seen dead in a pair of divvy monkey boots. He might not have managed any O-levels from school, but he was an educated man, with knowledge of where (but not what) the Stock Exchange was, and how far Buckingham Palace was from his council house, to within one-tenth of a mile. His dad had measured it in the motor when he was a kid, to show him how classy he was. And it was a nice motor, and all. He knew that you didn't put red wine in the fridge, or foil in a microwave, though he couldn't name a single variety of French wine and he didn't trust microwaves. This unique combination of culture and technology was pure English genius. Not like them northerners. They didn't know nothing. John Smith had memorised fourteen different sayings that he could recite at will, that sounded well sharp and happy-go-lucky, making him appear quite an alert character, despite the utterly dolorous and suicidal atmosphere in which he'd spent his entire life. He'd also memorised several terms from the financial world, such as 'investor relations', 'world indices', 'preference shares', 'foreign markets' and 'mutual funds', from a piss-stained investors' pamphlet which he'd had his nose ground into in an East End gutter during a particularly eventful Saturday when 'Man U' were down. He perfected a real cockney accent, quite easy living as he did in East London, and attended Upton Park on a weekly basis, with the rest of the Real McCoy Englishmen of this world. Upton Park was a fortress of Englishness; they would fight you on the beaches if you ever even thought about coming there, you soft poxy wankers.

Not far away lived another Englishman called John Bull. John Bull was short and muscular, with a skinheaded skull and a green windjammer, with high turned-up jeans and steelies. He was not shy about sticking the steel toe-cap into the boat race, was John Bull. He was Millwall. He'd never been up north, but he knew it contained a lot of big geezers who were nearly as hard as he was because they were braindead, but nowhere near as educated, and their dicks were a lot smaller. He had read that in a survey in The Sun. Southerners had bigger dicks. They'd gone round and asked blokes all over the gaff how big their hamptons were, and it turned out southerners' were massive, and northerners' were dead tiny. It made sense; northerners were too stupid to use rulers, so had probably fucked it up. Too honest and all. They didn't understand the appliance of science. Not like Chelsea, who lived across town, but who had taken the Stretford End back in the day. Not bad for a bunch of West End mouthpieces.

Bull and Smith were true Londoners – they didn't have no respect for fashions and politics – they just knew what sounded and looked right, and that's what they stuck with. Them Tottenham were trying to be Scousers or Mancs but the real London boys didn't give a fuck. They were Cockney Fundamentalists, suicide bombers of terrace style, and they didn't care, so long as the barbiturates didn't run out and the illusion could be maintained. Until one day, when someone pointed out that

London was full of backward, slovenly, wallowing, unoriginal skinhead punk puppets, who were in dire need of a clue, and all of a sudden, the whole stinking place erupted in a frenzy of shopping and preening, which lasted a while but was irrelevant as it was four years after the fact.

When the Cockney Fundamentalists finally managed to work out the basics of style, which initially took the form of the most obvious article of clothing able to be identified from the other end of a north-west football stadium – the Day-Glo diamond Pringle – they went to great pains to advertise the fact they'd finally arrived, while simultaneously pretending they'd been there all along. In Manchester in 1980, we had an expression for lads who neglected to attend the match in their new clean gear, with no intention of ever getting any of it dirty, especially in the course of fun and games with the enemy. For these merchants, the clothes were just clothes and the more noticeable the better, hence the ridiculous vibrancy of some of the colours. We called these lads Tonka Toys, as opposed to Town Boys, who were the denizens of the city centre, the Perries. These cockneys in their diamond Pringles were several notches in credibility below the Tonka Toys, who were at least part of how it all began. Being cockneys, though, they quickly mastered the genre and became its chief purveyors. Within a year, they had taken credit for its invention, dictated what the next big thing was, and declared themselves the top boys, over the likes of Everton and Man United. They stamped their authority on the issue, by giving themselves official names, like the Inter-City Firm (ICF), the Headhunters and the Bushwhackers. This proved how much better organised they were while reflecting the panache of the Capital.

The Government became involved. It became mandatory for all members of the ICF, Headhunters and Bushwhackers to attend weekly martial arts classes, as well as boxing, wrestling, and weight-training, by order of the Prime Minister and the head of the London Underground. The top lads from these clubs were also ordered to attend schools with the finest Milan and Parisian fashion models, to learn how to walk out of the tunnel onto the terraces at places like Anfield and Old Trafford, where they had a long history of being scrutinised and mocked mercilessly. The south-east hadn't spent the past several hundred years stealing every invention, archaeological find, and architectural innovation and bringing it to London, without letting this little blot on the north-west landscape get by unnoticed.

The television documentary Knockers, screened in the 80s and again in the early 90s, told the story of a group of Hammers fans out to make some shrapnel by going door to door selling cleaning supplies to women. To some, this may not have been the best advert for the hardest firm of geezers on the planet, but never underestimate the swag you can put your mitts on selling dishcloths and mops. One of West Ham's top boys owned an enormous castle in the Home Counties, with a large pool in its central courtyard. The sides of the pool were transparent, and could be viewed from a luxurious subterranean lounge beneath the castle. On a Sunday afternoon, it would be packed with the cockney cognoscenti, sitting at tables in the lounge, watching the sport: crocodiles versus rottweillers. This bloke would half fill the pool with water, so part of it remained terrestrial, as it were. Then, from two separate tunnels, the beasts would be released. The bloodbath was bet upon, and the resounding roar of the cockneys could be heard for miles as they cheered on their respective favourites, while tucking into pumpkin-lobster ravioli in pink sauce, Chateaubriand steak, followed by opera cake, washed down with that week's Beaujolais Nouveau or 20-year-old Pinot Noir. They were a proper rum lot of tasty-looking laughing cavaliers, untouchable and magnificent. The lad who owned the castle was the Official Hardest Man in Britain, and received recognition as such from Queen Elizabeth II (reluctantly; she's a United girl through and through, but it was for the good of England), on May 1, 1985. He was well top.

The cockneys not only became the world's leading practitioners of the fighting arts, but they also discovered new ways of interacting with their environment. Telekinesis, telepathy, gravity-wave propulsion, and electromagnetic manipulations hitherto unknown, all featured in their vast repertoire. In fact, members of the United States Government requested an audience with London's top boys, for advice on how to master and subdue an enemy. It is believed that the mysterious Philadelphia Experiment, which entailed the teleportation of a US Navy vessel from one coast to the other in an attempt to render military hardware invisible during wartime, was supervised largely by senior members of the Chelsea crew. The Star Wars programme is rumoured to have been designed and ultimately controlled by several Millwall heads, who revealed many secrets to the Americans, such as how close to their rotting tower blocks Buckingham Palace was, and the fact that you *should never put red wine in the fridge, because the French said so. A top-level West Ham think tank was credited with back-engineering captured UFOs in the New Mexico desert, by cracking the telepathic blocks the aliens themselves placed in the path of earthlings trying to discover their technology. Three of West Ham's top geezers offered to step outside with a top alien, a little fellow about three foot two, weighing around thirty-five pounds, for a set-to on the cobbles. When the alien acquiesced, and stepped towards the door, the three laughed, and decided to let him off; they were gentlemen, English and proud of it. They would never take advantage of a little chap like him, even if he wasn't from London. The ICF educated the Americans in many cultural fields, such as stating that Beethoven was a really good musician, that the game of chess was played by very clever people, and advice on pronunciation of the first ten digits, in French. America's cultural coming of age was facilitated by these fascinating and vigorous young men from the capital of England. Having officially named the phenomenon the 'Casual Movement', these young gentlemen wore Casual jeans, Casual jumpers, Casual shoes, Casual T-shirts, Casual hair, and exhibited a cool Casual attitude. They certainly had generated a mysterious je ne se quois, had they not?*

The three mobs received billions of dollars in payments from the CIA in exchange for their knowledge, with Chelsea's famous taking of the Stretford End often being cited as the most excellent example of the appliance of advanced technical know-how. Several of the main lads from these three exemplary firms received Congressional Medals of Honor from the President of the United States. When the Gulf War offensive was launched against Iraq in 1991, several top boys from West Ham and Chelsea directed operations from orbiting space stations high above the earth, using their advance knowledge to further the spread of freedom and capitalism across the globe. Millwall declined to supply their services, as they were opposed to the war, stating that it could only lead to 'a fractionized globe wherein civilisations are overly demarcated, leading to increased conflict and, inevitably, instability on the stock exchange, wherever that is'. That's right. Millwall didn't actually know where the Stock Exchange was, never mind what it was. But they did know of its existence, and at least they were opposed to the war, an attitude which turned out to be very fashionable, which is what this book's all about.

Soon after, West Ham also severed relations with the CIA, citing their English gentlemanliness as the reason; they didn't like being part of a bullying campaign against people who lived in the Stone Age, 'like northerners but with better weather'

Chelsea, being from outside the East End, had no such scruples. Chelsea declared that they would suck dogshit through a pair of Maggie Thatcher's old knickers if it meant a bit of success. After all, they were the Man United of the south. Success was owed to them, and they were prepared to bend over and take it hard up the passage from whoever would come along with whatever ridiculous and inappropriate agenda, just so long as they could pretend to have been a successful club for a while.

★ ★ ★

That, at least, is the Cockney Casual Foundation Myth. And as for the hooligans who follow the England national team, they embody the nationwide divvy (read: Casual) in all his glory. Scousers and Mancs receive hostile treatment from the rest of England's support for reasons that go back longer than soccer travel hooliganism or possibly even the game itself. Without seeming over-dramatic, the north-west has always represented a credible and intelligent cultural alternative to London, one that not only openly disrespects the 'authority' of Cockney Fundamentalists in matters of culture, but one which actually challenges it, and has done since the early days of industry. When the industrial barons of Manchester opened up their mills and crammed them with bread-and-water-supplied peasants, and cranked out goods and made themselves more money than any individuals thus far seen on this planet, including all the kings, emperors, sultans and Caesars, London was only too happy to rub its hands and rake in the taxes, along with the global market domination and enhanced credibility as a force to be reckoned with. The machines that were conceived and built in Manchester at this time were beyond anything before imagined, much less operated, independent of our then very grotty little capital. This triggered the single greatest population explosion since the shift from hunting and gathering 10,000 years previous, and it was all due to those machines. London saw in the magic of Manchester nowt but cash.

But when those Mancunian pioneers began to name their streets and their stations Oxford, London, Piccadilly and Victoria, London wobbled a bit. When those same individuals then began to import all the art and other cultural treasures, such as the great works of European painters, and the Hallé Orchestra from France, London erupted in a jealous frenzy, intent on preventing Manchester from gaining cultural credibility over the south-east. The first thing they did was impose a tariff on imported grain, making it scarcer and inflating the price, to the benefit of the farmers of the south-west, thereby enabling the wurzels to sell grain at higher than natural rates, and consequently stopping the industrial barons from supplying their peasants with 'free' food and water, as had been the custom until that time. The peasants now had to buy their own bread, and those barons were petitioned for higher wages in the face of more expensive corn, and the whole shebang generally fucked up Manchester's productivity, while the London snakes slyly grinned.

It doesn't take a genius to guess that people working in mills in the north-west of England must have been somewhat light-fingered in those dark ages, and that many of Britain's poorest peasants were walking about in cotton garmentry never before seen on the backs of average English folk (does this ring any bells?), and that in time it became known throughout the land that the denizens of the north-west were privy to something new and exciting in the rag trade. The rest of the nation's peasants caught rumours and hoped for a glimpse of these cool customers should they by some accident venture outside that north-west progressive zone. Unfortunately for the rest of Britain, the only travelling these simple folk did was when they were transported in the filthy holds of ships to America, where they operated those same machines, in newly-built mills in the north-eastern United States. They were the only people in the world who knew how to control these machinations wrought by the Mancunian visionaries, and were a valuable commodity in the building of the American Dream, out there on the frontier as ever.

Manchester was termed the 'engine room of the Empire', as it churned out ideas and products that gave Britain purchase on all terrains, across all continents. In time, north-west culture, especially its music and football, grew to be the most successful and powerful in the nation, if not the world, both in terms of glittering silverware and finances, with the help of the best-supported clubs in England, Manchester United and Liverpool. The resounding success of these clubs, coupled with the regional proclivity for sharpness of mind, innovation and style, set them apart from those other clubs, who were supported largely by young men considered backward and old-fashioned by the Manchester and Liverpool contingents. Incentive to travel to England games was very low, as the England team was not just unsuccessful – itself unacceptable to Mancs and Scousers – but the atmosphere at the games was crap. How can a young lad, raised amid the flowing pandemonium on Liverpool's Kop, or the effervescing, ear-drum smashing chants on Manchester United's Stretford End, extract even an iota of joy standing next to awkward-mouthed Brummies, substance-lacking arrogant cockneys, the ludicrous 'lad' mimicry of Leicester, or the harsh, inappropriate snarl of the Leeds sheepshaggers (hate-filled, Mancunian child-batterers)? It is fair to say that Mancs and Scousers are able to stomach the tones and humours of those such as wurzels from the south-west (despite the corn issue of old), Geordies, Mackems, and others from Sheffield, Lancashire, and Cumbria, for this crowd are down-to-earth northerners with a reasonable sense of humour, from places where technology is tempered with wine, laughter and song, and has been for thousands of years.

Those kids from the frothing cauldrons of Old Trafford and Anfield were no angels. The slums of Liverpool and Manchester are legend when it comes to tales of organised thievery, and the ability to seize something for nothing, even in the unfamiliar arcades of foreign countries. That dressing smart was only one aspect of what came to be called the Casual movement was lost

on the cockneys will continue to be a thorn in their side – they
were too busy admiring their nice new Pringle sweaters while
around the corner, Mancs and Scousers were having a jeweller's
or a sports shop off, as they had since the very beginning – and
for nobody does this fact burn more painfully than for the chaps
of London. Their response is to manipulate the rest of England's
support into believing Mancs and Scousers are not 'true'
England fans, because their clubs have been too successful, their
support too numerous, and their atmospheres too, too rare.

The fact is, many of England's travelling army find themselves dominated by the Cockney Fundamentalists, paying all
kinds of homage to the men from Waist Aim, Miwwoah and
Chewsoay, in some bizarre and unnecessary hierarchical dance,
designed by cockney conmen to soothe their own insecurity.
The boys from the north-west, from the only region truly fit to
be capital outside London, where the most successful and
honestly wealthy football clubs England has ever generated
reside, are incapable of bowing to these Pygmalions. Not only
are they not fooled by the tough-guy cockney accent, but the
undeniable fact, that the north-west are streets ahead of the rest,
will always prevent Mancs and Scousers from stepping into line
behind the cockneys, even if it means stepping into line in front
of everybody else.

The David Beckham scandal in the 1998 World Cup was a
perfect example of how the country can go wrong. Simeone
was a diving twat, and everybody saw it for what it was. Yet
everyone who wasn't a Man United supporter went ballistic at
Beckham's sending off and blamed him for the failings of our
sadly overworked and interpersonally estranged national side.
The visit of United to Upton Shitehole was typical of the attitude of sad cockneys with no life, hungry for a subject to abuse,
as they held up their plaques and chanted their patriotic hearts
out. Time, however, is the great healer. England supporters have
changed since 1998, and the whole Manc-Scouse versus
England thing has been digested by all, and even the Londoners
have developed an appreciation for the causes of it. They have
recently woken up to their own failings, and some have even

accepted their place behind Manchester and Liverpool in the line-up. But many haven't. If I were from London, maybe I would myself rummage through the vestiges of self-respect that were available to me, and try to convince myself, and others, that things were not as they really are. There are many sets of rules and many sciences in this world, but Londoners seem to think they're above them all. The bottom line is, if you haven't got a prize-winning cucumber down there, don't wear tight leather pants. The truth is this: *We from the north-west will never really be able to know what it feels like to come from a capital that is only just a capital. We only know what it feels like to come from a region that has done the work of a capital but remained a province. But this will not keep us down – for nature is as nature does.*

In the summer of 1979, when I was 13, my family and my cousins' family travelled to Lowestoft in East Anglia for our holidays. We stayed on a caravan park called Shitehaven which turned out to be full of cockneys and boring as fuck. At this point, we were wearing shortish hair, faded semi-flares, Levi's shoes, Gola trainers, cotton cricket jumpers, round-necked plain T-shirts with coloured trim, Adidas T-shirts, etc. A lot of the lads back home were wearing black Adidas trainers by then, but we were too skint to participate, hence the Golas (this was right before we decided to take without paying), and the Fred Perry was slowly trickling in. The cockneys on the campsite were something else, peacocking around in punk rock mohairs and John Travolta black cap-sleeved T-shirts, eliciting masses of giggles every time they passed my mother and auntie. The cockneys thought the women were giggling because they fancied them. It was a twisted and fitting introduction to the nature of the English condition; it put us very clearly in the picture of what *wasn't* going on in the capital in 1979.

There was a youth disco on in one of the dining rooms every night. We were forced to attend the first one by our parents, despite knowing on some gut level it would be full of Hersham Boys and other Fundamentalists, all labouring under illusions of southern superiority. Inside the disco, we slowly made the acquaintance of various cockneys, who were all still into the punk look. They had a brilliant sense of humour, and it was fascinating to listen to their stories of life in the metropolis, one of the world's greatest cities. They told us about punk rock in London and we listened with intent, as they definitely knew what they were talking about. Myself and my cousin Trevor had attended the youth club discos and various trendy cafes for those wagging school, mob-meets at fashionable shops and scally get-togethers at the footy back home, for the past several years. We had participated vigorously in the various dance crazes associated with the musical phases passing through Manchester at light-speed during those strange years. The local punk dance was known as The Kick; a frenetic arms-and-legs-kicking depiction of a vicious assault, which we preferred to the boring pogo. We had a number of rock 'n' roll dances – inspired by old films and the movie *Grease,* which everyone did for a nobble at discos. We had a post-punk New Wave dance, rocking back and forth, with occasional slow kicking, which we would do to songs like Elvis Costello's 'Oliver's Army', which many mods would adapt later that year to the sounds of Secret Affair and Mods '79, before they were murdered. And, of course, when we felt dead grown-up, we occasionally danced disco, to the black-American New York sounds snaking their way across the Atlantic. This latter musical form was a rare business. David Bowie and Roxy Music were merged among all of this, unaffected, undiluted and streamlined towards something totally unplanned and spontaneous... The Boys.

The fact that the cockneys were still pogo-ing to punk, even those several years older than us, was troubling. One night, I got sick of watching them making cunts of themselves and launched onto the dance floor, doing The Kick to Sid's 'My Way' just as it went into the faster segment. I was always a dab-hand at it, and though I hadn't done it in a year or so, I managed a great show, as Cousin Trev later confirmed. I went hell-for-leather for the remainder of that song and into the next, whatever it was. Trev laughed his bollocks off in the shadows while I did the business. A few minutes later, and he got up himself, and gave it plenty, as the cockneys watched. The following night, when the

Stranglers 'Go Buddy Go' started, some big cockney, about nine years older than us and probably the biggest, oldest kid on camp, in army pants and jumper, launched himself onto the floor and aggressively asserted his patch, awkwardly performing The Kick like it was the first time, ever – it probably was, for him. For the remainder of that week, we sat and watched cockneys try their luck at The Kick. Occasionally we would both get up and do it, when they lost their way, and then sit back down again to give our subtle judgements, like Little Caesars bringing civilisation to the barbarians. I don't know if such a dance existed in London at the time, but these lot certainly had never heard of it, and they were from all over the capital.

We decided at one point to have skinhead haircuts for a laugh, and T-shirts printed, despite it being a big no-no back in Manchester. After a trip to the camp barber, I made a Sex Pistols and a 'RIP SID' T-shirt (the 'I' forming the centre of a cross made from the two words, thereby getting two letters for the price of one), and I think Trev made a Buzzcocks T-shirt, from the camp pick-and-mix-letters T-shirt transfer counter. The cockneys were awestruck. Apparently it hadn't occurred to them to make such statements using the camp T-shirt transfer shop. We wore them every night at the disco but threw them in the bin before we left for Manchester.

If you are a Londoner, and have made it this far, please allow yourself a few minutes before continuing with the rest of the book, assuming you haven't already set fire to it or launched it through a window. London is a big place, and undoubtedly one of the world's greatest cities, and I believe its people are big enough to take this chapter on the chin without too much difficulty, especially as I have tried to be as amusing as possible. As a United fan, I am aware that a significant portion of our support comes from the London area and that over the years the Cockney Reds have provided the boys with no end of intelligence and physical support in their quest for Empire. When the Nameless Thing first escaped from the north-west, much of it flew direct to London, on the wings of the Cockney Reds. The lesions and slashes endured by the Mancs at the hands of the

Mickeys were analogous to the lesions in the muscle of a weight trainer, or the lesions in the muscles of a chick's wings as it pushes its way out of the egg; they make way for more muscle growth, more strength. Cockney Reds returned to the capital with their knowledge of our thing, and they allowed their London brethren to spread their wings – and finally the world knew about this thing of ours, broadcast from the capital of the world.

Cockneys, by which I mean real cockneys, and not some Home Counties dickhead with a half-mastered accent, are a source of pride for all Englishmen, including myself, and I love nothing more than to listen to those wonderful tones of proper cockney. The comedian Mike Reid springs to mind; an accent like that can only come from somewhere that's been very busy for a very long time. The British class system revolves around the way we shape sound waves with our tongues. Take a white man from deepest Salford, dress him up in a smart three-piece suit and briefcase, and send him into a professional building to speak with the people in there. They'll wonder what he's up to. Take an impeccably-spoken black man, dress him up in rags, give him a bottle of meths and sit him outside a train-station anywhere in Britain, and have him ask passers-by for spare change. They'll wonder how this poor chap ended up in such a state. I'm not saying Britain ain't got racial issues, but we judge by accent, above all else. When I say 'proper cockney', I mean those who, if put in a tailored business suit and sent into a professional building in Liverpool, would still come across like a gangster. In Manchester, there are people who'd be more inclined to compare the Union Jack to a bulldog's arsehole than a shining star, but cockneys are an enigma to us all, and that's not something I ever want to see go away. *You were the ones who sent the Nameless Thing worldwide.*

12

INTER-CITY INTERLUDE

Yer Scouse bastards!

—John–B–, to bemused Chelsea fans, wearing a flat cap,
pissed as a fart and somewhat confused, at Old Trafford

LIVERPOOL HAS ALWAYS been a loud city, and every
Scouser seems to know every other Scouser. All want in on
the conversation. Someone's always letting on to someone else,
usually across a crowded exterior vault, itself swarming with
more Scousers. There is much clamour, as that distinctive un-
English accent is slung around, like a rag soaked in human fuel,
splashing its enthusiasm on those present. The mouth of the
Mersey is always etched in the background, wide and flowing.
An armada of black cabs floods the streets like rolling pebbles on
an oil-hit beach. A constant, rapid interchange of ideas echoes
from the walkways and arcades, onto the ferries to Ireland and
Wallasey, and of course the pubs and clubs; all are saturated in
that Scouse sunshine, and the clatter of Liverpool beer on darkly
varnished tabletops, the patter of Scouse feet along the balconies
of inner-city flats, and the inevitable roar issuing from Anfield or
Goodison, exude a consistent spectrum of peculiar opinion.
Life's little ups and downs provoke the lightning impulse toward
humour, mocking this monkey existence, this smithereen of
temporarily conscious material called Humanity.

Mancunians have been known to write letters to the
Manchester Evening News, urging fellow Mancs to make a noise,
to be loud, Scouse-style. This is not a reference to the atmosphere

in the two cities' respective football grounds (the football grounds are no contest; United is King), but an observation of simple day-to-day life in the city centres. Walking around Manchester city centre, you might encounter the odd kerfuffle, but Liverpool is one *big* kerfuffle. Manchester has a big-city feel, with its sprawling and variegated architecture, but Liverpool is somehow more human. The greater anonymity afforded by the more metropolitan Mancs also confers a certain reserve in its denizens. Not so in Scouseland. Manchester's pandemonium occurs all around the inner-city, in the markets, the estates, pubs and factories. Once you hit the fringe of the centre, it seems to die. This is the cost of doing business. By mid–1981, the Nameless pandemic was simply another factor in the equation, but its ubiquity was the perfect compliment to a terrace-full of cheery Mickeys, all sporting wedges, chirruping across to each other like a clan of mischievous meerkats. The lads were every-where in the constant dark of Boxing Day clashes, filtering into the grounds, Mancs and Scousers, Scousers and Mancs.

While many north-west match-goers have fond memories of people-watching back then, very few decent photographs of these lads exist. Dave Hewitson described the difficulty of freezing these moments for posterity:

Cameras were a rarity, but someone would borrow one from their dad if they could be trusted. There weren't many teenagers whose first thought was to purchase a new Kodak Instamatic. Taking a camera to the match wasn't the coolest thing to do, and getting the mates to pose for a picture could be quite trying unless they had a few beers in hand.

Those who ended up with the camera weren't experts and many pics that did come back from the chemist were blurred or the lads were too far away on the picture. Luckily, a few pics have survived the years and can be viewed with interest. The clothes and styles are there for all to see, and the trainees are sometimes visible. Dates and venues of the pics can some-times serve to define a moment in time, and anyone who knows the script will always spot an out-of-order pic.

Munich 1981, for instance, was the time of the Adidas Trimm-Trab, and late 1980 the time of Adidas Tennis Comfort, a strap-over trainer. Another strap-over came in in 1983, Adidas Tennis Supreme. Those with the foresight to take a camera to the European games must be complimented. Without pictures, words wouldn't mean as much.

No wonder the bastards went mad for my Adidas Easy, acquired May 1981 from St Tropez. The bloody animals had never heard of them.

One reason for the strange absence of photographic evidence of these styles is likely to be that its proponents were mainly urban working class kids, whose parents only ever bought film for cameras during family holidays and Christmas. Most were at that age when appearing in a family photo seems uncool, so that added to the problem. Finding so few authentic pics actually serves to authenticate the roots of this underground movement. Punk rockers appear on postcards, teddy boys and mods featured in their own movies, as did the beatniks and the bikers. Hippies are practically revered these days, in the form of innumerable music videos, but these young Scousers and Mancs are an endangered species. Such is often the case with the animals bearing the coolest-looking pelts.

Money for travel to away matches was also scarce, and hitching was the cheapest mode of travel. The Liverpool Machine was now well and truly on the road, and tales of Transalpino rub-outs, stolen match programmes, women of the night, forged match tickets, hoisted cigarettes, perfume and booze, 'free' hotel rooms and bar tabs, plus, of course, designer clobber, became the norm. The jaded Scouse mind needed a new plaything, and the advent of sportswear provided it, according to Hewitson.

Liverpool has always had a reputation as the best thieves and scam artists in the country, and many European cities would be put to the Scouse acid test. From way back in 1976, when lads had returned with stolen leather box jackets (called

'Roxy jackets' in Manchester) to the zenith in the season of
1980–1981, the clothes really picked up, and this didn't
escape our notice. Because we'd been ragging Europe daft for
years, it was really the clothes that became a focus. Everything
else was old hat to us by the time we discovered Lacoste and
Fila. And then we fell into a deep fascination with all this
specially designed stuff. The arches in the insole of the
trainers, the extra row of stitching around important seams,
the composite rubber soles of the tennis shoes, it was a
science lesson as well as a Viking raiding party. Lads would
have conversations about specific aspects of a tracky top, or,
especially, a type of training shoe sole. There were so many,
and they were all interesting to us.

There were definitely competitors to Adidas during the
1979–1980 period, but by the beginning of 1981, Adidas had
regained its crown as the must-have name for footwear. The
new Adidas being sported on Merseyside by a select few had
never been seen before. They had obviously been acquired
from abroad, narrowed down to Germany after further
enquiry. One of these shoes was the Adidas Tennis Comfort,
with the Velcro straps. They were so original that the shops in
Liverpool would be inundated with requests for anything
without laces. As a result other companies began manufacturing strap-overs, such as Donnay, Patrick and Puma, but the
Adidas were the ones everyone wanted. People were trying to
buy summer tennis shoes in the middle of winter, and as soon
as it rained you ended up on your arse. These things really
were designed for dry weather, and we learned the hard way.
It was all worth it, to be walking around Anfield with these
gleaming strap-overs on, with all the boys staring at your feet,
and one or two daring to ask where you got 'em from.

The 1981 European Cup Final in Paris offered another
chance to experience some European hospitality. They were
giving it away, believe me. After a fruitless quest to locate
the (we realise now) mythical Adidas Centre, there wasn't
much to show for the visit to Paris, so we decided to steam
across to Switzerland for the England-Switzerland game

two days after our Euro conquest. The match was in Basel, right on the German border. A short twenty-minute walk across the border to the land of Adidas saw us in business once again.

We stumbled on new and amazing trainers, and vowed to catch them all, like a mob of professional butterfly collectors. Our prizes weren't getting pinned behind a glass showcase, though; they were going straight on the feet, and scuffed up all across the continent back to Liverpool. One of the best was the Adidas Grand Slam. A lot of money had obviously gone into the design process. Different coloured shock absorbers had been inserted through the body of the sole at the heel, the heads of which protruded on the outsides; one red, one white, and one blue. You could put them through the heel in whatever combination you preferred, as they offered different degrees of flexibility. I'm not sure if the different colours themselves possessed different physical properties, but the number of pegs you used would determine how the shoe felt underfoot. I remember having to pay £35 for them, and my arl fella said, "*How much*? I could buy a *car* for that!" A tool was included in the purchase, to remove the pegs. But after all that excitement, the Grand Slam only lasted a few months, before the heel wore away where the pegs went in. My mate Eric was on the same trip, and he bought a pair of Grand Prix. He asked the German shopkeeper could he pay in francs, and thinking he meant Swiss francs, she said yes. He gave her French francs, a blinding move, as it meant he'd copped for a brand-new pair of Grand Prix for about £2.50. That was our cue for a sharp exit across the border back to Swissy.

The England game was a predictable nightmare for anyone dressed decently; there were cockneys everywhere, knocking ten tons of shite out of anyone who wasn't a cockney, after the genteel Swiss failed to muster up any kind of firm. It happened in the ground, at the end where all the cockneys were, and lasted most of the game. We bunked into their main stand, and luckily I didn't have to work out which pegs to throw in my Grand Slam for giving it toes, as the cockney bootboys never sussed us.

While in Manchester innumerable shops were now stocked to the gills with much of this sportswear, Liverpudlians found scant domestic relief from their fever. Expeditions to Manchester had proved quite dangerous, but worthwhile, and then a shop opened in Liverpool that became a goldmine. 'In the winter of 1980, Robert Wade Smith attempted to have Adidas supply his Adidas concession store in Top Man with the trainer Forest Hills,' said Hewitson. 'There were five hundred pairs in the country at the time, which had been sitting in a warehouse for nearly a year. Eventually, in October, Wade Smith received just ten pairs, which went on sale for £39.99, a ground-breaking sum at the time. They were all bought within days. Wade Smith had proven his own hypothesis that the Liverpool punters were willing to pay a lot more for a rarer and different shoe. Now for the remainder: Wade Smith received the other four hundred and ninety pairs in the run-up to Christmas, 1981, and they were gone by Christmas Eve. His reward was a bottle of whisky. It was a repeat of the Stan Smith avalanche of two Christmases previous, with a shoe that cost twice as much. Only the Kio explosion of autumn 1980 had thwarted an Adidas Christmas treble during that busy period, and Kios were really a form of imitation Stan Smith.

'In 1982, Wade Smith opened his own shop on Slater Street, and the age of Scousers risking their liberty for trainers was over. The shop was broken into before its opening, on November 1, and seventy percent of the stock was taken, but this convinced Wade Smith of the value of the commodity, and he pressed on with his mission. On a voyage to Brussels, in search of a legendary trainer that threatened to put him out of business – Adidas Trimm-Trab – Wade Smith encountered some Scousers waiting for the ferry to Ostend. They talked, and on the train back to Liverpool, the lads appeared from nowhere, bearing many pairs of this sought-after shoe. Wade Smith haggled them down to £16 a pair, and started knocking the shoe out at £34.99. This was Wade Smith's Golden Fleece. He had truly become a Scouse Argonaut. After numerous arguments with Adidas bigwigs, Wade Smith travelled to Germany and established a trade link direct with Adidas. Wade Smith was now on the map. Before long, the shop was importing shoes from Germany, France, Austria, Holland and Ireland, and was selling tens of thousands of trainers. The years of 1981 and 1982 were to be the pinnacle for the cult of rare training shoes.

'It soon became apparent that Robert Wade Smith was able to get his own trainers. Now, all the scallies started offering him the top makes of sportswear, T-shirts, sweatshirts, and tracksuits. He sold four times the expected figure in the first year, and soon a larger store was needed. After a couple of moves, he settled in the Glacier-Chicago Buildings, close to Matthew Street.'

The Scouse hordes grew in number as they grew in experience, and the whole biochemical trip, the adrenalin rush, slowly assumed a different form. Scousers had become accustomed to persecution from cockneys and others due to their distinctive appearance, a persecution that became gradually tempered by the ridiculous attempts by other regions of Britain to effect a scally or Perry Boy appearance. The Liverpool Boys succumbed to the inevitable symptoms of their own jadedness. While designer gear remained an integral component of the Liverpool way of life, its chief proponents, the top boys, gradually relaxed their grip on the highest perfection, and allowed the general standard to slip diagonally down the seawall, coming to rest in the most casual of uniforms: Marks & Spencer crew-necks, Levi's jeans and Hush Puppies. In fact, anybody wearing anything too labelled up and brightly coloured beyond the summer of 1982 was considered a divvy, regardless of its integrity or its price tag. The post-Nameless Thing era was emerging, simultaneously in Manchester and Liverpool, as the battle-scarred originals retired to the nooks and crannies to do some good drugs and lick their wounds, nurture their memories and think about the future. As these monsters hibernated, the rest of England finally began to wake up.

The so-called scruff look was the endpoint that eventually epitomised the human being at the end of the 20th century.

As 1982 approached, the dress code on Merseyside went off in two directions. Whether this had anything to do with Liverpool's early exit from Europe is anyone's guess, or it could be that familiarity bred contempt, as every man, woman and dog was into the scally look. A new 'scruff' look took a hold, centred on cannabis, and pre-eighties progressive dinosaur music. It seemed that if you listened to Pink Floyd, Zappa, Gabriel's Genesis or Liverpool's very own Groundhog with their covers of the above bands, you needed a joint between your fingers. The 'history teacher on sabbatical' look was born, in the light of a cosy spliff.

At the match, though, the look that had been conceived three or four years earlier in Liverpool had now developed into a nationwide obsession. Every club in all four divisions now had its own mob of 'casual' dressers. The wedge was now the haircut of the masses. When rival firms battled outside the grounds it was hard to determine who was on whose side. The sight of six hundred Annie Road Enders at away grounds had inspired many.

The trainer trip had mushroomed, and the Scousers were rightly disgusted, after charging and robbing their way down that continental slope, all the way to the turquoise Mediterranean basin, many times there and back, all the while being attacked by their age-old Mancunian foe, only to be confronted by an entire nation who wanted to be like them. The Mancs were different; they *were* like them, but the cavemen in the rest of the country? Do me a fucking favour...

It's nice to hear of all the Mickeys who were taken in by the 'Adidas Centre', and the days they spent searching for the place, to no avail. Rumours of that type are difficult to forge, and even harder to spread, but you can manage it if you're determined enough to make fools of people. Making fools of people by telling lies is an age-old pastime, and one which I certainly have indulged in since I was a small child. The Adidas Centre! What a splendid place, and a real shame that it doesn't exist and was just a silly rumour spread by some faceless, mindless drone. Actually, I made that rumour up, along with a few others, and they spread it far and wide.

I'll let that Adidas Centre-seeking Scouse bastard have the last word: 'The last great revolution in men's clothing happened all those years ago on the streets of Liverpool. For the time being, there has been nothing to compare.'

★ ★ ★

Liverpool were the opponents for the Milk Cup Final in 1983, and a vanload of us took off from the pub at midnight. The colour scheme had become decidedly more subdued: earth tones, tweeds, faded Levi's, tan leather Adidas shoes in various styles, and Hush Puppies had made their first appearance since 1979. They were to become *the* footwear for the next couple of years. At Wembley it was early, bright and sunny. We parked the van and strolled into town. Our 300-pound driver, Col-H-, decided to get some kip, so it was just the twelve of us. The tabloids had the ingenious idea to issue paper hats for each team: red, white and black for United, and yellow and red for Liverpool. We were all wearing these red, white and black hats, and could see a lot of the yellow variety on show. A pub was open, and the twelve of us went in, to discover several main heads from both Liverpool and Everton, with their attendant crews, so out we went. For some reason we walked into the Tube station to find it packed with scallies, sitting on the floor, stood against the walls, so out we went. We walked down the main street as a crew of over 100 Scousers rapidly coalesced behind the twelve. There were some tidy lads in that twelve, Lenny, Oggy, Andy-H-, Phil, Mike-B-, and Goody quietly counted, 'One... two... three!'

We turned to face them, a sea of angry, hate-filled faces, jumping forward, chest-beating, baying for Manc blood. *As they came at us, we stood our ground. I hit one of them and knocked him unconscious, then stepped over him and steamed in. We were organised and up for it. One of the lads picked a Scouser up and just started using him as a truncheon to batter the rest. Most of us were capoeira experts, and the skills came in handy as we despatched them in droves. We had been to Chelsea and West Ham for formal martial arts training, and while we weren't as accomplished or as hard as the cockney supermen, we were still pretty tough blokes. I remember executing a multiple roundhouse, making contact with at least fourteen chins, seeing them fall like dominoes, and then launching myself off a nearby railing, doing a double somersault and landing with each foot on a Scouse head. Using my toes, I applied pressure through my Adidas shoes at precisely the correct location on their scalps to completely immobilise them, and delivered a chilling sermon to the sea of pleading boat-races arrayed before us. They cried and begged forgiveness and I jumped down and hugged more than a few, stroking their misshapen post-wedge fur, assuring them it was over, it was going to be alright.*

Actually, that's not true; what actually happened after the count of three was that we legged it down the street, across a junction, where the dibble materialised from nowhere and formed a barrier to prevent most of them from pursuing us, thank fuck. Looking back from the junction, we were amazed to see a crew of well over 100 Scousers being diverted in a U-turn, back to where they'd sprung from, swerving in unison like a vast shoal of fish in jeans and casual jumpers, topped with a sprinkling of yellow paper hats. Quite a few had penetrated the police membrane, and a couple of the lads jumped onto the railway lines to get away. I have vague memories of running into a café and trying to get behind the counter. It was chaos, all over twelve Mancs, but all over in a moment.

Down the road we went in another boozer and saw a load of our mates. It was Adam (one of the original Perries from 1979) and his brother John, Salty, and the Thompson Twins, with a full crew of lads. The afternoon passed in a beer and weed haze, as we sat in the beer garden, everyone drinking and smoking themselves into Wonderland, a solid United crew without concern. Some peeled off into London for a bit of opportunist this-and-that, and the rest remained on the substances. I may have had two pints that day, while serving in my capacity as Anthropological Gazetteer. I certainly wasn't there for the fun of it.

Liverpool won, despite Norman Whiteside scoring an early goal, and later as we threaded outward through the humans in our cosmic van, the Scousers' chances looked grim; a mob of thousands was bushwhacking its way from the stadium to the streets, over a terrible radius. No stone was unturned.

This was the beginning of the development of Salford Quays, when they tried to blow up a massive grain building at Salford Docks, but the thing refused to go down, and so remained towering, at a bizarre angle, for months and months, until they finally decked it. I could see it from my bedroom window, as we lived in Salford again at the time, a constant reminder of the tenacity of an old and wondrous way of life.

Everton were the visitors to Old Trafford in the spring of 1983, for the FA Cup quarter-final. Arriving at the packed forecourt, myself and *Boxcall giganticus* squeezed through the masses to the usual place; it was a habit, developed over years of waiting for the away fans to arrive, assuming they actually bothered. It became quickly evident that everyone around us was sporting tiny little Everton badges, speaking happily in Scouse accents. *Most alarming.* We cut through them and tried to pay into the Scoreboard End. No joy. The Scoreboard Paddock was already shut, too, packed with beer monsters like Jonah. United Road Paddock was the same story. We had to go around to the Stretford End for the first time in years.

Inside the ground, we were met by the novel sight of visiting fans not just occupying the entire Scoreboard terrace but the seating above it as well. This was the first time such numbers had ever been brought to face United on their own turf. There were over 58,000 people there that day, to see a last gasp Stapleton goal take United through to the semis. I was seventeen years old, sporting a brown chunky-knit cotton sweater with a fold-over collar, faded Levi's, tan leather Adidas shoes, an acid hangover and a psychedelic disinclination to want to do battle. Change was under way in Mancland. There could well have been murders that day for all that many of us knew or cared.

A few weeks later, early morning in the city centre on the way to Piccadilly station, Wembley-bound once more, to face Brighton and Hove Albion. I was with *Boxcall giganticus* and we'd been out on a major shicker the night before, as per every Friday. Still drunk, I periodically pulled my sovereign ring off and launched it up the street. It takes a long time to walk up Market Street when you have to keep stopping to locate a small piece of gold hefted from 100 yards away. The absurdity of the jewellery was becoming clear, through the onion-skin layers of my opening mind. The plain-clothes life was beckoning; the sweatshop labels were taking on a cheesy, worn-out appearance. At Wembley, they had erected barriers, checking for tickets, which we didn't have. The golden era was over. We retired to the same beer garden pub, but it was raining, and there was no one there. We went back to Wembley for the last twenty minutes, and witnessed a pickpocket going at it at the back of the lower stand in a tunnel entrance. Each time the crowd surged forward, he surged with them, his hands going like little blurs of dextrous dishonesty, in the private cavities of unsuspecting chappies.

After the match *Boxcall* realised he'd lost his return ticket, just as we were going into the train station. I did a bit of a cunt's trick by continuing into the station, leaving him to thumb a lift, which he easily did. He was driven home at 100-plus mph up the M1 by a bloke who was shitfaced drunk, which he thought was totally radar. During this period, *Boxcall giganticus* had gone out and bought the 12-inch single 'Rapper's Delight', by the Sugar Hill Gang, and we all knew every word of the songs on that disc. The wearing of tracksuits, sovereign and krugerrand rings, and rap music, combined to add momentum towards where our Thing was heading. But the glitter and the three stripes were about to become secondary to something else, something from within.

Mushroom season had been the one time of year when we all went totally bananas, but things changed. The previous autumn, I had undergone a serious episode of self-realisation under the influence of *Psilocybin mexicana*, with *Boxcall giganticus*, fittingly enough. Eyes were opening, and seeing, and digesting the world with renewed vigour. People were smoking funny cigarettes, and I couldn't shake that inhuman feeling from the psilocybin. It was an omen.

As the summer of 1983 developed, heating our section of the globe, the warm air wafted our heads out west, as product from Amsterdam overflowed, blown into the streets of Manchester. The previous few years' excitement had provided innumerable opportunities for transcendence through fashion and violence, but this was something quite different, and some would say superior, to the molecule called adrenalin. In 1983, the people responsible for this shady traffic were operating out of a sense of duty as much as anything else. The Dam was the reservoir and they were the conduits: bikers, students, chemists, hippies and, of course, gangsters. But at this point, it was really the bikers and hippies who were bringing in the good stuff. Superman acid, amphetamines, and myriad forms of chemically-enhanced cannabis were consumed along with lashings of cold lager. Visits to the UMIST campus yielded amazing prizes, undreamed by the Manc Perries, who'd previously waited all year for mushroom season to start, so they could assault their own subconscious. The summer world became purple-tinged, chemically animated and suddenly intellectually engaging.

On Saturday night, it became par for the course to transport oneself beyond the confines of a life in the north-west of a city in the north-west of a country in the north-west of a continent, on a tilted, spinning chunk of saltwater and rock, protected by a dynamic stratified air-mass that pissed on us most of the time – to a world phantasmic and gorgeous, populated by fabulous animals and human spirits: six-thirty, walking the streets, anticipation thick in the air. Seven-fifteen, an incandescent ball of human energy was uncoiling, sending euphoric waves surging out from the chest to the limbs and head. Seven-thirty, gaining on the peak, breathless, watching the contours on peoples' faces blaze like glazed purple fluid, the pupils maximised, taking it all in. Seven-forty five, up and off, totally gone, the personal identity disassembled and left behind like underwear on an incredible private beach, with bone-white powder sand, undulating aqua-green water, untold coves and gulleys, pulsating beneath a caressing all-wise sun. The weekly nine-to-five grind morphed into a ludicrous and inexplicable waste of time. The weekend, charged with an alien energy, took on new significance as the portal to another dimension, beyond the dreary reality of humping steel, operating a saw, weighing metal, packaging metal, loading metal onto the back of a flatbed wagon with a forklift, working an assembly line, stocking the shelves of clothing ware-houses, carrying furniture up umpteen flights of stairs, and all the while being paid peanuts in exchange. Is it any mystery why people choose to embark on more colourful and challenging expeditions in their spare time? People began to find alternative means of generating capital. So many, many ways.

Dave-D- was a regular uptown on a weekend, and he noticed that some places were off limits to us at the time. 'If you were dressed "normally" in lad gear in 1983, you were refused admission to clubs like the Hacienda, as the look had become synonymous with hooligan behaviour. Only those with purple spiked mohawks, gothic gear and other artsy-and-need-to-prove-it-type appearances were allowed into the mysterious depths of the club. They looked the part but were Dolly Dimple underneath. Sometimes, we could lie to the bouncers and say we just wanted to deliver a message to someone, but it was shit anyway, because none of the lads were interested and it was all the art school types, boring as fuck.'

Normal lads were confined to the commoner venues, and as the term 'lager lout' emerged, an alternative wild frontier was being explored by those who'd grown bored with it all. And plenty had.

PART 3

REASONS TO BE CHEERFUL

13

A SHORT HISTORY OF SUBSTANCE ABUSE AND VIOLENCE

It is easy to get a thousand prescriptions, but hard to get one single remedy.

– Chinese proverb

WE'RE ABOUT TO enter a time of change; a cyclic repetition ages old, whereby humankind indulges itself, becoming ever more potent, increasingly destructive, inventive, and, a lot of the time, very stoned. That's right; these lads grew older, wiser, more productive, and to succeed they injected intoxicants into the mix, which reacted splendidly with the tea-leafing and the knuckle. Scholars have speculated that the use of psychedelic compounds has catalysed human technological development. They say we used psychotropic plants way back in the mists of time. Consciousness-expanding chemicals have served as a tool for progress. But any tool, both metal and mental, can be overused. And in a world like this, who doesn't need to chill out at least a couple of times a week? Despite the whingeing from various right-wing groups about substance abuse, and whingeing from various left-wing groups about violence, neither is going away. Ever.

During the 80s there was one great discontinuity dividing young people: those who took drugs and wore the gear, and those who didn't. Those who didn't were the ones who continued to think inside the box, who probably went on to reasonably successful professional careers of one kind or another. Perhaps they even acquired a faith, one that carried them through the hard times, as is often the custom with steady, focussed people. We all need something, or someone, to lean on, even if it is the ridiculous notion of a bearded man in the sky who is all-powerful.

Then there are the ones that did. The ones who recoiled from the so-called real world, as they passed out of those school gates for the final time. These were the cherubim of escapism, the future pissheads and acid casualties. These ones didn't give a thought to marriage, mortgage, kids or career. They only wanted to think about dressing right, shagging, getting smashed and smashing in turn, in no particular order. Don't blame it on poverty or neglect. Blame it on DNA.

Every population is subject to genetic variability, which dictates the character of that population. Genes are responsible for an enormous variety of biochemical pathways, signalling cascades within the body that determine our personalities, our physical appearance, and how violent or introspective we might be. DNA transcribes soluble proteins, which react with specific regions of the brain, influencing our every thought. DNA transcribes protein receptors, distributed around the body, which bind chemically to both native and foreign molecules, creating a physiologic effect. Receptors exist in their millions, many attached to cell membranes, and others even free-floating in the bloodstream. When foreign molecules enter the body and are solubilized, either in the blood or the fatty tissue, they're free to bind to any receptor they have chemical affinity for. Some drugs share receptors, due to their possessing similar molecular structures, and therefore similar chemical affinities for their shared receptor. It's all dependent on electronic conductivity at the atomic level. A single receptor can metabolise thousands of molecules of a drug in under a minute. This velocity creates the rush we crave.

These receptors obviously were not evolved to interact with caffeine, thalidomide, heroin or amphetamine – they evolved to bind molecules produced by the body itself, called endogenous messengers. Endogenous messengers such as hormones (like adrenalin), neurotransmitters, endorphins and many other naturally secreted substances have their own receptors with which they interact exclusively, via the molecular topography at the interface between endogenous messenger and receptor. The two fit together like a lock and key, honed by billions of years of evolution. Each endogenous messenger has evolved to perform a function, be it fight or flight (adrenalin), painkilling (endorphins) or something equally useful. An adrenalin rush, therefore, is no different than a drug rush; it is the result of receptors metabolising the molecule in question at an alarming rate. When we introduce drugs, toxins and other compounds into the body, receptor interactions may trigger beneficial or harmful effects.

The molecules that compose opiates contain regions very similar to the 'active' regions on the endorphins – the region of the molecule that interacts with the receptor. An average dose of opiates binds the endorphin receptors at unnaturally high concentrations, far in excess of endorphin, and a 'high' is created from the resultant biochemical cascade. The fact that no pain is present increases the overall pleasure.

Psychedelic drugs are not so straightforward. Pharmacologists have not yet determined the precise mechanism of action for lysergic acid diethylamide (LSD), but it is believed to affect a large number of different receptors and consequent signal transduction pathways. The LSD molecule is relatively large and complex, possessing several potential sites for receptor interaction. When a young clubber scores some acid, drops it and waits impatiently for the rush, a dynamic and complex process occurs at the molecular level: in time, the tab dissolves, and billions of LSD molecules tumble through the body. These molecules interact indiscriminately with these various receptors, triggering many simultaneous signalling pathways. All this biochemical haywire produces the electrifying symptoms of an acid trip. The more of these various receptors an individual possesses, the more intense the trip, with the ratio of the different receptors present creating an individual's own unique acid experience. Higher chemical affinity for a receptor means a higher rate of metabolism and excretion, which is why a more intense 'peak' is often followed by a relatively calmer 'levelling out' period.

Biochemistry is a complicated field, and there's certainly more to an individual than how many receptors he or she possesses, or individual differences in brain chemistry. One thing is sure, though; receptors, and the attendant messenger molecules bombing around our cells like dragonflies, certainly influence our preferences, in drugs and in life.

Ancient humans were at the mercy of their genes and their resultant biochemistry, just like we are today. DNA resonates with its environment, creating a biophysical field within which the individual or the species operates, utilising whatever nutrients and other elements are available to it in that environment. The ancients existed in a seamless joining with dreams, with nature, and with other members of the tribe. The danger of inbreeding hung over the tribe like a shadow, and genetic variability had to be maintained. It was often all about location, location, location. They were entirely dependent on the natural cycles and their various biological products for survival. Eking out a transient existence on the frozen plains of the Pleistocene, they tracked the mammals on their migrations, and were forced to time the moment when they arrived in this or that valley, to coincide with the harvest of a sought-after plant, or the mating season of a certain wild ruminant. Losing the plot during the Ice Age meant extinction for the tribe, and there was much pleading with the gods above, those who controlled the forces of nature. This was, and remains, the way to get things done in a cruel world. It has been suggested that use of drugs like LSD takes a person back into that ancient mindset, where he or she becomes immensely aware of their place in this cycle, and the ways in which our existence is tightly dovetailed to ecological chemistry.

All matter is composed of atoms, which are configured into molecules, which themselves build the environment we see, smell, taste, hear and feel. The nutrient cycle – carbon, hydrogen, oxygen, nitrogen, phosphorus, sulphur, zinc, iron, potassium, calcium, sodium, and many more — consists of elements essential for the maintenance of our physiology, without which we would cease to exist. All of life hangs together in a complex dynamic web of disequilibrium, eating and being eaten in turn, as each species processes what it needs to survive, from the grass all the way up to the blue whale. All is one, but each one has its own requirements.

Another drug, Ecstasy, or MDMA, is metabolised via three different receptor pathways, producing a variety of metabolites. The molecular mechanism for its psychotropic effects is not well known, but the effects themselves are legend among ravers who first used the chemical in the 80s. A powerful sense of belonging, of being attached intimately to the world and the other living things in it, suggest that similar pathways to LSD are being affected. A major distinction between the compounds is that of dosage. LSD is thousands of times more potent than any other drug, and consequently doses of LSD are measured in micrograms (μg). Other drugs' dosages are measured in milligrams (mg). An average dose of LSD may be in the region of 100 μg, as opposed to an average dose of Ecstasy, which is 100 mg. If the use of psychotropic plants helped ancient humans to develop technology, then the use of LSD helped enlighten the Perry Boys of 1983 to walk away from the train stations and forecourts, to seek out answers to more spiritual questions. Later that same decade, Ecstasy helped late 80s football casuals to see beyond the blind territoriality and fear of violence. These two compounds conspired to put an end to much (but not all) of the trouble that had bamboozled police forces the length and breadth of the land. The reason for this transformation is obvious: *it came from within.*

When the Perries and scallies went travelling, pummelling their unsuspecting adversaries and sneering at their clothes as they did so, history was being repeated in an endless cycle, as nature intended. Tens of thousands of years ago, when *Homo sapiens sapiens* began to destroy the Neanderthal, it was obvious there was no contest — it was the nature of those first few encounters, somewhere in Europe or the Middle East, that determined whether our crew would prevail or not – and once we started turning the screw on them we didn't stop until they were gone forever. If the pioneering Perries and scallies had been made of different stuff, British style might have been extinguished before it started, by punks, mods, teds, skinheads and the rest of the apes roaming those dark satanic hills back in 1978 and 1979. But we *were* made of the right stuff, and that stuff is largely protein, hydrocarbons, polysaccharides and nucleic acids. Much of it is receptors. We conquered those apes with force, but at the molecular level there was surely a transmission of something more fundamental – that Thing which remained Nameless until the cockneys called it Casual.

Humankind is just another species of animal, whatever the chemical 'spirituality' of marijuana, LSD or MDMA might cause you to believe. The ways in which this material is processed depends on the DNA you carry; a sea cucumber requires this, and a cockney requires that. The elements in the nutrient cycle are literally as old as the stars. From the first level of the food chain, up to the apex predators, it is merely the flow of this material and the energy it creates that maintain your consciousness. There is no 'spirit', and you won't go to heaven when you die. You will be dismantled by biology, chemistry and physics, to be cast once more into the great mixer, to re-enter the flow of material and energy. Take a look at your hands, and behold those claws at the fingertips. Glance in the mirror and show your teeth. It is calcium. Look at your eyes, your ears, so watchful and sentinel-like. Cartilage, gristle – carbon, hydrogen, nitrogen – all made of the same few elements, older than the stars. You know what a scowl and a growl are, and the energy required to make them is your food.

Agriculture provided humans some degree of control over nature for the first time in history. Archaeologists studying the spread of agriculturalism from the Middle East across Europe employ a variety of devices to assess who was doing what, when, and so on. This is important information, as the shift away from hunting and gathering triggered the birth of the static community and mathematics, which, ten thousand years later, triggered the Industrial Revolution. The appearance of what archaeologists call the Linearbandkeramik (LBK) is one such device; the LBK represents the sudden emergence of a new style of pottery, one decorated with bands of narrow stripes. This suggests an awareness of fixed volumes, so it was functional as well as cosmetic. This trend spread with breath-taking swiftness across Europe from around 5500 BC, and describes the moving frontier of agriculturalism across our early world. Wherever this pottery is unearthed, it can be safely assumed that the population in question knew the score, and had turned to the brand with the stripes. It can also be assumed that as the frontier moved west, there was a good deal of violence occurring, as the cavemen were forcibly educated in the ways of this new stripey lifestyle.

Does this ring any bells?

Just as those practising the LBK vaulted over tracts of land with infertile soil, only for the brand with the stripes to reappear further along the line of migration, did the Nameless Thing move across Blighty's undulating landscape, ignoring this town, this city, but somehow infecting the lads of that city, where the soil was more fertile, where the membrane hydrocarbons were ripe for entering. And so did Tottenham become the first cockney mob, and so did Coventry remain mired in ska, and so did many others start the timer ticking and call it The Beginning, when in fact it was past the end.

Humankind enjoyed over 100,000 years in The Garden, and they were gruelling years, but still we refer to it as Paradise. When the monkey stopped chasing his lunch around and learned to keep it in a pen, or planted in rows in the ground, a lot of energy was saved and a food surplus created. This was good, but it also signalled the end of self-sufficiency. Humans can be forgiven for believing that they ceased to be animals that day, but it wasn't true. Some claim that psychedelic compounds played a role in this realisation, which is not surprising. Humans began to believe they had the power of gods, which placed them above the realm of animals, but this is all my arse. The animal we are continues to be, and its most distinct form of expression is in violence. One hundred and fifty thousand years of hunting and gathering was preceded by several million years walking upright, during which our DNA resonated with its environment and mutated, slowly assuming its present form. That we did violence on others is attested by the fact we exist today. The violence was never expunged from our genetic code, as it was a crucial component of the most important part of life: grub. To feed ever-greater numbers of people we needed ideas, which consciousness-expanding compounds in the environment allowed us to conceive, there by the campfires, out of our boxes. Trying to prevent violence and substance abuse in human society is like pissing against a hurricane.

Things have become silly, and it is time to trim the fat. An evolutionary endpoint such as this exudes fitness, muscle and stamina. It is streamlined and purposeful without trying to be, consuming all in its path. The ability to travel well, in fact preferring to remain constantly on the move, is one of its chief attributes. Armed with a panoply of razor-sharp cutters, scales and built for speed, the Nameless Thing thundered through the hearts of Britain's youth like a writhing, living arrow, launched under its own steam from the bottom of the sea, spilling blood and disappearing like a fishy Tube train. Isn't the aroma of hydrocarbons the greatest smell in the universe?

When I talk to the lads from 1979 and 1980, those who literally started the whole thing off, I am still struck by their sense of collective wonder at what it was that they invented. Once we had started the rest off on their journey, it took on a life of its own. Like the farmers taking the LBK to the cavemen, violence was its means but enlightenment was its end. The Scousers may have ignited it with their continental ragging sprees, but together we formed the dynamic engine of the phenomenon.

'Back then, 1978 and 1979, you'd get talking to lads on the terraces at Old Trafford or away games,' said Goody, an integral cog in the machine at the heart of the Perry Boy factory, 'and you'd say things like, "So are there many round your way into it, or what?" They'd reply, "Yeah, there's a few go to the youth club on a Wednesday, and everyone at school's wearing the gear every day now. There should be a few of the boys here today." It was obvious that a lot of these lads were chinning others into seeing sense. After a few months, you just took it for granted that to get this thing out there you were gonna have to be cruel to be kind. Wearing new kinds of trainers shipped in from Europe helped people to appreciate it, because they had an eye for that. We converted them, and they were thankful once they'd worked it out. At the match every week, there were more and more, with that proud look in their eye. Brand new lads, popping up like mushrooms. You'd keep your eye on the numbers, watching them grow like a farmer with his crop.

'It took off because it was a genuinely worthwhile way to be, but there was definitely a sense that if we didn't keep the lamp alight there was a possibility it would go out completely. But deep down we knew how right this was, by the way it made us feel. It made us feel proud, for the first time in our lives – and it was a guilt-free pride, something none of us had ever known. We were the lads who dropped out of school, we were too cool to do well in class, we were totally into this way of life, and it came before all else. Our enthusiasm drove us on because it was so strong. Knowing the Scousers were at the other end of the East Lancs Road was another factor, whatever they'll try and tell you. We fed on each other. It was us and them, and it was war, the days of the big crews. But it was more than just fighting; it was the only way to be. At the match, no one could laugh at us any more; no one could even try. The banter across the segregation took on a completely different feel, like we were untouchable. It was poetic justice to feel like that about cockneys, the most arrogant cunts of all. They were supposed to be the leaders, but not any more. We had a power over them and we rubbed their noses in it while we showed them the way to do it themselves.'

The big crews are now dead and gone, extinct like the big fish, the big lizards and the cavemen. Only the bones remain. The hooligan hardcore of the mid-80s onward were greatly diminished in number, possibly more ferocious, but forever pursuing a buzz that had atrophied and fossilised, laid down in the sediments of the north-west waterways from whence they sprung. Memories are short, and people today crave information on those early years, because deep down they know it was the Golden Age of Boys. *Perry Boys*. There were no mobile phones with inbuilt cameras. There was only the unknown, the dark, and the primeval climax when two tribes on a strange and vicious frontier collided on monkey island, Earth.

It went like this, according to 'The Satisfied Customer', a lad who liked to travel a lot, to meet interesting people, and to throw himself into life with both feet: 'We were coming fast across the car park in numbers and the train was pulling in. There must have been four hundred of us, and the Dibble was nowhere. They were chanting as they come off the train, and we could tell by the noise there was a load of them and they didn't know we were there. I can't begin to describe the buzz of these moments, knowing you were about to go into a crew of lads who themselves were up for it, but probably having the element of surprise as we knew they hadn't seen us. Now you're jogging, breathing deep, savouring the moment, into the right position, the one giving us the greatest ambush impact, breathing, breathing like a drug-rush kind of breathing, but even better. Their chants are getting louder, and there's lads bouncing up and down on the spot, pumping their chests with their fists, giggling, bursting out laughing, grinning from ear to ear, they can't believe it's gonna happen like this. There's a full crew here, and only the lucky ones at the front will get to experience the best bit. We even back off a bit, to make a bigger circle for more of the lads, and to give them the chance to come out at us and make it a proper fucking off. Their lads don't know what to expect, so it's fucking brilliant when you manage to meet 'em like this, and make it real.

'The footsteps are now as loud as the chanting cos the chanting's dying down a bit, and they're going to appear any second. We know the station and can hear where they are, down that last little lot of steps and now they're within fifteen feet. One last look around, and the laughing's stopped, and it's

pursed lips and steel eyes, the proper fucking rush with the pit
of the stomach nearly killing me. We've got to end this soon,
because we're all at our limit, and then they appear. It's their
lads. I'm almost weeping, sobbing with the pleasure of the
release, and the adrenalin has turned me into a monster with
the strength of ten men. Everyone's in that state, bouncing and
shouting, terrorising them. They sense it's on top, big time, and
they think about running back inside but their way back is
blocked by their own mob, so they start to come out and growl
at us. I don't remember much after that, just running in, feeling
ten foot tall, landing with my hoof right on someone's crutch,
and diving right over the guy to punch a lad behind him. I
know I went down but sprang back up instantly, like Zebedee,
grabbing someone by the throat and nutting him in the face
about four times. The rest is a blur, and back in the pub I just
want to sup a pint and enjoy the tingling. Another job well
done, thank you very much.'

This is a real phenomenon, as real as a gambling, motor racing
or base jumping addiction. The young men involved often wore
the clothes simply because it was the accepted thing to do, but
many began as trendies who became ever-more engulfed in the
thrill and danger of the violence. This author can attest to the
thrill of approaching Lime Street station, aware that individuals
carrying Stanley knives were waiting for him, and knowing he
would be requiring an injection of energy from a gland in his
brain as he alighted onto the platform. Adrenalin is a major
player, when it finds its way home to a specific receptor. The
physiology of all living things is to blame, not football, politics
or the economy. It's that DNA and those receptors, those little
protein machines. Receptors evolved over billions of years; they
are not going anywhere, and to deny them their fill is to try to
drive a car without spark plugs. Even viruses (which are non-
living particles) and bacteria possess receptors. Receptors
perform multiple roles, and often some of those roles have unintended consequences. The fact is you cannot amputate such a
fundamental piece of the human physiology, for it is in the
DNA, that molecule which expresses all proteins as and when

needed. Without receptors, you wouldn't be reading this book; in fact you wouldn't *be* at all. Through attending football matches, the working class youth of an entire nation developed an addiction to the lock and key interactions of adrenalin and its receptor, just as they later developed cravings for other molecular interactions, when the mind drugs came rolling over the Dam. The signal receptors amplify is the essence of what makes us alive. It is the particle-wave duality inherent in all time, space, mind, matter and energy. It is being.

14

THE DAMBUSTERS

Ye shall know the truth, and the truth shall make you mad.

—Aldous Huxley

COLONIALISM IS AS old as life itself. Bacteria, life's original travelling crew, began colonising various foreign materials almost four billion years ago. Slime moulds, algae and fungi soon followed suit, spreading the contagious spores of expansion across the globe, transforming communities and incorporating themselves into the more fundamental strata of living systems at the ground floor. Animals and plants also indulge in this most ancient of processes. Ants control silkworm life-cycles, while ivy and alien plant species spread into and choke native species that obstruct their march on the environment. This tendency is heritable, passed through DNA down the timeline, and has consequently passed through The Word of humankind. Colonialism is as natural and old as the hills, but it has also become a conscious idea, one which has been refined over thousands of years. The Sumerians, Babylonians, Egyptians, Greeks and Romans all received wisdom from their predecessors, and honed the skills further, going on and conquering those not yet in possession of the knowledge of organised mayhem. These people brought unfamiliar inventions upon their victims, steamrollering across the world unopposed, passing the baton through the millennia to the next member of this exclusive club, from the slopes of the Middle East to the fabled archipelagos of Europe.

But in the late nineteenth century something happened, a mutation in the genetic lineage of 10,000 years, unknown since the end of the Ice Age. *Manchester* happened. *The Industrial Revolution* happened. Truly programmable machines were witnessed on this earth for the first time, machines enabling one person to make things in hours that previously took many people many years, machines to transport people and goods to points distant in hours, distances which previously would have taken days, or even months, to traverse. The city itself became a spontaneously self-organising unit. Social strata were expressed in precise locations, as the backstreet squalor of the peasantry became automatically segregated from the gleaming high street of the new industrial barons, the kingly thoroughfares of Manchester. It's a curious truth that the geographic site of emergence for a certain technological phenomenon seems to provide a launch pad for subsequent improvements in the same direction, and that its initial perpetrators are endowed with some ineffable advantage over the rest of the herd from that point on. And on. It's a strange fact that people across the world simply accept the reality that Manchester United are the world's biggest football club, with the biggest following, and with the successively most expensive, most technically advanced and largest stadiums seen on the club level in Britain, ever. The Mancunian Tower of Babel looming high over the city attracts them from far and wide. Nobody gives a thought to the fact Manchester isn't the capital of England. There's an obvious parallel in Barcelona.

Mancunians are not Scousers or Yorkshiremen. The accent stands crisp and inscrutable, like a diamond on a mountaintop, colourless, devoid of character but loaded with Englishness, while remaining somehow Celtic, or northern, even comical, yet respectful and serious. This is due to location, location, location, my sons and daughters; we are situated smack in the middle of Great Britain, and this is reflected in the speech patterns of thousands of years' worth of migrations from all corners of these precious islands. Manchester was not called the engine room of the Empire for nothing; we built the fucking machines, invented

the machines that allowed us to literally steamroller the world.
We punched holes in foreign walls, releasing floods of beneficial
materials, such as cotton, steel and intoxicants, which enabled us
to prosper and mutate,

Those who travelled to see the machines often remained,
from all corners of the globe. This tendency to absorb cultures
was reflected no better by the fact that at one point there were
at least eleven breweries in town. Manchester is a beer-savvy
city. When I first started going in pubs, aged sixteen or seventeen, blokes would often point out that in London the table was
laden with golden lager; in Dublin Guinness blackness was
uniform; in Glasgow it was dark pints of heavy all around; in
Yorkshire, best bitter flooded the tabletop, smoothly brown; but
in wonderful Manchester the glasses packing the clustered tabletops contained liquids of all possible colours and combinations,
reflecting the myriad accents, as well as the hybridised local
accent, bang in the centre of the British Isles. It was a cultural
revolution waiting to happen.

'In the 70s, the country was rocked by United's ferocity, as
the Red Army voyaged far and wide, exacting world-renowned
carnage on all corners of the country, establishing a name that
to this day is discussed the world over,' recalled Tom, a Man
United bootboy in the olden days. 'Its followers were drawn
from all over the UK. The backdrop to all this was a fast-moving
kaleidoscope of changing fashions, Northern Soul included. The
all-night, speed-fuelled dance clubs were dens of iniquity and
havens for the multitudes returning from away match mayhem,
where they could dance to the latest soul until the sun came up.
In the background, the drinking dens and shabeens of Moss Side
and Cheetham Hill were gaining popularity among the blacks,
the descendants of those people colonised back in the days of
Empire. The black kids were undergoing the same types of
changes the white kids were undergoing. While the Manchester
clubs led the way in the 70s, the rest of the country stagnated in
their flares and platform soles, with no direction.'

Tom went off and lived around England, but the novelty of
Manchester's nightlife never wore off. 'We had places to go after

we'd turned places over, places that contained thousands of lads and girls, decked out in skinner gear, all of a like mind, all hip to what was going down, and what music was the very latest. Other places didn't. They had to make do with pubs with decent jukeboxes, which was alright, but hardly the same thing. No disrespect to others, it was just the way things were in different places. There was us and there was them.'

The 70s slowly ended, amid that doldrums period in which nobody seemed to have a clue, even the Scousers. In the 80s, things hadn't changed much, and only a combination of John Lennon's death, black American disco, New Romanticism and beloved Bowie and Roxy Music kept things ticking over, as musical tastes started to incline towards a 60s' retro sound, fuelled largely by kids who'd received Beatles albums for Christmas following Lennon's tragic end, as well as charts hits like Tight Fit's 'Back To the Sixties', which everyone loved. Unsurprisingly, Manchester quickly self-organised into a hotbed of 60s-style trippiness. The rest of the country stagnated in the current garbage music trends, like Wham!, Spandau Ballet, Simple Minds and Michael Jackson, while clubs in the centre of Manchester were playing Led Zeppelin, The Doors, The Rolling Stones and Bowie to crowds of adoring stoners and dancers, high on speed and grass, tripping on what was dawning as a new possibility. This was chiefly due to the large student presence in bars and clubs around the university area, where long-haired biker types sat drinking cider, stoned and whizzing on high-grade amphetamines and acid from The Dam.

Dave-D- was a regular in the university bar on a Saturday night, savouring the dawn of a new flavour. 'UMIST earned a reputation as the place to score acid or speed among the ex-boys of football by 1983, and it wasn't unusual to see a good few lads in straight jeans and Adidas merging and discussing events with the smellies on a Saturday night'.

A strange animal was being assembled in these academic Frankenstein avenues; bikers, hippies, and students, being assailed by Perry lads for that stuff that did yer 'eads in. This led to much larger numbers of people making the trade route from Amsterdam, and the gentle tide of recent times suddenly became a tsunami. It was another Manchester hybrid, ironically conceived in the shadow of UMIST's Barnes Wallis building, named after the man who invented the bouncing bomb – The Dambuster.

Dave continued, 'This was an era when the Hacienda was off limits to anyone who even remotely resembled a football type, with the result that for a year or three the ultimate goal was postponed. The football lot in Manchester at this time were maturing, some even getting into their twenties, and a few pints and a spliff in the beer garden and a night out in town once every few weeks seemed to be enough'.

It was another doldrums, a short-lived intermediate phase between two high energy eras in which young people in Britain and the world would be forever changed. As ever, there were those for whom a few pints and a spliff wasn't cutting it. These lads insisted on intensity, on being terrified, even, by their drug trips, and this became a fashion in itself. It wasn't enough to smoke pot for pleasure; the act was elevated to the status of an ordeal, an internal voyage upon which it was everyone's divine right to embark. They were like Aztecs to the sacrifice, bearing the might of their minds upon jaded shoulders, sculpted from the previous few years' battles and styles. People of working class character suddenly woke up to how intelligent they were, something they'd always known but somehow hadn't realised the power of. Exploration was afoot. People were set in motion, as Dave-D- remembered.

'Around 1983-4, a lot of people jumped on a very profitable bandwagon, which entailed moving down to London and signing on, only to be housed in a hotel at the government's expense, as you were supposed to be in the capital looking for work. With the system being as it was, prior to proper computers, people were able to sign on at several places around Greater London simultaneously, be assigned to multiple hotel rooms, and collect dole money from several cheques. These characters would return to Manchester for the weekend, with amazing stories of their exploits. They would send you postcards telling you that they'd been pissed and stoned for days on end, and still there was no end to the money. It was outrageous.'

Mark-L-., United supporter and occasional writer, describes the downward arc of colour and the upward curve of individuality that accompanied these changing times, wherein the movement truly was set in stone: 'The lads at the match were dictating the look and the attitude, instead of some cockney media who had spent three years telling everybody to be New Romantics or Nutty Boys. The national newspapers failed to grasp it all, and described the UK as going "designer label mad" with identikit Casual looks on the fashion pages. They weren't totally wrong in that they recognised the fact that a designer fixation had started, still evident over twenty years later, which ultimately led to the stagnation of the scene as labels and/or money ran out.

'Nineteen eighty-four onwards was perhaps the best example of Casual behaviour, as the Mancs, and in particular United, broke off at a tangent from the polarised, money-obsessed, cockney-driven, one-style-fits-all direction. They created their own 'dressed down' style which ultimately led to Madchester, and the Indie look becoming the prevailing street fashion in Manchester, Britain's best city. Again, the 'look' rather than the label was of more importance, and the evolution spawned flared cords, cord shoes and tweed jackets, perhaps with a dash of goatee chucked in. This was the look that went to Turin in 1984 and fought the ICF on the cross-Channel ferry in 1985. Despite the college-professor appearance, the age-old Manc motto, *minimal cost with maximum attitude*, the original pure Casual catchphrase, was still very much alive and kicking. Nobody else in Britain really took to this look, and it eventually evolved into the fully matured Madchester style, which still pervades today — the Indie look in its modern form.'

The mid-80s was considered the height of the Casual movement. The clothes were still enough of a novelty for most English lads, and even the football crews maintained high numbers, in the face of other attractions. Some of the individuals involved in the football at this time had matured and

developed into even cannier versions of their previous selves, if
that were possible. Many had seen several decades of terrace
activity. A mysterious example is Martin-X-, who helped me
with the research for this book, only to disappear without
receiving even a 'thank you'. He told many tales of ingenuity
and change from this era.

'If there is one thing that pisses me off, it's the Scousers
claiming only Liverpool fans were going abroad in the 70s.
United had a large support from the sixties onwards in Europe,
from Benfica to the Anglo-Italian Cup in the early seventies, to
Ostend in 1974. The whole early eighties thing was an important part of my learning, and still shapes my attitude today. I still
go abroad and bring back clothes when I can, and spend the
Euro away matches that I get to at clothes shops rather than in
the boozer. I'm self-employed, and still have the "get off your
arse and make it happen" mentality.

'Even though United always had a large hooligan following,
a lot of reds still had their eye on a wage. We all loved to travel
to away games for the crack, and I well remember the Persil
ticket offer from British Rail. If you collected the tokens off the
boxes, you could send them in and get rail tickets, buy one, get
one free. National Express did it, too. I remember we used to go
into the local Co-op and rip all the tokens off the boxes, to send
in. I remember in 1984 going to Tottenham, in the days when
you needed to be mobbed up or you got a hiding, and these
cockneys sussed us on the Underground, cos we were wearing
semi-flares, totally a Manc thing at the time. Back then, you
didn't have to be close enough to read the little two millimetre
badge we all used to wear to work out who was who.'

Heaton Park is said to be Europe's largest municipal park,
and covers a large tract of north Manchester. Several neighbourhoods abut its perimeter, such as Prestwich, Crumpsall,
Bowker Vale, Whitefield and Blackley. The park attracted people
from all over Manchester back in the early 80s, with its boating
lake, animal petting zoo and Heaton Hall, a grand mansion
with a museum and café. The vast lawns in front of the Hall
would be mobbed with families eating ice cream on a hot

summer's day, or browsing the petting zoo. There were dingoes
and wild boar and foxes in the little zoo. In among the families
would be groups of girls from all over the place, and it was our
job to get to know them. There'd be other little crews of
Perries there, too, from surrounding neighbourhoods, notably
Salford, Crumpsall and Blackley, which often led to skirmishes
and face-offs, especially if girls were involved. The park had
large areas of open grazing land, with herds of bison, yak and
other livestock, as well as a large blue concrete paddling pool,
where people took their little kids to play in the water. The
greenery was intersected by wide footpaths, down which the
ice cream vans would coast, with little refreshment kiosks here
and there. There were rolling lawns with bowl-like depressions
in which people could picnic, among the odd cluster of rhodo-
dendrons, leading down to the boating lake, where skiffs and
motor boats could be hired for a few shillings. One entire side
of the park runs along Bury Old Road in Prestwich, site of the
Ostrich pub, our local.

Our local overlooked a sacred spot; when the Pope visited
Manchester in the summer of 1982, he spoke in Heaton Park to
a crowd of hundreds of thousands. There remains to this day a
commemorative stone on a plinth at the place where His
Holiness stood. That stone is smack in the middle of a giant
magic mushroom field, and the Prestwich Boys owned and
revered every mushroom on it. This sacredness is fuck-all to do
with Christianity.

Most of us were proficient star-trekkers by the time we were
in our mid-teens, having undergone voyages out to the further
tendrils of the Milky Way on the wings of the toxic fungus. We
were like a tribe of Mexican Indians, worshipping the mushroom, and the assortment of totem creatures and animals it
spawned in our fevered imaginations. There were plenty of
woods around Prestwich, the Clough being foremost, and the
fabled hollows and pathways were an established mystical
stomping ground by the early 80s. Long before lads in Prestwich
encounter marijuana, they are familiar with this much more
potent entity.

As they grew older they perfected the art of powderising and freezing their enchanted little friend, guaranteeing that none went to waste. The lads around Prestwich began to formulate their own alternative version of reality, based on the chemical visions they perpetually experienced. All over the city, in 1984, people seemed to be losing their minds. The need for fear generated a large catalogue of fictional characters that were said to police the underground world in which we lived, as well as heroic figures that were constantly at war with them. A body of men known as 'The Stewards' was created, a form of intoxicant constabulary that was said to keep tabs on our alcohol and drug consumption: anyone not drinking or taking enough drugs, especially acid, was punished severely. Leaving beer in your glass upon exiting a pub, or doing just one hit of acid when two were available, resulted in an immediate Stewards' Enquiry, and the wrongdoer would be hauled off in a flash for questioning. If a bottle of wine or a joint were discarded not fully finished, a Mobile Incident Unit would be assembled for forensic study of said article, and the Enquiry would begin.

'Basically, everybody urged everybody else to get as fucked-up as possible, all the time, or else face the Stewards,' remembered Dave-D-, who was often referred to as 'Doctor'. 'It was a grown-up version of the Bogey Man, if grown-up is any way to describe these proceedings. And then there were the enemies of The Stewards, a courageous band of men, led by Doctor Bernard Watson, a scientist and voyager of the far cosmos. Doctor Watson and his boys were capable of ingesting vast quantities of intoxicating substances with little ill effect. They lapped it up, and The Stewards monitored them closely, unable to believe they could live so far out on the periphery of human tolerance. A lot of the lads started to call each other 'Doctor' as a greeting and a mark of respect after various exploits. The familiar places where people would meet to get wrecked took on new names to reflect their significance.

'There was a little mob of lads who were known as the Bong Gang, who were legend in their fondness for the water pipe. There was a group who hung out in the deeper nooks and cran-

nies of the plumbing system at Prestwich Mental Hospital (very
appropriate), unbeknownst to the staff and residents/inmates. A
few liked to do their cosmic travelling in a local cricket pavilion,
which was christened the Mind-Warp Pavilion, after a line in
the Bowie song 'The Bewlay Brothers'. Others still favoured
Prestwich Clough, a small wood not far from the centre. There
was a stepped, concrete waterfall there that resembled a half-
buried Mayan pyramid, which came to be known as the
Fountains of Venus. Many all-night campfires were enjoyed
there. The old landfill, a quite spectacular glade overlooked on
three sides by steep hillsides covered in trees like a crater,
became the Valley of the Quarks. A dirt-track through the
Clough was called the Path of Excess, after a line in a William
Blake poem. It led to a small recess where stream water
collected, called the Well of Wisdom, also taken from Blake.
There were the lads who hung out at the old reservoir on acid
all night, walking round the vast concrete bowls and bizarre
pieces of abandoned machinery from a bygone age. One piece
of machinery was called 'The Brontosaurus'. A nearby brick-
built cubicle was called the Tardis. A railed-off square protrusion
about halfway along one of the giant bowls was known as the
Royal Box, and lads would sit on those railings, admiring the
view from the highest point in Manchester.'

One night in spring 1984, three extremely drunken lads took
some luminous green paint, and wrote huge words around the
concrete bowl, including 'The Doors', in honour of the 60s' rock
band, executed in the style the band themselves used on their
album covers. The letters were fifty feet high. We were like the
ancients, assailing the heavens with our symbols and messages, in
the hope of an answer from the forces of nature. The older lads
around town, the borderline original hippies and 70s' wallas, must
have sensed that change was under way; the Perry Boys and scallies were on the move, from the football terraces, to the woods, to
the cricket pavilions, to the magical and secret places of the mind.

'They invented another fashion from nothing, like they
invented the football culture,' recalled Glen, one of the older
lads. 'It was the same set of lads. When the incentive to keep

going to the football, done up in their togs, had worn off, they turned it all inside out. Where before it was all about what you wore on the outside, now it was about what you had to offer from the inside, how original and clever you could be after a few tokes and a couple of tabs. A bunch of style boys suddenly became poets.'

The drugs, music and psychotropic literature all contributed to an atmosphere of fantastic revolution and possibility. It was very unusual not to be intoxicated somehow, and the idols of decades past revisited the minds of the young. The focus for robbing moved from clothes to other things. An anonymous quote says that those who were never caught will never have bragging rights to their secret crimes, and unfortunately this is the case here. You are only reading half a tale, and I must apologise. My tendency to be light-fingered was accompanied by a lightning hand, and innumerable books and bottles of wine and brandy were deftly whisked from beneath the noses of bookshop and off-licence owners within a considerable radius. You could fill an Olympic-sized swimming pool with the booze I walked with. Books also. I never saw the point in nicking stuff just to sell it to buy booze. All I ever asked for in this life was a good drink and a good book, so I just cut out the middle man and went straight for that. My salt-of-the-earth parents were confused and angered by the transformation in their son, who appeared to have been possessed by a screeching gargoyle. It seemed I was either being thrown out of the house or leaving voluntarily every few days, while embarking on mayhem around Manchester. If the shop was open, I swept in and did my magic trick, making goods disappear under even the flimsiest shirts. One day I obtained *Lord of the Rings* for a laugh to entertain my girlfriend, wearing a thin cotton shirt that miraculously camouflaged the doorstep-thick tome. She threw it over a railing, so I made her climb over and retrieve it, giving her a push and leaving two big green hand prints in oil paint on her arse: I had stolen a gallon of paint earlier and given a local public building a new coat, daubing 'ACID' and 'LSD' all over the walls, as well as myself. She was wearing a new, hundred-quid white suit, and it was ruined.

If the shops were shut, then it was smash the front window
and straight in, grabbing all the bottles of gin and cigarettes on
hand. One night, myself and a lad whose brother called him
Bilbo Baggins, steamed an off licence in full view of about
twenty people queuing at a bus-stop. They looked shocked,
apart from one lad stood laughing his balls off as we disappeared
through a time warp between buildings and were gone. I went
home to bring my stereo to Bilbo's flat, so I could play him a
tape by the new California band Green On Red, and while I
was carrying it, drunk, along the road, two lads pulled up in a
car, and offered to give me a lift. As I jumped in the back seat
they said, 'Just go and check that boot's locked mate,' and when
I jumped out they fucked off with my stereo. I walked, sobbing
madly, back to Bilbo's, and we went looking for them in a motor
with a little posse, but they'd vanished. Only the thought of
more mayhem and outright hammer could relieve the pain of
insanity inside.

I had several run-ins with my old feller, culminating in one
completely arseholed day when I came home and swore at my
mother ('Fuck off!'), then crashed out. The old feller came home
from work and steamed into me and gave me the monty,
punching and kicking, the lot. Then he packed a case and pissed
me off out of the door. I declared I was off to party on Jim
Morrison's grave, fuck this for a game of soldiers. I turned up
round the corner at Kenny's with a black eye, to see if he fancied
a trip to Paris for some bohemian adventures among the poets
and artists of the Left Bank. Kenny's mam steamed me again, this
time verbally ('You've gorra bloody good mam and dad, you
'ave, and you'd better start appreciatin' them, and get back round
there *right now* and apologise!'), and sent me back round to our
house with a flea in my ear. So much for the rebel without a
cause. I went back in the house. My folks were gutted, angled
silhouettes, protruding grimly from the chairs in the gloom of
the lounge, as I plodded darkly up to my room. I opened the
suitcase my dad had packed, and there in the middle of my
clothes was *John Lennon in His Own Words*, a book I had often
read, before embarking on the insane drug trips and destructive

riots of late. My dad had put it in there, a gesture of brotherhood in a world we cannot control. It woke me up, and I went downstairs and had a laugh with my mum and dad, the two people who have always been my best friends as much as my parents. They are as honest as the day is long, and so am I, believe it or not. I really love my parents, as they have always refused to make excuses for my behaviour and forced me to take responsibility for myself. It took a long, long time, but it paid off eventually.

The first game of the 1984–85 season, United played Watford, and me and Kenny went in the Scoreboard Paddock, pissed as farts on Tennent's Super. I climbed up into the rafters and hung high above the crowd, before letting myself drop. By some miracle, I landed on Kezz, who was there with the Thompson Twins and a load of other nutters. I was paralytic drunk, and went on to climb the railings between us and the edge of the Scoreboard End. Then, for a laugh, I started chanting, 'Liveeerpoool! Liveeerpoool!' at the lads in the Scoreboard Paddock. The Watford fans looked puzzled, but the United lot were familiar with such nonsense by then.

But it was only just beginning.

While the national papers finally began to feature the stories of young men in the capital who spent 'fortunes' on their fashionable clothing – a whole new 'London' phenomenon in 1984 – the youth of Manchester began to evolve once more, this time wending their way into the nightclubs and pubs of Britain's second city. John-Q-, one of the Prestwich elders, who had lived the entire gamut of music from the late-60s to the mid-80's, was relieved that the world had finally caught up with him. At least part of it, anyway:

'By now, most of us were worldly enough to know that we lived in a nation of lunatic working class whose movements were media broadcast to the masses via a group of middle class drips with useless college degrees who failed utterly to understand what was going on until it was almost over. So, when a lot of young people in Manchester in 1983 and 1984 started to take acid and speed together with a lot of weed, and dance all night under the consequent effects, they did not expect the national media to get wind of it for at least five years, which is exactly what happened.'

When the lad fashions receded into their faded denims, suedes and tweed, and the aroma of marijuana smoke began to cast its magic tendrils through the air, people's taste in music began to take a turn for the different: Bob Dylan, John Lennon, Roxy Music and David Bowie were not cutting it any more. Something with a bit of serious psychedelic clout was called for. People were starting to get uncontrollably fucked-up on mind drugs collectively for the first time since the 60s, and festivities were in order. John-Q- had a massive record collection, full of bands you'd never heard of, playing music that frightened you to death, it was so good. Rebellion was the central theme. The Doors' singer Jim Morrison became a regular discussion point with his refusal to play by the rules, the acid intake, and outrageous exploits under said influence, though the music didn't frighten like some. Bands like the Soft Boys, whose singer-songwriter Robyn Hitchcock was revered as a Lizard King-Monty Python hybrid and psychedelic icon to the growing self-awareness, were played endlessly, sung out loud by people who revelled in the craziness of the lyrics and the tunes. John-Q- regularly held taping nights, when he would make cassettes for people hungry for samples of the new sounds. And the old.

'Syd Barrett, the Moody Blues, Robyn Hitchcock and the Soft Boys, Frank Zappa, Daevid Allen, Kevin Ayers and Talking Heads became the only stuff worth listening to, as it brought on that much-sought experience of being scared shitless in your armchair. By the mid 80s, a slew of American, Australian and European bands had flooded Manchester's record stores with psychedelic music: Magazine, the Only Ones, Green on Red, Plasticland, Thin White Rope, the Naked Prey, The Creeps, the Crimson Shadows, the Rain Parade, Lipstick Killers, the Dream Syndicate, the Beasts of Bourbon, Lizard Train, the terrifying Sky Sunlight Saxon, and many, many more. I used to make tapes for all the lads, and they'd all be pissed and stoned in the pub the next day, singing the songs, lyric for lyric. When they should have probably been in college, young lads were dedicating themselves to learning every word of Robyn Hitchcock's *Black Snake Díamond Röle* album instead. They were daft but they were years ahead of the game. More than a few of them owned musical instruments, or could sing. If only they'd've put down the bong and left the acid and speed out for a while, they could've made it. As it goes, the Manchester bands were OK, but I'm sure a lot of potential stars around at the time missed out, due to their own utter craziness. That's the way it goes, though. The Roses and Mondays are the exceptions that prove the rule.'

Music, drugs and associated equipment became the objects of desire, as the clothing took a back seat: plain lambswool sweaters and T-shirts from Marks & Spencer, frayed Levi's and Hush Puppies. The small-scale pipelines were apparently still largely responsible for bringing contraband into Britain and selling it directly, which was reflected in the high quality of the merchandise. There was one crew of lads who specialised in bringing acid in, sellotaped under their top lips, and they were always available, knocking out the good stuff in the pubs and streets. There was still a dazzling array of smokables available in Manchester, myriad types of lysergic acid and regularly changing forms of amphetamine sulphate.

'One week it was large pink crystals,' remembered The Satisfied Customer, 'the next it was white powder, the next it was fine-grained yellow "champagne", followed by large unprocessed granules that resembled brown sugar which sent you into a three-day trip, hallucinating and hearing things and going right off it. The fucking doctor had to come out and administer a sedative one day, after I'd been up for three days straight and was completely radio-rental off my rocker on that brown granuley shit. Everyone was into it. It was Speed City.'

The return to mind drugs was well under way when the hippie convoy rolled into the outskirts of Bolton, at Edgeworth, in the early summer of 1984, for a festival. The hippies were engulfed as hordes of young scallies descended upon their camp, demanding acid, speed and pot. The Satisfied Customer recalled, 'The marquees and tents were raised and the two very different tribes went at it, dancing and tripping into the night, out of our minds, eventually becoming One. It was chemical exploration, and we all became united in a tide of high-grade shit. Some of the young Perry lads were getting up and having a bash on the guitars and drums, as they were trying to form psychedelic bands of their own at the time. The hippies were surprised at how knowledgeable they were about music, acid and the history of the hippie thing. We discovered that we were actually very similar to them. A young girl ran away with the hippie convoy and we didn't set eyes on her for three fucking years.

'One day at Edgeworth, after five miscellaneous acid hits and a lungful of black from a caravan called The Tardis, I forgot who I was, and spent half an hour walking in a nightmare dreamscape, struggling for purchase on my identity. I never did completely recall who I'd been before that particular dosage. When I hitched home that night, my family seemed to recognise me, so I played along with it and just took it from there. No-one's ever said owt, so I assume that must have been who I was.

'The annual beer seminar was held in Prestwich in May 1985, which I attended faithfully. An old-fashioned United dinosaur was manning one of the booths, and he cheerfully told me some stories from the old days, about when United went into the Second Division and took the piss. It was free ale all day. I ended up bladdered, and crashed out in a field in Prestwich Clough. When I woke up, it was twilight, and I trudged home, having missed the European Cup Final. It was the night of Heysel, when Liverpool and Juventus met with disastrous consequences. It was the beginning of a time when politicians were forced to become more involved with what happened on the terraces. The supporters took the blame for a wall that collapsed, but things were to happen in the future that couldn't be quite so easily blamed on hooligans. This wasn't for want of trying, though.'

At this point, a lot of the boys were trekking off for cosmic adventures abroad. I certainly had my share of adventures, always ready for learning something new. But it was a great pleasure, back in Manchester, to have a chinwag with some of the voyagers, and catch up on developments on the building sites of

Germany, the kibbutzim of Israel, or current quality of the product in Morocco. Between 1985 and 1987, I enjoyed several eventful trips to Israel, Egypt, Canada, and back to Egypt to check that the pyramids were still there. I never took more than the absolute minimum amount of cash, but managed to see huge areas of those countries, stopping in London for a few months here and there. All the lads were bubbling with stories, and it was always a laugh to bring outsiders to Manchester to show them how we lived. It wasn't until I met lads from other parts of Britain that I realised how mental Mancs were, and that's saying something.

By 1987, the Electric Banana, a new club off Albert Bridge in the city centre, was playing all the psychedelic sounds, simul-taneous with a constantly moving wall-sized projection featuring bacteria, scientists, irregular blobs, dancing girls, etc, while the groovers danced to the electric tunes of this great era. The Electric Banana became The Asylum, but the bowls of Rizzla papers were still sited along the bar, and herb was smoked openly by paisley-wearing regulars. The club was lamented deeply when it was burned beyond repair in a fire at the end of the year. John-Q- was a regular on the scene, often discussing obscure sounds with the DJs.

'By then, others had begun to cater for the psychedelic craze, and things were moving into second gear. Everyone had been at it for a few years, and the clothes had gone very trippy – lots of paisley and bell-bottoms worn with long hair. The draw was still cheap, and it was common to hear about people smoking "star-spangled bongs", a bong filled with ice-cold whisky or brandy, loaded with a combination of different product; a bunch of grass, studded with Leb and Moroccan black, with some hash oil thrown in for good measure. They were getting themselves into some right states. Any club worth its salt at this time featured at least a partial concession to psychedelic music, and the Madchester bands started to spread their message, becoming acknowledged as *bona fide* additions to the growing catalogue. The smiley face began to shine, and the term "acid house" was used to describe proceedings, but it really hadn't even started yet.'

This was the Nameless Thing Revisited, a bunch of scally-wags simply indulging in various experiments in recreational and full-time hedonism. The bagginess of the clothes, the long hair, the laid-back attitude, all seemed set for an eternity of stoned-out bliss, a wonderland that couldn't be spoiled. Or could it?

15

ACID HOUSE, RAVE
AND TECHNO

I'm so mean I make medicine sick.
—Muhammad Ali

EVER SINCE I was a small child, living in that brickish labyrinth of many stories and storeys, I was aware of a certain class of citizen which it paid not to fuck with. In the part of town where I lived, there were individuals said to belong to The Families, groups of men and women who over generations had coalesced into an underground society, so tight you could not insert a razor blade between them. Once again, the media of the time was hopelessly ignorant of the situation, choosing instead to report on the power moves executed by crafty cockneys, while refusing to admit to any organised criminal presence in the north, as it didn't fit into the land of make-believe which they populated. But there was always someone in Salford who knew someone who would blow your kneecaps off, just like in East London. It was that port-city thing, generations of foreign DNA tadpoling its way into the community and making diamond mongrels, the hardiest of the species. The area had earned a vicious reputation for bloody violence and murder over many years, the bulk of the activity centring on the docks, always a traditional battleground in which hard men fought out their animal claims to rank over the industrial human group. The shotgun mobs were well known, and The Families had controlled that part of Salford forever. Only established members of other

Salford Families dared to challenge the authority of whoever ruled what patch at any given time. And then the shit would hit the fan. But they were English, and that meant something special; our hard men went at it without weapons when necessary, often inflicting horrendous and life-threatening injuries upon one another in their various bids for supremacy.

Gang-related violence among the young population is part of our nature. In Salford and Manchester, there were large violent gangs of young people on the loose long before the football hooligans and the Families of today. When the industrial revolution caused the population of Manchester to explode in the mid-nineteenth century, street gangs emerged from the multi-layered squalor of the cobbled streets. Peter Walsh, in his book *Gang War*, documents this emergence from the smoky mills and chaotic brothels and beer houses:

> In the midst of this unstable mix came the Scuttlers, strangely dressed youth gangs that appeared suddenly and aggressively around 1870 in the poverty-stricken Rochdale Road area. Their name may have referred to the sound they made when they ran in their clogs, like scuttling insects. The cult spread across the Manchester-Salford conurbation and was unique to the area, where there was a huge demand for juvenile labour. Most of the gang members were aged between fourteen and nineteen; anyone over twenty was a veteran. At any time there were twenty or thirty gangs, with names like the Bengal Tigers, the She Battery Mob and Buffalo Bill's Gang. They were style conscious, their clothes an outlandish affront to older generations. Boys and girls wore bell-bottomed trousers, pointed-toed clogs, silk neckties and long fringes plastered over one eye, topped with pointed caps pulled down at a jaunty angle.

Mark-L-., who lived and loved the times, strings together an interesting thread of commonality, from the Scuttlers all the way to the subject of this book. 'Some of the descriptions of the

Scuttlers, particularly the long fringes, could be used to charac-
terise the appearance of the much later Perry Boys. A typical
fight could entail between two and three hundred fighting but
although the battles were terribly fierce, only a handful of deaths
were reported in the Salford and Manchester papers. The
Scuttler fights were reported in sensationalist tones, but they
neglected to mention that the violence was largely targeted at
other gangs rather than innocent members of the public. Again
comparison to the behaviour of today's hooligan gangs is in
evidence in this fact and also that they were prepared to travel a
few miles to take on rival gangs in foreign territory. Ironically,
we consider the fact the Perry Boy thing is even *remembered* to
be a sure indication of its significance, but is it, really? Why is a
youth movement that started nearly twenty-eight years ago of
any relevance today? I mean twenty-eight years! Taking that
period back again, from the birth of the Perry Boy, we'd be back
in the nineteen fifties, a time when Britain was emerging from
the poverty of World War Two, and rock 'n' roll was the big
thing. Many people involved in the early eighties style-hooligan
revolution in north-west England probably think this is proof of
how very different we were, but there's always an exception that
raises questions. Not a lot of people realise this, but when
Bolton beat United in the FA Cup Final in 1958, just months
after the Munich air disaster, the young people of Salford
prepared a very special welcome for the Bolton team coach
when it passed along Bolton Road in Salford on its way home
with the FA Cup. A huge mob of kids assailed the Bolton coach
with a variety of missiles, chiefly stones, and there was uproar
about it. Bolton's coach George Taylor described Salford as "red
Indian territory", and the incident went down in folklore as
"the Cheyenne Ambush".

'The fact is, Salford has always been home to a lot of ener-
getic young people who are compelled to organise and cause
disruption to the usual daily flow. Where there is football, in
Salford, there is trouble, and before football there was trouble.
It's not about football, it's about trouble, and Salford is a place
that causes it. From those lads who started the last great style-

hooligan trend, to the rowdy kids who peppered the Bolton bus, all the way back to the Scuttlers, nothing has changed. The Scuttlers were not a dubiously named modern-day homosexual soccer firm, but the feared gangs of Manchester and Salford in the Victorian era that fought out to-the-death turf wars around the Docks area. The different crews had names such as the Ordsall Lane Gang or Hope Street Gang and battled with bottles, knives and heavy belt buckles in the shadow of where Old Trafford now stands. It is strange to relate such similar activities and attitudes from over a hundred years ago, but there has clearly always been a need for young lads to dress up and have a go.'

Many cities claim themselves as England's number one farm for hardcases, but these claims can be neither substantiated nor refuted. We are surely all equals, but even the 'cockneys sense that there is something rare and precious in the air in Salford, something that speaks for all of us and refuses to be stopped in its tracks, something borne of innovation and change. Perhaps there's the stuff of fiction or romance about it, but just as everyone is scared shitless of West Ham and Millwall due to the London docks image, so they are too of Manchester United. The association with Salford is a big part of it, but which came first, the chicken or the egg? I apologise to other men in other cities suffering from symptoms of the Peter Pan complex where they, too, sit and dream and make ridiculous claims about being 'harder' than everywhere else, as there are too many places to mention and too little time. We all like to imagine that our troop is the handiest in the jungle. Being the 'hardest' is only one piece of it. Being the most adaptable is by far the majority of it, and herein lies the kicker, so to speak. It is the call of the wild, the response of Life to a new world called Industrialism. We got the jump on the rest of yiz, and yer know what that means…

The 70s saw a mass migration out from the inner-cities to the suburbs, garden cities and New Towns, a one-way flow of human traffic that would forever alter the character of many cities, Manchester included. Back in the 60s, things were still relatively undisturbed. People lived a natural life, in communi-

ties that had developed over vast time periods, laminated by the
organic, four-dimensional onion skin of time and place. The
soils were made of our ancestors, our food and our hearts.
Commerce was unchanged for millennia; there was a little shop,
or a yard, or a market stall, where you could go to buy specific
things, often on tick if need be. The big-box stores of the present
were non-existent; only the one-off corner shops and places like
Woolworths were required. The rows of shops, each specialising
in something different, like a butcher's, newsagents (with big
double-decker bubble-gum machines outside), pie shop, pet
shop, carpet shop, chip shop, were always packed with people
busily getting in the grub and newspaper. The main drags, like
Regent Road, Chapel Street and Bury New Road, were lined
with stores, and the natives moved along the swarming pave-
ments like ants. Lower Broughton Road on a Saturday
afternoon was abuzz with its greengrocers, bookies and hazy
pubs such as Poets' Corner and the Royal Archer. A constant
stream of people from the flats poured both ways across
Broughton Bridge to buy that week's food and get the beer in,
mobbing the public toilets halfway across, which themselves
resembled the Old Trafford latrines on a match day, such were
the numbers. It's impossible now to imagine people actually
queuing in droves to have a quick slash. The place was alive.

Everybody served a purpose, and those that didn't were
marked as having strange ways. The steel and glass of Salford
Quays was a futuristic unknown, and the soot-darkened warrens
of back-to-backs that hemmed in the docks were a magical
cacophony of sound and activity. The 'sunrise to sunset' cobbled
play-streets of Salford were decorated with multi-coloured
chalk, and on occasion ribbons and flags, and people kept
chickens in their backyards. Women pushed prams through
puddles to the Flat Iron market, and men were invisible during
daylight hours, immersed in whatever labour had engaged or
kidnapped them.

One night in that maze, and beyond, to the ends of the earth,
many little angels were unexpectedly woken up in the middle
of the night by the adults. They were excitedly brought down-

stairs and put in front of the telly. It was difficult to make out
the images on the screen; a glimpse of a human body part here
and there, and a lot of darkness. The picture was distant, and
strained. Eventually, the sight of men in big puffy suits with
goldfish bowls on their heads appeared. They were moving
about in a fashion most peculiar. *The Eagle had landed*. Man was
on the moon.

It seemed there was a parade of some kind every other week
back then: baton-twirling, bugle-blowing, Union Jack-waving,
oom-pa-pa-ing, big base drumming, uniformed red and blue
soldiers, steaming down the main drags, bringing the traffic to a
standstill, drawing crowds of thousands, who cheered and
smiled, in their suits, ties, pretty dresses and shoes. Whit Week
was always a big deal. We kids would get decked out in new
clothes: shirts, elastic ties, short pants and socks, with new shoes.
My mother even bought herself a blonde wig one year. Whitsun
was the first time I ever heard the word 'blazer', as myself and
cousins all got one. I remember the parades down Regent Road
and Littleton Road, the masses of adults, often the Scouse arm
of the family descending on us, which always meant plenty of
drinking. Every Sunday we'd go to my nana's in Kersal. There'd
be about ten cousins all eating their Sunday dinners from plates
on newspaper spread across the floor, like a litter of puppies,
while an elected auntie watched over us all. The rest of the
adults would be in the Racecourse pub, where they had pewter
tankards hung behind the bar.

Having no car, we walked everywhere. I covered miles, the
stench of the factory at the UMP (Universal Metal Products),
the looming but fascinating Ward and Goldstone's plant, and the
monumental motorbike shop, Queen's Park Motors, under its
ornate façade with the towering minaret, covered in tiles like
fish scales. Salford Town Hall stood opposite this fanciful structure, with its lanterns either side of the front doors. The AEU
club round the corner, where I tasted my first Guinness froth as
an infant, seemed to be a second home for my mum's family. My
granddad was something to do with the union, and everyone
knew him. When he died in his 50s of cancer, there were said to

be thousands of people at his Salford funeral. Not bad for a Scouse, eh? The Maypole pub had an actual maypole outside, and right across from it was the chaotic market, looking more like something from Morocco than Manchester. Through the market, the maze of two-up, two-downs and across the big roundabout, you hit Trafford Road. Ordsall always had a heavy-duty atmosphere, and the enormous factories, grain warehouses and illuminated billboards for cigs and whisky at the docks made me feel like I was in New York, especially at night, with the brand-new adjacent Precinct lights blazing like the stars. I would pretend that the curved glass Manchester Liners building, with its name illuminated in red along the rim, was Old Trafford, and that the sign actually said 'Manchester United'. Funnily enough, Old Trafford today resembles that extinct structure. The docks possessed me, and I yearned to get in there and feel the pull of the oceans. There were Navy ships and submarine shows there, and I was amazed at the height of the subs' towers. The storage structures, office blocks, cranes and stacks of undistinguishable material were penned in behind an ageless brick wall that ran for a mile or more along Trafford Road. Its occasional large gates were the entrance to my own personal Willy Wonka factory, more transporting than any chocolate bar. It was like Aladdin's Cave.

My Uncle Norman, who lived all around Ordsall and Weaste, was a hero to me. A sailor in the Merchant Navy, he'd been around the world several times. His muscular arms were covered in tattoos from all continents, and he had more stories to tell than a million books by scallies like this. He had a reputation for being able to look after himself around the area, and that's saying something. He went into construction and worked on the doors, always a colourful character, with his red hair and handlebar moustache. Tales of him taking on several at a time and winning were common round Salford. He was taken by cancer in his 40s, and it wasn't nice to see a man like that reduced as he was, but he went far longer with the Big C than the doctors predicted. After seeing him during his last Christmas in extreme pain in their house in Weaste, I took a taxi home and sobbed my heart out like I'd never done before. I remember his funeral, at St. Paul's church in Salford Precinct. The yard outside was packed with hundreds of people, all kinds of people, but especially tidy-looking blokes from the construction and what-have-you in the area. They were jammed in all around the sides and back, paying homage to their Norman. It was quite an army.

The sight of the swing bridge down the bottom end always set my nerves on edge, for beyond lay the real Theatre of Dreams. The big roundabout at the top end of Trafford Road was reputed to be the largest in Europe, and served as a baffling compass with which to orient yourself. The gasometers off Liverpool Street, and the bristling balconies of Regent Square, were town direction; the hulking Clowes pub with its revolving door was the docks direction down Trafford Road and Broadway; the brick facades and white window frames of distant Sutton Flats above the jumble of streets, was Langworthy Road direction; and the old London-style flats on Eccles New Road, with lawns out front behind tidy low walls, pointed to my other nana's house in Weaste, on the banks of the Manchester Ship Canal. We went to my nana's every Saturday, and continued to after she and Granddad were flirted to the eighth floor of Newbank Tower in Greengate, which was very handy after a weary trawl through the department stores of town, looking at carpets and furniture we couldn't afford.

But it was what lay between these points that came to symbolise change in the area more than anything else. Hanky Park, where my mother came from, was an intricate maze of earthen streets and pathways, a life-size jigsaw puzzle made of rock, cobbles, brick, stone, slate, and terracotta, perplexing to outsiders but reassuringly familiar to its swarming inhabitants. This little world was effectively vaporised, all memory of the ancient community razed like a rainforest, making way for harsh, grey concrete in the sky. Salford Precinct slowly rose like a Martian fighting machine from those extensive mineralised mists during my first years on this planet, and the hazy doings of those plodding, grinding monster cranes and diggers was a constant source of awe and fear in me. The natives were blitzed,

confused, like an undiscovered tribe being displaced by
Amazonian logging companies. The many towers, that came to
dominate the Manchester skyline even more so than the city
centre itself, seemed to look down and mock, the million
windows watching, as the demolition ball chased them out of
their warrens, brick dust on their heels. I remember the first
time I went inside one of the towers, and looked out of the
window. It was Sutton House, the first, and possibly the highest,
in Salford. I was with my Auntie Joan, who was visiting a mate
of hers up on the top floor. From the window, the people and
the cars were microscopic; the cars resembled multi-coloured
biologic cells, rounded and shiny.

The estate became legend, and for years the Precinct
symbolised all that was wrong and cool with Manchester:
poverty, violence, drunkenness, gangs, Manchester United and
hundreds of people in designer gear going about their daily
business. It provided a mainframe permanence through which
many lads and lasses would pass, going up, going down, going
to OT, to Europe, to Australia, never to be seen again. The truth
was, most people who ended up on the Precinct were stuck for
life, in resigned despondency. In time, attempts were made to
civilise the flats and the people in them, but it wasn't easy.
Security guards were installed during the 80s, but many left
their posts within hours. A source of amusement for locals was
to drop refrigerators, washing machines and television sets from
the higher floors, preferably when the security guard was stood
outside having a fag to calm his already ramped-up nerves. The
Satisfied Customer witnessed a particularly alarming incident
in the mid-80s:

'This one security guard had already had a right good hiding,
and it was only his second night on the job, but he wasn't a bad
bloke. He was stood there, having a smoke, after some nutter had
threatened to bring his python down from the twentieth floor
and stuff it into his little lodge in the foyer, when a fucking big
fridge landed about two feet from him. The fridge exploded,
and I think he might have actually shit his pants. We didn't see
him again after that.'

During the mid–80s, as the whole 'lad' culture was formalised in the retarded national media, a number of notable individuals operated under cover of fear and underworld connections. Some of these individuals were from the Manchester area. Several were connected to the notorious organised crime families tightly dovetailed to Manchester. Many of the old-fashioned British gangster types were superseded by a new breed of villain, and the use of handguns replaced the familiar shotgun of yesteryear. As a glut of contraband flowed into Britain from Amsterdam and other continental locations, these individuals secured and locked down the inflow streams, distributing the product as seen fit around Manchester and the north of England, establishing a formidable drugs and arms supply centre.

Brian-W-, a shopfitter who worked in Manchester city centre, ran into an embarrassing situation one afternoon in a city centre pub. 'I was with some lads from work on our lunch hour,' he said. 'When I went for a piss, I walked into the toilets, and there was these two blokes there. One of them had a big leather bag zipped open on the floor, and the other bloke was having a gander at it. I didn't hang about long, but it was long enough to spot a couple of fucking machine guns. A few months later, I saw the bloke again. Another feller asked him where he was off to, and he said, "London, a bit of business." As he said it, he patted the breast of his suit, to mean he was carrying. Guns got popular and that was that, I suppose.'

Certain parts of cities become dangerous during these transitions, and the infrastructure rapidly withers like a dying leaf. The new breed of gangster in Manchester provided a form of policing in the inner-city, in areas deemed unworthy of attention from the police in uniform, and to a large extent this helped keep the undesirables under control. It was in cities and towns that *lacked* a strong mafia presence that muggers were able to operate with impunity, without fear of being brought into line by some locally respected individual. In many ways, the gangs were the cream that hadn't flown the nest, those that were able to modify their environment to their own ends. Many people in places like Ordsall were thankful for their presence, as without them the petty criminals and muggers would have been rampant. The areas neglected by the police evolved into fortress-like no-go zones, where blood relatives and familiar faces alone were welcome. The ability to operate illegally with little fear of prosecution created a powerful underworld in a city that was ripe for the picking.

Many stories circulated, such as the one about the gangster in the long coat, who carried a shotgun. One night he walked into a Salford pub to collect his protection money. The landlord was there, with some members of his family. He refused to pay. During an argument, the landlord whipped out a knife and plunged it right through the gangster's hand, pinning it to the bar. The gangster pulls an axe out from under his long coat and brings it down on the landlord's head. He got his fucking protection money.

This was the type of thing that happened in the Rainy City, and people proudly presented the latest morsels of mayhem from the gossip mill, the dregs of the grapevine, if you will. Some would swirl the rumour around their mouths for a moment, before spitting it out. Others would digest the infor-mation, pondering on it for longer than was healthy. The spitters and the digesters formed two groups, an audience for the mayhem, segregated by opinion, like a football crowd. But in time, the line between 'control' and 'out of control' became blurred, and both the Mob and the men in blue must have been scratching their heads at the level of lunacy afoot. The faceless drones, the Perries of old, the bad lads and the loveable rogues, were galvanising into such numbers as to create a visible alternative to law and order. As our delusional Chief of Police, James Anderton, went down in a religion-crazed haze, Madchester rose on the horizon like a sunrise in the west, a weird ball of energy drawing all into its sway, into its dance, into its consciousness. The grassroots heads were clamouring for a taste of the nightclub splendour, and they broke the padlock on sanity.

As a backdrop to all this druggery and skulduggery, which presumably wasn't just happening in my neighbourhood, other forms of more organised self-expression were developing. Gradually, new bands emerged, playing an enticing combination of 60s' psychedelia with a more modern 80s' electrifying dance beat, a parallel to the evolution of the Boys from more modish and traditional beginnings at the end of the 70s. Manchester bands began to make retro music for a while, before realising that the genre was actually superior to anything being produced at the time, and suddenly it exploded in a fruity, modern form, championed by the Stone Roses, Charlatans and the Happy Mondays, among others, in a fantastic complement to the light shows, dancing and drugs in the clubs. The ex-football boys weren't surprised at all.

'We'd been waiting for something like this for a long time, when it finally broke,' said Glen. 'That the chief initiators were of the laddish breed went without saying, but the rest of the country was only just grasping the football side of things. It's amazing to think that, while certain cities were exploring the "new" Casual styles, those old styles began to mutate once again, and trousers went bell-bottom, jackets became faded denim, hair grew long and wild and ultimately everything went very, very baggy. T-shirts, pants, shoes, hair, life, voices, faces, attitudes – all became really laidback and of a distinctly intellectual nature, probably a reflection of the superior marijuana and other drugs with which the city was being flooded at the time.'

Who was doing the flooding? That's a good question, and one that appears to have influenced the course of things considerably.

The fashions changed rapidly in the north-west, and people, including gangsters, were forced to adapt to what had become credible and what had not. The same people who, years earlier, had prized expensive tracksuits now prized expensive cars. Accessories to the fashions took a sinister turn, coincident with the sudden emergence of the Yardies, Jamaican gangs that began to invade the English inner-cities, bringing handgun culture with them. The shotgun wallas were done. This was do or die, and Salford rose to the challenge, as did Moss Side and Cheetham Hill, by equipping themselves with an arsenal of illegal revolvers, automatic pistols, assault rifles and fully automatic machine guns, by any means necessary. The Yardie menace was easily repelled in Manchester, due to the gangs already having had access to firearms for several years. The Yardies were forced to position themselves outside Manchester, probably the only major British city able to successfully exclude them by force.

Glen described the irony in the situation: 'This was not a victory for law and order. Manchester and Salford were simply defending their turf. It was the biggest market outside London, and there was no way those players were going to surrender their place at the head of the billion-dollar checkout line. Kids like myself had always known about the situation in inner-city Manchester, but now it seemed the situation was being glamorised, televised, and the nation was learning about the true extent of Manchester and Salford's involvement with the British underworld.'

The media had a field day with the news of an organised crime presence this large. Between Moss Side, Cheetham Hill and Salford there was an abundance of cheap-thrill material to slap on the television, and people devoured it. There were regular news reports and documentaries, in which anonymous 'gangsters' were interviewed, their faces scrambled by computer, providing the public with inside information on the gang scene. In the eyes of many, this was betrayal, and the identities of these 'grasses' needed working out.

'Someone realised that if you squinted your eyes while looking at the television, you could see through the computerised shield,' said the Satisfied Customer. 'The face of the person became a lot clearer. If you were in a boozer somewhere, and something like this came on, everyone would instantly squint, like they'd been impacted by some poison gas, all staring at the telly. It was dead funny. Squinting was a sign you knew the score, even if you were just a day-tripper.'

It became commonplace for young men to leave Britain for foreign climes, often settling there for years, even for life. North America and Australia received large numbers of young people seeking new decent lives, ones that Britain couldn't offer them, and families and friends were left behind as the lure of sunshine, opportunity and money drove them on into the unknown. It was a sad phenomenon, one that broke up working class families who mistakenly saw it as a blessing, as they were so used to being shat on by the system. The cultural landscape of Britain was changing once again, largely in response to years of unemployment and poverty, endured by intelligent people in a country blighted by ignorance and neglect. These emigrants were often people who simply refused to live beneath themselves, precisely the type of people a country needs if it is to improve itself in a meaningful and just way. Unable to prosper in the impoverished British environment, they sought friendlier climes, more responsive pastures.

Travelling abroad was on the increase, and it wasn't just the concert swag boys and grafters who were spending months away on the road. Some took off for Tenerife and parts of mainland Spain, while others went on a grand tour of Greece and Turkey, on the piss for weeks and weeks on end. In early 1988, I flew to New York with Dave Leckie, a mate who'd already been to Florida in 1987 while I was in Canada, and we went back down to Miami to sample the delights of college America's famous 'Spring Break'. It was mayhem, and I was very sorry to come home. America had cast a spell on me; back then it wasn't somewhere you considered going for a three month jib, but we'd managed it, and I wanted more.

Many of the young men who flew the nest during this time were surprised at the way things had altered each time they returned to Manchester. 'People who had warned me of the evils of drugs like acid just a year ago were now acid dealers, hanging round in the clubs and pubs, wearing the baggy clothes and talking the lingo, with a glazed look,' said Paul -L-. 'It was weird. The former lads of yesteryear would give each other the knowing wink, but the entire place had been colonised by a new breed, one that was driven by the yuppie drive for success and a reckless need for good times and loud music.'

The gangsters and the yuppie dealers consolidated their respective skills, bringing it in the back door, totally devaluing

the acid and speed, cutting it to within an inch of its life, but at
this time a new compound was filtering into the market, one
that would change everything. 'The many herbals of old were
replaced around 1985 by a generic green hash product called
Sputnik, which was neither one thing nor another,' said Paul.
'We just thought it was Afghani cos of its name, but who knows?
Its quality went up and down, due to animal tranquilizer or
something a bit hallucinogenic, that was either shite or fucked
you right up. The past few years of speed and acid had seen a big
downturn in the quality, thanks to the hunger for money.

'The numbers of small scale operations involving students
and hippies had disappeared because of the new breed. The
opportunists saw possibilities in the popularity of the drugs
scene in Manchester, and they chopped their product up with
anything that came to hand, knowing everybody else was doing
the same, and that only those in the know could get decent gear.
If you were "from the neighbourhood" you could still find the
nice tackle, but most of the Johnny-come-latelys had to be
content with diluted shite, as demand threatened to outstrip
supply, as amazing as that seems.'

But something novel was in the air, something that rendered
the acid and speed issues defunct; a molecule that came to be
called Ecstasy, a drug that possessed all the beneficial properties
of LSD and amphetamine, and more besides. By some remarkable coincidence, the effects of this substance were tailor made
for the type of music flooding the clubs of the city. The fertile
nature of the creative mind responded hugely to the compound.
It was the roar of a new germ, one that had been unexpectedly
placed in proximity to the precincts of another germ, the
Nameless Thing of yesteryear. So-called indie bands sprouted
like Technicolor mushrooms everywhere, all frantically trying to
express their own unique version of what Ecstasy had revealed
to them about themselves, all striking the same familiar series of
chords, a tune that echoed in the nooks and crannies of the
mind like birdsong or the rustling of leaves. It was a primeval
organic experience, one that took the user to deeper places than
anything encountered before, at least as long as the rush lasted.

The speedy, complex nature of Ecstasy, coupled with its tendency to place the user in a state of empathy, enabled a self-created world to spring into being, beginning in the clubs that played the right music and provided the best light shows. The compound facilitated apparent heart-to-heart communications between users, resulting in an intimacy and lack of paranoia. The clubs were redesigned to accommodate this fantastic quality, with the installation of special rooms, chambers and furniture, in and on which those affected could sprawl, hug, talk and share together.

The talk turned from 'acid house' to 'raves', and hundreds of young people bamboozled the authorities when they began turning up spontaneously at deserted warehouses in rural outposts, having received printed leaflets containing directions to the latest rave. Entrepreneurial members of the citizenry seized the opportunity to rent warehouse space from owners, or else to simply stage parties in abandoned industrial plants without permission, selling hundreds of gallons of water and thousands of hits of this bizarre and powerful chemical. The acid house was maturing, and the novel locations caused more to become curious, as increasingly larger numbers of people drifted down the motorways in search of a rave, homing in on service stations, where messages were disseminated by the organisers to avoid detection by the authorities.

Some found the experience so disconcerting that they never went again. Jeff, a clubber, described the first, and last, warehouse party he ever saw, when he went along with some of the lads from work who were closely connected to the scene: 'I was a bit nervous about even meeting them, cos they told me to be in some pub down Salford, and I knew it'd be dead shady. I went out on my own earlier and got a few scoops down me, for Dutch courage. I walked from town to the pub, and when I arrived, it had graffiti on it, saying things like "Young Firm", and "John-M- is a grass", proper dodgy territory.

'The place was heaving with headcases, and I was relieved to find my mates,' said Jeff. 'There was this big skinhead in a red one-piece Adidas ski suit, bopping about round our table, and he

threw a big plastic bag full of Dennis the Menaces at one of my
mates, who put it in his pocket, and made it clear he was selling.
The ski suit alone was amazing enough, never mind the rest of
the malarkey. A line formed across the pub, and he was doing a
roaring trade. It was obvious there were others at it as well, but
they all seemed to be part of the same crew, as they weren't
arguing or anything. They were rolling unbelievable joints and
passing them round the entire boozer, and the place was full of
smoke and noise. You could hear conversations about this and
that, and believe me it was all business. I was shitting it, thinking
someone was gonna mistake me for a copper any minute. In no
time, I was totally wasted, and that was before I did an E.
Someone leaned over and said something about the Dibble, but
I thought he asked me, "Have you ever flashed yer teeth at a
cripple?" Someone gave it a loud Long John Silver, "Ooh-arr,
Jim, lad!", and within seconds everyone in the place was doing
it. I thought I was going mental.

'Everyone headed out about eleven o' clock, givin' it the
"Ooh-arr" across the car-park in a giant happy mob. We started
driving along the M602 to the party, then on to some other
motorway. One of my mates told me we had to first go to some
junction in the sticks to direct operations. We swung onto some
crossroads with a couple of pubs. What looked like hundreds of
young people were gathered there, waiting patiently for us. It
was insane, like a potentially dangerous football crew that had
decided it wanted to love its opposition. My mate told me to get
out and help him direct people to the warehouse. I asked him,
"What, do we just walk up and down, telling them where it is?"
He turned round and said, "No, you twat. I give you a fucking
wheelbarrow, you on yer hands and me holding yer feet, and
you sing it to them while I push you along, you daft cunt." I was
pissing myself laughing at that, and he gave me a load of leaflets
to dish out to the punters. They were all downing pints of
orange and zooming off, big time.

'We got to the place and I did an E, my first one ever. It was
a weird, triangular white tablet, and it totally took me to the
races. I felt like a ten-foot-tall pink foetus, with a giant dewdrop

hanging off its nose, reflecting all the colours of the rainbow. The rave itself I cannot remember properly, as I was bollocksed on the gear. I just remember a mad mixture of *Emmerdale Farm* and *Star Wars*, as I kept going out into the countryside for a piss, completely absorbed in the trip.

'On the way home the next day, we stopped at a pub some-where. When we got in there, there was a big mob going berserk. My mates must've known what was going on but they didn't warn me, the bastards. I wasn't sure if they were the same ones from last night or not, until I heard that bleeding "Ooh-arr, Jim lad!" coming from a few corners. They took over this pub and gave the landlord a chinning. One lad had a screwdriver out and was taking a big old-fashioned map off the wall. People were helping themselves to pints and cigars and bottles of whisky, while the landlord was pushed into a corner with his fat lip and purple eye. I never went to another rave with the lads from work after that. I stuck to the clubs in town. That was one hell of a way to discover the warehouse scene though.'

There have been many descriptions of what a proper MDMA rush feels like. Apparently, the doses were subject to some vari-ability, which caused the effects to be different in kind and not just in degree. The first flash of a true hit is said to come upon the beholder quite rapidly, if it is a high dose. The user may suddenly find himself somewhere, such as in a bathroom, watching an amazingly shiny chrome tap slowly drip funny, fat dewdrops into a cartoon-like and acoustic wash-basin, or else under a streetlight, gazing at the texture of the paving stones, feeling like he'd been thrust into the animated landscape of a *Dick Tracy*, *Hudsucker Proxy* or *Batman* movie. Any aspects of the user's personal build, such as tallness, chubbiness or shortness, may be manifest explicitly in the objects he sees around him. It may seem difficult to breathe, mainly in response to the high drama of events unfolding within. Mention of a type of car, a colour, a species of flower, or a region in a far-off country, and the unconscious suddenly takes control, rapidly taking the user to the precise moment in their life when they were first introduced to that particular phenomenon or colour, an experience that can be massively enhanced in the pres-

ence of family members or old friends, with whom one shares
common past experiences.

It's as if the mind is mounted upon some wild trolley and
fired at almost light-speed down a vast network of corridors,
each of which is lined with open doors, and a glimpse into each
door reveals, in luminous colour, the first time, the initial exposure to a specific thing or opinion you have developed over your
lifetime, in an instant. As conversations move along, those under
the influence can be seen swooning with amazement every few
seconds, as the trolley sweeps them on super-greased trackways,
through the filamentous matrix of the unconscious, back, back,
to the beginning of each and every line of enquiry they have
ever embarked upon. The corridors are surely the neural pathways of the physical brain itself, and the rooms are the precise
locations in that fabulous network of specific neurons responsible for a unique recognition – the actual individual brain cells
that were involved on the day those molecular memories were
born. If LSD is able to dissociate the user from his or her
personal identity, thereby causing untold personal tremors, then
MDMA takes that state, rinses it in even more vivid colours, and
proceeds to wring the whole thing through a most alarming
mangle, where it separates the various starting points of the individual's personal development, and delivers one to the doorstep
of doorsteps.

It's good shit.

The consciousness-expanding properties of MDMA were
matched only by its stimulant properties, which were becoming
a growing component of the music itself. This latter trended
heavily towards faster and more complex beats and rhythms,
which only skilled musicians or electronic instruments could
truly express, and a mass of anonymous players entered the
game, bearing weird and wonderful stage names. DJ's became
ever-more important to the overall experience, and the ability
to rig up a tight visual accompaniment to whatever sounds were
playing became crucial. The thing was now totally fluid,
unbounded and moving through all the barriers, all the senses.
People called the thing 'Techno'.

Clubs began to specialise in Techno, and the resident DJs, witch doctors of the sacred substance themselves, competed for the title of Top Shaman, each one vying for maximum credibility in the darkened sanctums behind innumerable unassuming facades all around the city centre. Manchester was by no means the only place this was happening, but it was the only place it was being executed so professionally, and by so many. From Acid House to Rave to Techno, the shoals of smartly-dressed lads on the coral reef terraces were slowly trawled into the scene.

Phil Thornton gave a diagnosis for the easy transmigration from the football terraces to the clubs in his book *Casuals*:

> Previously, dancing was something you did for one reason only: to cop off at crap clubs. Now it became an enjoyable activity in its own right. 'E' loosened limbs and attitudes alike. Unlike the ritualised, elitist Northern Soul and rare grooves scenes, you didn't need to be the best mover, you didn't need to know the release date and catalogue number of the record you were dancing to, all you needed was to be part of it. It was instant acceptance, no holds barred, transparent togetherness. To be part of an acid house night at its height, whether at Shoom or Land of Oz in London, or Hot in Manchester, was to be a part of something special.

Indeed. The Satisfied Customer more than agreed: 'We were in the clubs to knock out the product, get shickered and high, and hopefully cop a bit of a fright off the light show. We didn't even know the name of the fucking club half the time, never mind the DJ or the tunes he was banging on. The irony is that while we looked down our noses at the punters who we considered divs trying to be cool, we ourselves were too cool to even admit that we liked the music. We'd try to convince ourselves it was all about offloading the product and winding each other up by unexpectedly zapping purses in each others laps for a laugh. The truth was, we were addicted to the whole package, and couldn't wait to get stoned and see them strobes going off and on, in and out. Some of the musical breaks in the indie songs would just go on forever, strobes at it and everything. When the song found its way back to the verse again, it felt like a century of mad light-surfing had passed. I'd give my right arm to relive those years.'

What had been an age-long problem in British society appeared to be erased overnight. The Casual crews of the mid to late 80s were refusing to take life seriously as a result of the compound, and levels of football violence dropped precipitously, while the Government turned their attentions to this new 'problem' – people loving and accepting each other rather than slashing each other up with Stanley knives. The song was still the same, only the words had changed. Anything the people did would be wrong in the eyes of those who sought to control them, so the party just carried on. The Salford Mob stormed Manchester like they were the RAF, and the flood came bouncing in. Gone were the days of intense nostril burn from amphetamine sulphate, as the cosy nights of Ecstasy washed over everything like the radiation from a love bomb...

16

BREAKING THE LAW

That's it. Boxing Night's knackered.

—Uncle Norman, having inadvertently punctured the
curled paper tongue of a party horn

THE ENTIRE TENTH floor of the tower-block had been sealed off, and there were no balconies. A couple of dozen sentries were stationed at the bottom of the tower, on every other floor, and along the hallway outside the lift. On floor ten, several DJ stations were set up, and each area was playing a distinct type of Techno or indie music. The floor was packed: girls, lads, dogs, everybody dancing like crazy to the sounds, gazing out of the window towards Old Trafford or town, or somewhere else. Once the rave started, a steel gate was set up, excluding the rest of the world. At one point, several police had attempted to gain access to the floor, but a police dog had died after contacting the steel gate barring their way; the gate had been hooked up to the electricity supply for the tower, and was live. The dog died in a second. The police were unable to penetrate beyond the live gate, and the Salford ravers knew it. As the party raged on, the music issuing from the open windows to be heard for miles around, a police helicopter hovered outside, just feet from the windows... Is the situation under control?

I know, you've heard it before: the clubs were packed with students, bricklayers, shop girls, football hooligans, drug dealers and factory labourers, and everybody loved each other and it was X-cellent. The absolute saturation of this craze meant that even relatively straight pubs hosted weekly DJ nights, during which a lot of Techno was played, and the strobes were working overtime along all the major thoroughfares of the city, and the people smiled and raved and grooved and became quite mental in the way they never seemed to stop dancing, even when they were at work. The place was literally awash with the stuff, which changed the entire character of Manchester, and the foundations were being laid for the mass marketing of the city as a place to get down to some serious partying, but partying with verve, with awareness, and with an inextricable football component. It was E, fanny and United. The Perry Boy had risen like a phoenix, above the city that formed his fabulous plumes.

At Maine Road for the 1990 FA Cup semi-final against Oldham, Dave-B- and I had tickets for the Platt Lane, which was Oldham's end. On the way in, walking past United's several crews who were spaced along the road leading to the hovel, I told Dave, 'Don't be taking the piss in here. They might be sheep-shaggers but they're still human, and we could come unstuck, you never know.' There were two tiny pockets of reds at either side, towards the back, and when we gave it 'United!' prior to kick-off, a preposterous little firm of sheep-dippers jumped up and started giving it the big one, coming up towards us. All the lads must have been Anthropological Gazetteers by then, because we just stared at them like scientists studying a Stone Age tribe, one we thought had become extinct hundreds of years ago. Our addiction had progressed to other forms of molecular interactions, and this firm was a joke anyway. The Oldham Casuals faltered in the face of this bizarre response, and quietly sat down. I turned to Dave and said, 'What I said earlier about them still being human beings… you might wanna strike that from the memory banks.' By the end of the match, a thrilling 3-3 draw, the entire end was half-full of effervescent United fans who'd emerged from the woodwork as the game progressed. It was actually a great example of how things had changed, not counting the impotent little monkey show earlier.

The more traditional sounding bands, like the Stone Roses, Charlatans and Inspiral Carpets, kept Manchester's feet on the ground, and helped Mancs remember where they were and who they were supposed to support. The late 80s roiled to a frothing, twisting turn of the decade, and after United won the 1990 FA Cup against Crystal Palace, the World Cup in Italy began in earnest. Italy's 'Toto' Schillaci and Cameroon's Roger Milla were the darlings of the world press, as the song 'King of the Road', by the other Roger Miller, was played on all radio stations. Salford's New Order were appropriately chosen as the national side's official songsters, and a hot summer burned along ('Burma', as Dave-B- put it), with almost everyone willing England to do the business in Italy while wearing the white strip all the time, every day. The clubs were packed with people wearing the kit, and sponsors Umbro (and Persil) must have made a fortune. Inevitably, however, England's luck ran out.

'The night England were eliminated on penalties in the semis, people went out and smashed German cars, which were owned by English people,' remembered The Satisfied Customer. 'Fuckin' idiots. We were all dead choked, though, because for a good few of us, it was the first time we'd even wanted England to win something. It wasn't like United losing a big game, but it was fucking horrible. Two of the lads in the pub ended up knocking seven shades of shit out of each other in a fight over a big Union Jack, after the Germany game. Everyone was depressed for a few days; the World Cup Final, on the Sunday, between Argentina and Germany, went almost ignored in the pub. The George Crosses and the Union Jacks were removed from sight again, and despite the pain, we had put another notch in the bedstead of experience.'

Wild rumours, fuelled by hallucinogenic drugs, began to make the rounds in Mamucium. Questions required answers: why are we so far ahead of the rest? Were we the Clangers and the rest of the country mere Wombles, only distantly related to us? Was Old Trafford really built by alien technology? Was Alex Ferguson christened with H_2O from Loch Ness, while the music of an alien piper played by the banks? When the world's very first Inter-City passenger train rolled in, and the Scousers alighted in ancient G-Mex, were they steamed by a crew of

Victorian scuttlers with their flat-caps pulled down at a jaunty angle over one eye? Did the fish-eye lens of the architects of Christmas past ever realise that Manchester United would allow two magical goat-men called Ryan Giggs and Paul Scholes to play their fiddle in the park? These were the questions asked by the children suckling at the two-breasted hill, and they receive no answer.

Down among the tower blocks of Salford Precinct roam the shaven-headed scallies, walking their bull terriers, smoking big joints and admiring the solid lines of the architecture, made in the 60s and 70s and well-preserved to the present, outlasting anything put up across the city in Manchester. The towers on the Precinct were built at the same time as United's first cantilever, along United Road, by the same firm. The blokes on the job would be shuttled from the one site to the other; it was one big project, and the majority of those working on it were from Salford. Salford and Manchester United have always been one and the same. The flats have that same superior appearance as Old Trafford – sealed, solid, glazed and timeless. The stone blocks for the towers seem to have been unleashed from the depths of the English crust, cut, hewn, polished and shaped by the finest of men and machines, before being slotted into place in the multi-storey mayhem. It's the fixed point on the radar screen of the British Isles, the bull's-eye. There is a dynamic quality in the air there, a mixture of technology, danger and pheromones. This area has always seemed rich in a certain type of person. They're all either master thieves, expert criminals, violent animals, or else they specialise in electrical engineering, cantilever bridge design, or some other complex form of materials technology.

The scaffolding business was understandably booming during these high-energy projects, of which the Arndale Centre in town was one. To a small child living in Salford 5 and 6, the whole world appeared to be an endless steel matrix, held together by industrial fasteners, while giant cranes reached dizzy heights far above, controlled by inscrutable men in the sky. Every time you closed your eyes, you saw it: the Etch-a-Sketch effect, a mass of juxtaposed lines, intersecting each other at impeccable right angles, embedded in a grey background. There was so much scaffolding in this quadrant, the pattern burned its way into your developing brain, like a blank Etch-a-Sketch screen, some lines more distinct than others, lending depth as well as gravity. The three interlocking sites, Salford Precinct, United Road cantilever and the later Arndale Centre, became home to thousands of scaffolders, bricklayers and other tradesmen from the area. The hive of industry was a playground, an immense entrepreneurial climbing frame for the Salfordians.

Dave, now a retired scaffolder, was on all these jobs, and remembered the many characters of the time: 'There was one bloke, we'll call him Mack, and he was the biggest fence in Manchester. He was the Godfather of the scaffolders. He was hard as nails. They called him The Bear and he was one of the most feared men in Salford. Every shop around was selling his knock-offs. Anything you wanted, you'd go up to him and let him know, and he'd instantly direct you to this place or that, and tell you to mention his name. Everything was cut-price, as it was all knocked-off gear. He worked on the scaffolding all through that time, and he had some right jobs off. It wasn't at all unusual for him to phone the office and ask for tons of gear to be delivered to some place, and for the dispatcher to say, "Mack, we haven't got any jobs on at that site." He'd tell them, "If you know what's fucking good for you, you'll have that stuff there tomorrow morning." They were all scared of him, and he always got his own way. He did loads of foreigners, big jobs, using the firm's poles, and never paid them a penny. He used to drink with his henchmen in a boozer ran by a popular Manchester boxer near Strangeways prison. One time, he did a foreigner for a Jewish feller in Cheetham Hill. When it came time to pay the bloke was struggling to come up with the money. A few days later, Mack turns up at the boozer in a fucking Rolls-Royce. It was the Jewish bloke's, and that became the payment. The funny thing was, he did the entire job with bent stuff.

'Many a week he'd turn up for a day or two but get paid for the entire week. Nobody dared say anything to him. One

winter's morning, we were working at Carrington. He phoned
to tell me he was having the day off. The van crashed on the way
to work, and it turned out there was a chance it was down to
negligence on the part of the company. The following day, Mack
turned up in a big Mercedes with his brief. They took the
company to court and he ended up getting fifteen grand out of
it. He hadn't even been in the fucking van!

'There was another bloke, a Scouser called Tommy. He was
the best thief in Manchester at the time, and the stunts I saw
him pull were legendary. We used to be on these big jobs,
driving in past the security lodge, on Trafford Park and Ordsall.
The guards would tell us, "You thieving bastards won't get
anything out of this place, yer know." They all knew about
Tommy, and he took that as a challenge. He was the sort of
bloke who'd nick mop buckets or a lump hammer if there was
nowt else there. On this one big job, at Colgate-Palmolive in
Ordsall, he had a brainwave. The security guards were giving us
loads of stick, all the "You'll get fuck all off here" and all that.
Well, when you drop a pole off the scaffold, you drop it so it
sticks in the ground, and you take it out and throw it on the
wagon. These twenty-one-foot poles end up with soil plugs in
the ends, which eventually fall out when the soil dries. Tommy
was removing the soil plugs from the ends, and completely
packing the poles with tubes of toothpaste, then replacing the
plugs. We're talking thousands of tubes here. It went on for
weeks, and every night these guards were boasting, giving us
the shite when we went through the gate.

'One Christmas, we worked in the place where they made Ye
Olde Oak Hams. They were dead popular at the time. It was
another security guard job again, with all the usual bollocks
between us and them at the gate. I was dropping multi-tip four-
wheel wagons off, and the lads were filling them with flat boards
off the scaffolds at the end of the job. Well, Tommy asks for an
entire wagon of his own. He's stacked the flat boards up at each
side, then sawn a load of boards in half. He put these towards the
back of the wagon, and stacked them to look like it was packed
with flat boards. The entire middle of the wagon bed was jam-

packed with Olde Oak Hams, right on top of Christmas. We made a bleeding fortune.

'On another job, we were working with a big painting firm from Salford, providing scaffolding so they could paint the ceiling of a massive warehouse, one that supplied the big supermarkets. Most of the gear was on shelves, but the cigs and spirits were locked in cages. Every once in a while, a painter would go and tell the security guard he'd dropped his brush into a cage, and the guard had to let him in to get it. The bloke would go in and look for his brush for a bit, and then come out with it. His mates were still up above the cage, working on the scaffold. The security guard would lock it again and be off, and there'd be all these bottles of whisky and brandy rising up in the air attached to fishing lines they'd dropped from the scaffold. The place was massive, and a lot of brushes got dropped on that job.

'Another bloke at ICI in Fleetwood was caught nicking mercury from the place, which was a big deal then and is now. They knew the stuff was going through the gate but they couldn't work out how they were doing it. Finally one night this feller drops his bicycle, and he can't lift it back up again. He'd only found a way to dismantle it and fill the insides with mercury. Unbelievable. But that's the way they are, this lot from Salford – and the Scousers. They'll always work out a way to get round a problem. Ask them to solve a maths equation and they'll get bored with it, but ask them to work out how to rob something and you're guaranteed they won't rest till the job's done. They're like a gang of squirrels after a nut.'

These tales define the generational nature of the region. It's the DNA, that functional, informational molecule, shooting its way from one decade to the next, cradled in the loins of the *fathers* of those that became the Perry Boys. There is no standing up to the tide of nature, for she does as she does. Sociologists tell us that hardcore urban environments are detrimental to the psychological well-being of their inhabitants, but it appears that every cloud has a pewter lining: if you can take back enough from the society that robbed you in the first place, then the world is your crayfish.

Kenny put it this way: 'It really did sometimes feel that Manchester was a separate race of beings, from those early days at Old Trafford, dressed in the Perry gear, to the later days of Techno, still dressed in Perry gear, but finally with a soundtrack to live life to. I suppose Arsenal have got their Emirates Stadium now, and Chelski have their sugar daddy, but here in Manchester we were the originals. We had the best stadium then and we still do now. We wore the best clothes, and had the best bands playing the best music. Only the Scousers ever beat us to the punch with anything, and that didn't last long.'

The vast number of young men available for mayhem in this area is far beyond anything expected by rational statisticians. It appears that Salford has always contained a surplus of crazy individuals, each one capable of effecting major changes in a situation, all cohesive and organised by means of some primeval telepathic vibration that shudders through the labyrinth at a moment's notice. A crew of hundreds can be summoned in a heartbeat, football or no football. The powerful crime bosses in the area that includes this arena of towers are well aware that they control the single largest instamatic crew of men in England, unrivalled elsewhere. They have used this to their advantage in taking control of much of the city, but the road to that control was long and hard. The MDMA explosion definitely contributed to the arrival of the pecking order in Manchester. Salfordians loved Ecstasy, and they began to enjoy it in earnest, right from the beginning. But many already existing modes of life were exposed along with the rave culture, and the rest of the country was shocked by the reality of what went on in the underworld of this fascinating city, a community where individuals used their expertise to steal everything, from handbags and cars to electricity and gas. In Salford, you didn't just worry about being mugged, you worried about whether the nutters down the avenue were tapping into the gas main again, and whether it meant the street was going to go sky high. If they'd been up all night at a rave, you just had to hope that they still had some of their wits about them. They paid for nothing.

From the summer of 1989 onwards, warnings were issued to

pet owners, specifically the owners of small dogs and cats, to take care when allowing them to roam outside. Many were disappearing, and the police had determined exactly where they were destined. Following a raid on a suspected drug dealer's flat on Salford Precinct, a most terrible contraption was discovered: an exercise machine for a pit bull terrier. The machine was a kind of treadmill, with a small platform attached to the front end upon which a small dog, or cat, could be fixed. The pit bull could be made to run long distances, in pursuit of a quarry it couldn't hope to catch, for many hours at a time. Finally, as a reward, the dog would be allowed to attack and devour the small animal that had been presumably quaking in fear for hours, thereby ending the life of the hapless family pets captured by these criminals. The Salford lads involved in this type of training believed that it gave the pit bull an added *whoof* when it came to taking on a rival. It was a coldhearted thing to do for an Englishman, especially one who peddled vast quantities of 'love drug', but it was what was going down.

Certain advertisements started to appear in the *Manchester Evening News*:'York Stone flags wanted. Good prices. Call 061…' These were ads from builders who were supplying the London Docklands site, and smaller local developments, with authentic York stone flags to pave the courtyards and streets. Such adverts probably appeared in many local newspapers at the time. The price offered for a half ton, or hundredweight, or whatever, of this precious commodity was quite handsome, so the lads set about the task. The first order of business was to get one's arse down to the motor auctions at Belle Vue and buy an ex-Northwest Gas van, of which there were many, all sprayed a familiar mid-blue colour. They were about four hundred quid. They lasted a few weeks or even months, until the axle finally croaked due to the weight of the flags. It was very common to see blue ex-gas vans patrolling Manchester (whose streets had a lot of decent stone left on them at the time) containing three lads, all scallies, on the hunt for stone.

Andy was a large and active stone-lifter, and was running with several gangs of flaggers. 'There was one little crew of

Salford lads, who'd nicked fluorescent jackets, helmets, ribbons, tripod lights and wellies, who'd turn up anywhere, at any time, and strip loads of flags from all kinds of surfaces at any time of the day or night, and claim to be legit blokes just doing their job,' he remembered. 'One day I saw them in town, right off Deansgate on a Saturday afternoon, nicking a load of stone, plain as day. Nobody batted an eyelid. Later that night, I ran into one of them in Band on the Wall. He'd eaten a quarter of Sputnik and was dancing on the stage. He probably went home and shit the bed or something, he was that out of his face. The blue vans were at large for at least a year, until all the stone had gone. It was funny that on the streets of Weaste and other Salford strongholds, the York stone remained. Even the bravest lads were not prepared to rob the stone from certain streets.'

Post offices were a target at the best of times, but somehow it seemed to keep getting worse. Gangs would hit both main, large and small, local post offices daily. In one attack, a man was beaten senseless with his own prosthetic leg. In another, the raider appeared to have been captured, until he kicked the panels out of the wall under the window and escaped into the jungle. It was starting to look too easy, and this caused more and more to try it, often with success. Banks were the same. While there was an air of optimism and belief in our energised lifestyle, a dark assault on the city's infrastructure continued, and all it did was entertain people.

Benny-S- was alcohol-crazed and out of control on the streets of Greater Manchester. He told a cautionary story of what Ecstasy did to put him on the road to reform: 'I'd wake up every morning and leap off that piss-drenched mattress, slam the door of my flat shut and head out for a day of business. Any cunt stupid enough to rob my flat deserved to get his legs broke, with me personally doing the breaking. Many a time, I wished I could leave the window open to air the mattress off, but no such luck where I lived – the ground floor. Me and Billy-J- had a system for post offices that was foolproof. We'd wear rubber masks of Idi Amin, Donald Duck, Ronnie Reagan and Arabs or Maggie Thatcher. It was wintertime when we went at it. We

used to arrive at the post office door right as the guy was
opening up. We'd steam straight in, turn the lights out, close and
lock the door behind us, and even adjust the little paper clock
in the window. Whoever was behind the counter was taken by
surprise and got a few hard bangs to let him know we weren't
pissing about. This was when the Ecstasy was coming in, and we
were all well on it all the time. It was making us think differently, though. I felt sorry for the people we twatted for the first
time in my life.

'One day, we did a post office in the afternoon, right before
it was due to reopen for afternoon traffic. We did a line of whiz
apiece in the motor, and left it running, as it was a nice area.
Billy gave me a lump hammer and said the lock'd be like paper.
I was sweating like fuck in the mask, and got side-on to the
door. I gave it a belt, right over the lock, and the door juddered
open an inch. The door was vibrating, just a blur, when Billy
steamed through it and I followed. Bill gets a shooter out and I
nearly shit my pants. Fuck-all to do with me. It was a nightmare,
and it was the E that caused it. Billy's got the bloke against the
safe, kneeing him, with his gun against his shoulder, mumbling
threats. He was trying to tell Bill that it was on a time-lock, but
Billy wasn't having it. I grabbed Billy and dragged him out of
there. He was fucking furious, but that was that. It was the last
time I ever did a job. Ecstasy put me on the straight and narrow.'

Most people didn't enjoy such chemical epiphanies. There
was a moment during this period when anything that wasn't
nailed down, and was worth a wank, was nicked in a heartbeat.
Ambulances attending incidents around Salford had to be
locked at all times, as a trip up in the lift to attend to an injured
person usually resulted in the vehicle's entire contents being
stolen within seconds; not just drugs, but blankets, stretchers, air-
supplies, radios and even seats. There was no regard for public
safety or general infrastructure; these individuals were engaged
in a war with ordered society, and were taking that war to the
authorities on a daily basis. Even fire doors became a target.

'Little crews of lads would hit a tower block, with a couple of
vans parked outside, and have off with as many fire doors as

humanly possible,' explained one regular raver of the time. 'There were complaints from residents in some towers that hardly a fire door was left in the entire block. There were reports from office blocks of computers, monitors, desks, chairs, even a newly delivered rolled-up carpet being hoisted from the entrance lobby within of minutes of it being delivered. This was in Manchester city centre, as well as the surrounding areas. We all knew each other, and it was a case of "Where you going tonight? OK, see you later," as we passed each other during the day, up to no good. Banks were closing down and moving out of the area because they'd been robbed that many times. It was abnormal. Pubs were used as HQs for this mob or that. Everyone was part of this larger thing, it was just loads of headcases on the rampage. No police force in the world could have been ready for us when we finally went ape-shit. In the circumstances, I'd say the Old Bill round Manchester did a good job keeping up with it all, and were probably the least envied force in Britain at the time. Greater Manchester Police must be the top boys in the country after all they've been through this past thirty years, with the footy and then the rave scene. It was everything that wasn't nailed down, I swear. People going into petrol stations to pay for petrol would come out to find their cars had disappeared into thin air in seconds. It definitely wasn't Cornwall.'

A notorious road junction just outside the city centre in Ordsall was the site of many a surprise attack on motorists. The traffic was always high-volume in that area and it took several traffic light cycles to get through the lights. A couple of kids, one on a mountain bike, and one creeping along on foot, would work together. The kid on the bike was a spotter, looking for women motorists careless enough to place their handbag on the passenger seat. He would signal to the other kid, who'd creep along, on all fours, until he reached the car in question. Then, suddenly the kid would stand up, smash the side window, grab the bag, pass it to the kid on the bike who'd circled back around, and off it would go. The older lads got the plastic and the kids got the cash. In that part of town there was no danger of have-a-go Seb Coes thwarting the plan. And if there were, then more senior members would be quickly on hand, as there was more to these kids' exploits than just two scallies and a bike.

For a time, there was a network of communication that enabled lads in the clubs in town to phone some young kid, who'd go out and steal a car to bring the lads home in. It was a dial-up car thieving taxi service, ran by modern day Fagins and their scally protégés. Thievery and mischievery involving motor vehicles is something all of England can relate to. Many people in Manchester know someone who's walked into a garage for a quote, only to be confronted by something irregular. Whether it's the sight of two car halves being welded together, registration numbers being ground off, or simply a clock being turned back, these things are endemic to the territory. All manner of theft occurs, and it seems that just about any part of a car may be targeted.

A popular story began to spread at this time. It went like this: 'A bloke I know, who drives for the Post Office, stopped and went into a place for a few minutes. When he came out, and set off again in his vehicle, the interior seemed dead cold and windy. After a quick inspection, he realised that in the time which he'd been away from his vehicle, the windscreen had been nicked.' These reports filtered in with some frequency. Post Office vans were particularly vulnerable. It was obvious windscreens were the new prize, and hordes of light-fingered professionals were on the case. One can only imagine the number of windscreens that were stolen at this time, as everyone knew someone who knew someone it had happened to.

Another one was airbags. The problem with the airbag thieves was that they were so quick and so good at it that there was no way to tell you'd been robbed unless you had a mechanic go in and take a look at your airbag. There were reports of airbags being had away in minutes, in cars that were left unattended outside supermarkets and shops. A more obvious crime, such as the one that found the victim's motor on bricks, wasn't quite as nebulous in nature. When they nicked your wheels, you knew they'd nicked them, and it seems that everyone was prone to having this done to them at some time or other in Manchester.

There's the tale of the guy who bought his son a top-of-the-range motorcycle, one that was coveted far and wide. He installed an incredibly thick and impenetrable door on his garage, confident the local mob couldn't affect an entry. The following morning, the bike was gone; they'd come in through a small window that the guy had not given a thought to, dismantled the entire thing, and moved it bit by bit through the window. One bloke bought a new car and made a lot of noise about the state-of-the-art security system he'd installed in it. He was quite explicit to all and sundry, saying nobody, not even the local villains, would be able to get around this system. The first night he had the car, he parked it in his garage. The following morning, he got out of bed, and looked out of his bedroom window. There was a strange object sitting in the middle of his driveway. He went outside to take a look at this thing. It was the alarm system from his car, sitting there, good as new. The garage was empty. It was obvious that some very naughty boys were using these vehicles (and their respective security systems) to keep their hand in, presumably between more serious ventures. These 'local villains' are not amateurs.

Sometimes, the heavy mob would steal cars in a much more direct fashion. It was not uncommon to hear stories of how people with expensive cars have been literally terrorised off the road, and battered horrifically for the keys. In one incident, a man was run over several times by his attacker, who came to steal his car early in the morning, knowing he would be going out to work. This happens a lot in winter, because people start their cars and let them warm up for a while. It's easy to jump in and burn off without a struggle. This guy saw his car being nicked and ran out to stop them. When they do it the other way, the story is very straightforward; a car will pull up alongside, and possibly begin to side swipe the targeted vehicle, while its occupants gesture for the victim to pull over. Guns may be brandished and loud threats issued from the gangsters. It is difficult to escape from these people once you are in their sights. They are not there for the fun of it. The sum total of all this skulduggery must surely amount to astronomical figures, and those profiting from it are in control of a veritable empire of crime. They have made it clear to the authorities that coming after them is a wrong move, as was discovered in 1992, when riots broke out in Salford lasting several days, in the wake of the arrests of a gang involved in vehicle theft. The riots presented an opportunity to settle several scores simultaneously for the local mob. Businesses refusing to pay protection money were selected for burning, and fires raged for days as attempts by firemen to extinguish them were met by gangs of youths throwing pool balls and other missiles. Someone fired live rounds at the police; a van carrying several officers was hit by a bullet from a high-calibre handgun, which penetrated the van, bounced around the interior, and exited at the opposite corner. Officers involved in this incident understandably took leaves of absence, due to stress. Greater Manchester Police appeared in the media to reassure the people that the situation was under control, and that they weren't dealing with a no-go area. To prove it, they proudly displayed a freshly painted white armoured personnel carrier (presumably borrowed from the Army), complete with the Greater Manchester Police crest emblazoned on its side. And through it all, the raving went on.

By 1990, everybody with half a brain was earning money one way or the other. If they weren't working, nicking flags, grafting, or living as fulltime gamblers, they were dealing E or being drafted into the secret army that was growing by the day. A new club opened every week, and on Saturday nights you were spoilt for choice: will it be the Continental or will it be the Cyprus Tavern, or maybe that new 'un that opened on Thursday?

When the shootings had started, a year or two earlier, the media had referred to the 'gang war', that is to the competition for territory by the black street gangs of Cheetham Hill and Moss Side. It was partly about a new drug that came in the form of a rock, which allegedly caused instant addiction in users and so was hugely profitable to the gangsters dealing it. The media performed their usual half-hearted job of keeping the populace informed. Unfortunately, society sometimes fails in its civic duty to diagnose its own pathologies. When the media become confused, the populace become confused, and then things can take on a life of their own. This was one of the factors that contributed to the rise of the big gangs in Greater Manchester County at the end of the 80s; the media didn't know what the fuck was going on, but thought that they did.

Occasionally, there was a shooting in Salford, rather than Moss Side, and with no way of working this into their 'black gang war' hypothesis, the media slowly worked up a murky picture of what was developing in Salford. Just as the average age of the black kids being shot, and arrested for shootings, was worryingly low, around twenty-one, so was the average age of the lads in Salford being arrested for the same. The victims of the Salford Mob, however, appeared to be a mixed bag, which should ring bells. The people being shot in the black sections of town were the same people who were doing the shooting, excepting those unfortunates who were caught in the crossfire and were completely innocent. In Salford, the people being shot might be drug dealers, shopkeepers, pub bouncers, building contractors, or young men with 'no fixed address' (the standard answer given in response to the question posed in court, 'where do you live?'). This mixed bag usually had one thing in common: they were all at some time or other living or doing business in Manchester, and many of them, though by no means all, had criminal records. It slowly became obvious to anybody with a working memory that there were people in Salford who had their fingers in a great many pies, and were capable of murderous violence to consolidate the viability of these pies, which were juicy indeed.

As the years rolled on, and the shootings continued unabated, the 'gang war' hypothesis lost its allure, and the grim reality of inner-city life for many of Manchester's black population more resembled that of the South Bronx than Great Britain. This wasn't a war. It was just life. Peter Walsh's book *Gang War*, was a timely account of the situation, all the more authentic for its preserving the atmosphere of the moment, capturing the sharp aroma of conflict between the newly established black crews in south Manchester. They put Manchester on level par with some of America's cities, handgun-wise. The statistics for Salford were more stable; the shootings didn't exactly go up, or become worse, they just kind of happened once in a while, whenever something had gone wrong somewhere and someone had to be disciplined, or killed. For the most part, though, it was as it had always been, and all, young and old, pulled their weight.

John-D- was a dealer around Manchester at the time, and described one scene as something out of *Oliver Twist*: 'There was this woman who had a madhouse, a factory. All the truants would go there to get stoned. Loads of kids, wagging it in her gaff. One day, I went to pick some gear up, and she had all these kids arranged around a big table in the kitchen, grinding away with mortars and fucking pestles. It was like a sweatshop. Half the E they just cut to fuck and got as much beadage as they could. The shit stuff mostly went out of town and to people they didn't care about. It was full of travel sickness pills, icing sugar, Marvel powdered milk, you name it, everything was going into the pot and getting ground up.'

* * *

On a glorious evening in spring 1991, Manchester United were to face Barcelona in the European Cup Winners' Cup Final. They had qualified for the competition by winning the FA Cup the previous year against Crystal Palace. I did not attend due to personal issues at the time, but watched it on television in a pub. There were a lot of Manchester City supporters out that night, obviously convinced United couldn't pull it off. City fans had been enjoying something of a resurgence at the time and their boys had fallen into the habit of doing Ecstasy and going to the match, spending the day laughing and just being happy campers. When they played Crystal Palace a week or so before United beat them in the Cup Final of 1990, many attended dressed up as the Blues Brothers, in shades and suits, all loved-up and brothers-in-arms with the south Londoners, wishing them all the best for the Wembley date with the mighty reds. The number of City supporters in Prestwich that actually attended

matches definitely seemed to exceed that of United at the time.
I was one of the few people who continued to take the weekly
punishment at Old Trafford, or wherever, to watch United
beaten 2-1 by Derby County, to draw goallessly with outfits
like Wimbledon, with average home crowds of around 40,000;
42,000 was considered not a bad crowd in the 1989-91 seasons,
and I remember seeing a fair few 38,000s here and there along
the way.

Part of the problem was that large numbers of lads had flown
the oceans, mainly to Australia, and were simply absent, working
on building sites in Sydney. Once in a while you would see
someone who'd come home for a spell, and there would be a lot
of boozing and welcome home-ing. I personally was going
through a stay-at-home spell, which was unusual. I had just
done a two-year City and Guilds course in Signwriting at
Central Manchester College and was revving up for another
voyage. All I now required to make some cash on my travels was
my Bundle, the brushes and mahl stick of the signwriting trade.
A source of income at the time was painting signs for all the
clubs and other businesses opening around town.

The Blues were everywhere around Prestwich at the time,
always tripping on acid or E, always singing, and in the 1990-91
season, they finished fifth in what was then the Barclays First
Division, one place above United, setting off wild celebrations
in all the pubs. It was a sad time. Many of the United lads in
Prestwich seemed to have given up on football, possibly as a
result of being too distracted by other things too often. Twenty-
two men kicking a bladder about a field wasn't their idea of fun
any more. But this was in between those phases, those high-
energy eras that go down in history. Nobody talks about the
dark years at Old Trafford around this time, which the 1990 FA
Cup win pulled us out of. People only want to talk about the
glory days. Where were they when we were getting beat at OT
in front of 38,000 people, though? That's a question for *all*
United fans, not just the bandwagon-jumpers of the 90s.

Anyway, there were loads of blues out that night, salivating at
the prospect of United receiving a leg-slapping from the

Spanish giants. Someone forgot to pack the kits for the boys, and out they roved in an unusual all-white strip, brought as spares by Norman Davies, one of the Old Trafford staff, and my hero-uncle's namesake. Mark Hughes fired in the two goals that saw us lift our first European silverware in decades, and the pubs erupted, not to mention Rotterdam. All the rats who'd bailed out were suddenly back on board ship, and the full United complement was in force again, singing and dancing to the karaoke for all they were worth. Lenny Norbury, a loyal red through the hard times, with painted face, sang, 'We went down to Wembley one fine day in May…' into the microphone, as leagues of bitter blue bastards sat around, heads in hands, inconsolable. Their nightmare was only just beginning; little did they know. United went from strength to strength, and the rest is history, but that night (or perhaps the year before, when we won the FA Cup) was the turning point. The James song 'Sit Down' became inextricably linked with the occasion and with United's successes in the future, after the crowd sang it out in Rotterdam. That night seemed to put the icing on a very strange cake that had been baking for several years. It brought a continental atmosphere to Manchester, and a cockiness that had been there all along but was now worn on the sleeve with a wink, instead of just whispered as a joke between friends. We could feel the strength ebbing into the city, and the whole lifestyle was mutating accordingly. The mix of honest and dishonest geezers blurred more than ever, and all was well.

'One or two of the lads were caught bringing in the goods around this time, and sentenced to years inside, along with others who were punished for crimes of violence and stealing, the usual story,' said The Satisfied Customer. 'One lad got involved in heavy stuff and sent down for years after shooting someone dead in a gunfight, and other "friends" got long stretches for attempted manslaughter and smuggling speed through the Channel Tunnel. A couple were involved in robbing in town, computers and furniture from the office-blocks. There was indescribable drug traffic. The rest of us were coasting along, biding our time before we'd saved enough money to launch off on a new trip. Everyone slowly drifted away from the fixed, central point on the radar screen, out into different ventures. Some slipped off altogether. Since the early 80s people had been jetting off, usually with no money, for months away in the sun. It all just became a lifestyle of its own, mainly due to the fact that we were too good for the jobs and wages offered us. It was partially a result of attending mad schools where no-one gave a fuck, or a thought, to what lay ahead in life. I think the teachers gave up on us, we were completely uncontrollable. It might have appeared that we would come unstuck in the cruel world, once we were out of school and on the scrapheap. But we didn't fold, we stuck our chins out and simply employed aeroplane fuel to get us to where the good times were at. We did not resign ourselves to being losers. We'd finally grown up to the point of knowing there was no prospect for you in England if you didn't work at it or just fuck off somewhere better. Most of the lads I know who left school the same year as me eventually ended up doing something with their lives, many attending universities or learning valuable trades, or starting their own businesses.'

The tendency to travel to faraway places had been with me ever since the night I went to stow away on a ship to America as a kid, but ended up at Old Trafford instead. However, in life, I did end up at my intended star-spangled destination. Many others ended up elsewhere, as the seeds of our time were scattered far and wide.

PART 4

THE BOYS THAT GOT AWAY

17

HIT THE ROAD, JACK

The time is now, and now is all we have.

—Neal Cassady

KIDS ARE DAYDREAMERS, always off someplace in their minds, very rarely in the physical present. They dream of jungles, deserts, volcanoes, desert islands, tropical oceans, crocodiles, sharks, and, if they're British, often wish to live somewhere hot and home to exotic animals, plants and slimy things. I was always a tremendous bookworm, often buried in a stolen book, experiencing the intense colours, sounds and aromas of distant rainforests, ancient ruins and primeval deserts. I always knew I was destined for one of these places, and had a feeling it might be America. In fact, in 1985, many maturing young animals were struggling free of the withering sac of yesteryear to plop juicily on the alien shores of unsuspecting lands.

The romance and heroism of travel sits high in human story-telling. Scarcely was there ever a hero who did something worth a wank, who didn't travel some distance from his homeland to accomplish it. When, as drug-addled teenage Perries, many of us began to read works such as *On the Road* by Jack Kerouac and *The Teachings of Don Juan* by Carlos Castaneda, we plotted our escape from Mancland to see the wonders of the world. The earlier trips to the Continent, in search of rare and endangered pieces of cloth and leather, were usually shortlived. This time, we were after a more permanent adventure, one that would enable us to avoid the so-called 'real world' forever.

The previous few years had seen numerous misadventures, involving jail cells, hospital visits, violent encounters, accidental overdoses and crazed rampages that should have ended with most of us being institutionalised, or plain dead. A couple of the boys had already started their great escape, having been to Israel, Turkey and Greece, returning with many tales of mayhem. It sounded magical, living on a kibbutz among the endless dunes. To be blasted by that desert sun and made to work ourselves to the bone was like joining the Foreign Legion. It became a plan; a voyage into the unknown. For many Perry lads in 1985, a morning of graft, robbing or dealing might lead to a city centre boozer for the rest of the day, in other words business as usual, but for some, it led directly to a travel agent. Nobody gave a toss about personal safety, especially after several years of battling with alcohol, poverty, drug addiction, vicious psychos and just life itself, so they travelled with a one-way ticket and next to nothing in currency, relying instead on their wits to see them through. Their Manchester training had served them well.

Israel was favourite if you fancied staying away for a long time and reliving the voyages of Sinbad. Israel became the world's only Jewish state in 1948, but had received waves of Jewish immigration since the twelfth century. The persecution of Jews globally had led to a population of millions in the tiny country, and those who'd made the trek were not fucking about any more. Surrounded by nations that openly declared the destruction of Israel to be their aim, the Israelis organised themselves into the most formidable military presence in the Middle East. There were guns, and soldiers, everywhere, but there was also an urgent need to obtain blood from a stone; the swelling numbers of Jews heading 'home' to the Promised Land required feeding. The desert, they reasoned, could be manipulated into yielding food, with the help of technology. They employed their natural intelligence and talent for getting things done, and conceived the kibbutz system. The kibbutz was something very interesting, and a life model that suited certain personalities perfectly, especially those who liked to be on the move through hot climes, interspersed with long excessive nights of feasting and mayhem in a desert setting.

The kibbutz became a major target for lads in search of communal drunkenness and psychedelia. Kibbutzniks were also known as 'volunteers'. Emerging from the portal into the Tel Aviv night, greeted by hot air and the sight of palm trees waving in the tropical wind, was fantastic. The Negev desert was a fabulous land-scape of craters and mountains and all manner of wild animals, and there was cheap vodka, plentiful herb and beautiful women. It was Paradise all over again. And just like the original Paradise, there was a Scouser in it. There was much discussion of the evolution of the Nameless Thing between Mancs and Scousers, and the more recent drug culture. There were other English trooping about this foreign pasture, too. It was a mish-mash of the various stages of that evolution, with some, like the cockneys, right up to snuff, and others not quite getting it yet, as late as 1986.

The Israeli commanders commanded their desert strictly during working hours, but once the bell had gone we were on the rampage. Kibbutz work in the desert often meant olive orchards. Anybody recognised as hard working was put on a 'mickey', a tractor with a platform that was able to erect itself, hydraulically, with hydraulic clippers to prune the branches of the olive trees. You were left to your own devices, you and your mickey, and it felt like you were enveloped in the turquoise Mediterranean myths, happily toiling away, dreaming alone. The amazing blue desert sky often contained tiny silver triangles performing incredible manoeuvres high up there among the wispy white clouds, tumbling, spinning, shooting straight up and then falling back down. The triangles were Israeli Air Force jets in training. The local fauna was a little different than the cats and dogs of Blighty, too. You might stumble on a giant, lemon-coloured owl on a bough, which frightened you shitless, as you ploughed through the olive trees on your mickey. Porcupines, gazelle and even leopards weren't out of the question, either. The place was highly conducive to many encounters with mili-tary hardware and wild animals.

Some obtained the cushy jobs in the kitchens and were able

to sneak vast quantities of beer from the fridges into volunteers' huts. The young Israeli kids were quick to mingle with us, as interested in our girls as we were in theirs, and wasted no time in letting us know that they were big friends of herb. We spent our time in a turquoise haze, getting smashed and working in the fields, writing letters to friends back home, telling them what they were missing, there in the baking Mars landscapes. Such letters were responsible for kick-starting a mass emigration of English lads, out, out, to the far corners of the planet.

Aiden-H-, a sticky-fingered Scouser, flew home the weekend of the 1986 FA Cup Final between Everton and Liverpool, and then back to his kibbutz on the Monday. 'It was all just lads from England, everywhere. Of course there were arguments, as Scousers and Mancs found themselves living in the same room, but once we'd shared all our impressions from that era, it became a trip. For the first time, sworn enemies became roommates. It was funny to see guys from all over England wearing the styles we'd started all those years ago. It made you realise what an important contribution to British sensibility we had made.'

Neither Scousers nor Mancs realised at the time that these styles represented an evolutionary endpoint, that the cut of the cloth would persist into the millennium. Armageddon was writ in The Book by the ancient Hebrews, but were there any references in there of this evolutionary attainment? Were silver spacesuits around the corner, and if so, were they so different from what we'd introduced into the mainstream?

English lads were everywhere you went, and it was party time in the sun. We'd roam the Stone Age streets of Jerusalem, where the Arabs had been taught to speak cockney by the cockneys. The Dead Sea tasted like curry and saw hordes of floating scallies giggling and sploshing, walking on water. Israel's buses always had a couple of British Casual-types sitting at the back, and there were hilarious, excited conversations about everything, from the sweets we ate as kids to the first time we set eyes on a Fila tracky top. It was beers a-plenty, standing around blazing oil drums with the Palestinians, discussing politics until the early hours. Jerusalem was made of enormous stones, walls that loomed on all sides, and which had little spiral staircases disappearing into them. There was a myriad of alleyways, their cobbled and crazed trajectories leading into dark and aromatic courtyards. Windows in the stone, containing no glass, emitted a distinctive orange glow, and it was like living in the Bible under a million stars. Just blocks away, however, were modern multistorey concrete apartments. Given half the chance, Israeli developers would do the same to Jerusalem's ancient neighbourhoods as the British Government did to Salford. It is a worldwide phenomenon, and a natural one, unfortunately. Every population has its crushers, men who value not history and tradition but instead worship the dollar and nowt else. The Leftists who dreamed up the streets in the sky had much in common with the Far Right exploiters who simply wanted to pour concrete and receive payment forthwith. They both delighted in the destruction of traditional ways of life, specifically those that weren't geared towards upward mobility.

Many a night was spent exploring Israeli and Arab cities, and it was fantastic. The age of the civilisations in that part of the world is remote enough to effect a gut-level reaction in the beholder; it contains the remnants of the world's first static communities, the fall from paradise once more. Somewhere among the tumbledown rocks of those ancient towns and cities, surely lived the first person to mass-produce a decent sweater or pair of sandals.

After a few months of paradise in the wilderness, seeing herds of wild antelope, porcupines, giant eagles, scorpions, snakes and unbelievable canyons, mountains and endless expanses of sand, it was time to hit Tel Aviv, to run amok, among falafel stands, cafes and bars. The food was top notch, and healthy, which was a novelty for an army of fish and chips-fed English boys and girls. The bars had English names, and were full every day of lads on the piss, loads of little crews from different kibbutzim. There'd be a mob from all over Britain, but all thinking as one, as they'd been grafting together in the sun for several months. Many unlikely alliances were forged, and groups of mixed Middlesbrough, Scousers, cockneys, Mancs, Geordies, Mackams,

Brummies, Leicester, Yorkies, Scots, Welsh and Irish drank together, shouting, screaming, watching football on the pub telly, breaking into spontaneous song. It was absolute shite. Nah, only joking, it was a riot. Whenever the Mancs and Scousers got together, there was always a prolonged debate about the origin of the Nameless Thing, while the rest sat and blankly stared, listening with empty eyes. If just Mancs and Scousers were present, there were no debates any more for the benefit of the audience, just long, hard verbal tennis matches, where stream-lined wit was belted across the table back and forth, back and forth, back and forth, as the top seeds pushed each other to the limit, officiated by interested cockneys. There was little in the way of fighting, though; the two enemies couldn't ignore their similar histories in the face of the hordes of English Casuals, and a grudging ceasefire would ensue, much to the fascination of our cockney observers.

The Chernobyl disaster occurred around this time, and there was some concern about radioactive winds in the north. Katyusha rockets were more of a concern to some of us, cour-tesy of the Hezbollah, while the grizzled inhabitants assured us that they had a fixed range, and the topography in southern Lebanon meant that they couldn't hit us, as there were no decent launching sites available. We began to doubt the Israeli claims that we were safe after one or two little incidents. One dark night way up north, we decided to have a walk around a kibbutz perimeter fence, which was the border of Lebanon. Among our group was Gary, from Oxfordshire.

'There was a deserted watchtower and we climbed up the fence next to it,' he recalled. 'Within seconds, three army jeeps descended on us from different directions, and a load of Israeli soldiers jumped out, ordering us down from the fence, pointing machine guns. We got a stern warning about messing about on the fence, and were amazed at how quickly they'd got there. There must have been a camera somewhere, but even so, it took them less than a minute to arrive.'

Every Thursday night, droves of English from all kibbutzim in the surrounding area would descend on a little town called

Kiryat Shmona, which had been hit by more katyushas than any other town in Israel. It had a square with a couple of bars, and it would be party time for the boys and girls. I used to bring my passport and leave it with the guy behind the bar, in lieu of payment for my drinks, when I was skint, which was usually every week. Little did he know I didn't give a fuck about my passport.

'One Thursday night, we arrived back to a mass of kibbutzniks all crowded in the main square of the kibbutz,' said Gary. 'Apparently there'd been a breach of the fence. It was three years to the day since a group of terrorists had penetrated the fence and killed several people on the kibbutz, in the nursery. We just stumbled through the crowds to our room and crashed out, totally oblivious English pissheads, while the soldiers searched the kibbutz for the Hezbollah. No wonder they patrolled that fence so avidly.'

Eilat, on the Red Sea, was more the ticket, away from such northern trifles. Across the desert they streaked, those cheeky chappies, headed for the Middle East's answer to California. A big Mercedes taxi would take you hundreds of miles for about a fiver, full of Arabs, babbling away in that crazed tongue. Eilat was a different world, on the same latitude as Los Angeles; brand new, concrete, potted palms, with little shopping centres sprouting up here and there, built by the drunken English Perry-spawned mobs. There was an airport bang in the middle of town, and jumbo jets would zoom in, between the buildings. My first night in town I met two blokes from Salford in the Red Lion pub. I figured that was good luck, meeting someone from the old country like that, but it was not to be. Later that night they murdered an Israeli heroin dealer and were sent down, and the key lobbed away. Very weird. There was a whole other breed of English down there, those that had left the security of kibbutzim for the sake of freedom and mayhem.

Bernie, a young scally from London, sporting a curly wedge haircut and all the trimmings, loved it: 'Most people were sleeping on the beach, or on the grass at the side of the road. It was just accepted there, partly because of the weather, and partly because they knew we were building their fucking city for them. It was like the frontier, and it was brilliant. Most of us worked in construction, or out in the blazing melon fields on the edge of town. The temperature at that latitude was sky-high, but you got used to it, the dry heat. There was a café at the edge of town, called the Peace Café, where everyone would go to find work in the mornings. They sold beer round the clock, and anyone not being picked up for the day would simply start drinking there and then. We were right off the radar. Most of the work entailed grafting your bollocks off digging trenches, carrying bags of cement up countless flights of stairs, or carrying flaming buckets of red-hot asphalt up ladders, in two hanging buckets, balanced on a pole across your shoulders. It wasn't easy work, and a good few lads sacrificed the wages for the comfort of serving behind a bar, or working in a hotel.'

At the end of each day, we'd head to the Tropicana or the Red Lion. The Red Lion played music videos and films. They played the Talking Heads film *Stop Making Sense* literally every night as the lads rolled in. There were dozens of English lads all over the place, boozing it up, getting into fights with the locals and each other, singing, dancing and laughing in the sun, while Middle Eastern music blared all around. There were a fair few Israeli women and other girls off the kibbutzim, so the leg-over was quite possible. Everyone was a Casual-in-exile. There was a fifteen-strong mob from Leicester, complete with a Baby Squad group. There were West Ham and Arsenal, Middlesbrough and Sunderland, Celtic and Rangers, and a good few Yorkshire lads who seemed to have no affiliation. For a short while, I worked at the Eilat Aquarium, and was able to spend my lunch hour watching ten-foot tiger sharks race around a large tank, or observe clownfish lurk among the corals.

One day, I was working with a writer called Robyn, who was a mate of one of the band The Clash. We called it a day at twelve and went on the piss, discussing London, Manchester, music and mayhem. I told him, 'If anyone ever asks you, "D'you know Eilat?" tell them, "*Know* Eilat, I fucking *built* Eilat!"' He laughed his bollocks off as we threw ham butties to the sharks.

Gary the Blue from Salford was a Red Lion regular: 'It was daft, down there on the Red Sea. It was the hardest work I've ever done; digging ditches for melon farmers in the middle of nowhere, with only warm water to drink. There'd be loads of lads, all trying to be cool as fuck. Loads of different little mobs that all knew each other from off different kibbutzim, out on the piss. Every night it was straight in the Red Lion. The first one didn't touch the sides, so you'd order another pint of liquid engineering and into the shitehouse for some Andrew's Brain Salts. Enough sulphate'd go up my bugle every night to paralyse a full-grown walrus. There'd be music on every night, and by ten o' clock the place was alive. Rows about football, with the older Leicester lot all clustered at the bar, looking moody as fuck, treating their Baby Squad lads like shit. One night we chased one of them and poured a two-litre bottle of piss all over him, the poor fucker. There was this one main crew, Mancs, cockneys, Yorkies, Scousers, walking about giving it the big lad one. The locals used to leave food and drink out everywhere outside shops, unguarded, not to mention clothes and stuff. It was robbing, robbing and robbing again, but the Israelis were no mugs, so you had to be careful.'

This was where the tales of Egypt started, from deranged lads who'd just returned from a trip up the Nile with a wild look in their eye. Egypt sounded totally insane, and was the next port of call on everyone's list. Meanwhile, I contracted an infection in my leg, working for a fisherman on the Red Sea, and spent a week lying in the shadows of some tunnel, unable to walk. My leg had a blister the size of a football on it, trembling with its liquid load, and my feet swelled to twice their normal size. There were loads of little sores around my legs and feet, weeping and bleeding constantly. The flies were all over it, disgusting little bastards, and I had a raging fever. Finally, I managed to make it to a clinic, where a doctor popped the blister, and quietly informed me of a cheaper clinic across town. I had to sit outside in the hall while they wrote up my bill, and I hopped it, literally, out of the door without saying goodbye. I struggled across town, cursing all the while, towards the other clinic. When I arrived, it was the same doctor! How he'd got there I don't know, but he treated it and let me slide on the money. Nice guy. He gave me some advice: May to September was known as the 'septic season' down there, and infections such as this could turn gangrenous, and then... he made the international symbol for knackered – the slice across the neck – and I took notice. The leg was packed in ice for a while, and I took a temporary job in a hotel, cooking eggs and vacuuming rooms.

The first time you see Cairo, you immediately think that somebody has spiked your water, it's that psychedelic. It is the world's most central city, a global analogue of Manchester in the British Isles. If Old Trafford is our monument, then the Great Pyramid is theirs. Middle Eastern meets European meets African meets Mediterranean meets Asian. There are huge ancient streets, like chiselled black canyons, bearing facades both alien and elaborate, wrought iron balconies, cartouches, arabesques, and all the while the music is wailing, those strange desert pipes. Cairo's version of Salford's high-rise slum clearance programme is its concession to globalisation in the form of concrete blocks of branded hotel chains. This is the council estate equivalent, towering disharmoniously in the urban desert haze, full of jani-tors and caretakers, wearing Adidas and Nike. There are modern flyovers that curve off between fabled and magnificent hotels, multi-storey buildings with gigantic Coca-Cola signs illumi-nated on them, written in Arabic. Minarets, spires and mediaeval towers protrude from the confusion of the streets, silhouetted against the indigo night sky, often ringed with green neon lights, with the Koran broadcast from loud-speakers at the bizarre pinnacles. There are cats everywhere, and a species of enormous rodent that resembles a rat but is the size of a dog, running wild among the parked cars. The bazaars are loud and plentiful, and the purveyors of spice, perfume, gold and silk attempt to entice Westerners with free cups of tea and 'special' prices. The kids beg for 'baksheesh' and the traffic is an atrocious stock car race, conducted with all horns sounding, all day and night, and there appear to be no lanes marked on the roads. Every car has a million tiny dents in it, from the daily lunacy of the average drive. Beautiful women pass you by, veiled, with black-edged smiling eyes, and the men stand about in their robes, drinking Turkish coffee, smoking water-pipes, gesturing wildly. The coffee shops are decorated with endless mirrors, like old English gin palaces, stark and simple, everything glazed and immaculate. The lifts in the buildings are ancient trundling wooden boxes, fronted by sliding iron gates. And running through it all, the river meanders, splits, widens and disappears over the curvature of the globe, into Africa one way, the Mediterranean the other.

There are a few rules in Cairo if you're English. Everybody must get stoned, the pyramids must be climbed (and a joint smoked on the pinnacle) and the Sphinx must be given a coat of looking at. There are no ifs or buts about this. Everywhere, the boys ploughed about the city, stoned as bastards, before heading for Dahab, in the Sinai Desert. Going to Dahab was Rule Number Two.

The bus to Dahab was knackered and always packed. You would stand for the fourteen-hour overnight journey, and in the morning behold the Red Sea once again, with the mountains of Saudi Arabia in the turquoise distance across the Gulf. In July 1986, Dahab was a small settlement at a desert oasis. It was the most beautiful and amazing place that any young, working class traveller had seen in his life. You slept in small huts made from palm fronds that had dustbin lids for front doors. The sea was fifteen feet from the door, and it was the most alarming combination of different shades of green and blue, even at close range. The only fresh water was obtained by lowering a bucket on a rope down a hole and drawing it back up, full, from an underground aquifer. Dahab was like being shipwrecked on a desert island. The place was basically a cluster of small cafes, with generator power, and fresh fish, caught daily, along with salad, to eat. The cafes sold herb as well as food, and had top-of-the-range sound systems. There was a small trailer owned by the police, and even they had a smoke once in a while. The music played all day and all night, and there were little booths and alcoves with Bedouin carpets in them, open to the stars, where people would lie and take it all in. The women were there, English girls taking a break from the kibbutz for a couple of weeks. But the main attraction was in the water.

All the cafes rented out snorkelling equipment dirt cheap. You were not ready for what lay beneath. There was a vast submarine cliff face, most of which was alive with vibrant, brilliant coral and its attendant ecosystem. Fabulous fish were everywhere, clownfish and anemones, giant clams, lion fish, scorpion fish, some fish with leopard markings, some purple and yellow. The colours reminded me of United Road Paddock back in 1980, everybody sporting the tracksuit of choice, swanning about, being admired and admiring in turn. It was unreal, especially after a few bong hits, stuffed with ripe African bush. The time passed too quickly. You'd be in there for three hours and it would feel like twenty minutes. At night, the sky was awash with millions of stars, with a shooting star every few seconds. Behind the stars, you could see the astronomical spirals of the Milky Way, ghostly and immeasurable, while the orange moon reflected itself in the undulating waves. It was a nice way to relax, after a hard day's snorkelling, with the music going and the herb taking you out there. There wasn't much demand for booze in Dahab; our Western anaesthetics were unnecessary.

'Soon enough, we were on a bus back to Eilat, with a big stash of pot that we had to smoke before hitting the Israeli border,' remembered Yorkshire Pete. 'The ride was beautiful, along desert cliffs overlooking that Red Sea, which by the way is bluer than owt you've ever seen. We just about managed it, and entered the country quite the worse for wear, especially as the driver had almost driven us off a fucking cliff and into the sea on the way, trying to avoid a camel. Someone made a stupid joke about having a bomb to the friendly customs officials, and they gave him a thorough going-over, and just five days to get out of the country. He stayed for another four months. It was the usual round of working and boozing, and back to Tel-Aviv to find a moshav to work on. A moshav was like a kibbutz but you were paid slightly more and had to fend for yourself.'

There was a whole other breed of English on there, including more excellent cockneys and other lads and lasses from all over Britain, as well as Scandinavia and Australia. Dave from Bournemouth was a regular participant in the goings-on. 'We would have drinking competitions, the north versus the south,' he said. 'I lived in a house with a cockney called Doug, Yorkshire Pete, and Ian from Manchester. The house was a total party day-in and day-out, with plenty of shagging and general chaos; we would make up a big batch of chocolate milk, with about four bottles of vodka in it. Vodka was about ninety pence, so it was flowing. Everyone was invited, especially the birds. There were these Danish birds that were great. One day cockney Doug was shagging one of them right in front of everyone who was sat round the table downing the vodka milkshakes; a guy from Manchester just walked up and lobbed his cock in her mouth, and she had it and all! Every Saturday we started drinking at about eight in the morning and it went on until the early hours of Sunday. We'd make these layered drinks by pouring orange juice into a glass tumbler, then pouring vodka on top of it through a handkerchief, creating a two layered drink, with the orange on the bottom and a distinct line separating the two. In competitions, this line had to be perfect, or you'd have to neck it in one and start again. It got harder the more pissed you were. The cockneys beat the northerners in the grand final after a Manc cocked one up, big time, and more or less collapsed on the spot. We also had fly-eating competitions, in which you had to eat as many live flies as possible. Yorkshire Pete and a Boro lad ate about fourteen each, before deciding to call it off. It was disgusting. It was a common event to wake up in a strange girl's bed – there were lots of strange girls – or in your own bed next to a big lizard that had crawled in for warmth. Nobody gave a monkey's about anything, ever. We were all about the same age, eighteen to twenty-one, and this was mid-1986, when people weren't really travelling like they do today, so only the nutters were there. It was my kind of town.'

Everybody seemed to return to Eilat periodically, working their balls off again, and 'old' friends would reunite and swap stories. I was sleeping on a post office roof at this point, right next to a warm air blower. One morning, the builder I'd been working for let me down by not turning up for work, and he had my bag with all my clothes. All I had were a shirt, a pair of shorts, some sandals and my wallet. The next morning (builder failed to show again), after a late-nighter on every substance known to *Homo sapiens*, I woke up on the roof feeling brand new, to discover some thieving cunts had taken everything, except my shorts. I walked up the road to the Peace Cafe, bare-footed, potless and shirtless, thousands of miles from home, laughing my cock off.

Stuart from Salford was in Eilat with his mate Gary, a rare Man City boy embedded in the red extreme of the Manc spectrum. Stuart, a Salford red, enjoyed the work, rest, and play in that dehydrated hellhole. 'We was the main boys, right. All them cockneys and what-have-you, they was turning up wearing the gear we was wearin' about five years previous. It was dead funny to be sitting outside a mad bar, all spliffed up to fuck, with all these English who had finally managed to get a fucking clue an' had gone out and *bought* – not nicked, *bought* – these shirts and trainers an' that. The Scousers and us were well laughing, cos we'd been on the rag for stuff like that since the day Elvis died. But it's interesting to find out that everyone's the same under-neath. Even the lads from places you think are backward.'

One day, myself, Stuart, Gary, the Yorkshire lads, and Cockney Bernie, all went to the British Consulate to ask some questions. Some of them had been nicked, some had no visas, and one was wanted by the Eilat police and wanted to know if they could get him home, as he was skint. I had no visa, it had been nicked, and had lost all my possessions, including my passport, weeks earlier, but had continued the party dressed in just a pair of shorts and whatever cash I had stuffed in the little inside pocket. Most of the time I was barefoot, unless someone lent me some shoes. The others had dragged me along with them as it was clear I'd lost the plot. A few of us had spent at least a few days in the mediaeval Eilat jail by then. It was a rotting little sinkhole, with crumbling brickwork and bare light bulbs, with bars across the front of the cells, like an old cowboy film. The food wasn't bad, though. We knew we had to get away from the place before someone did something totally sick.

'It was this big white mansion overlooking the Red Sea, tea and tea-cakes, fucking cream teas, little finger in the air tackle, out on the back patio,' said Gary. 'The woman there was an eccentric, living in the days of the British Empire, and she had a fucking crocodile in a cage down the bottom of the garden. While we waited for her we went and had a gander at it. It was an eight-foot jocker in this cage about three-and-a-half foot high. Stuart, the cunt, gets this piece of thick grass, and threads it through the top of the cage down to the crocodile's face, then just rams it right in its nostril! The croc went radio rental and ended up stood right up with its teeth bared, stock-still like a statue. When the posh bird come down to interview us, we all had to stand together in front of the cage so she wouldn't see the fucker and turf us all out. It looked off it.'

Chris from Stockport was a regular in the migration between the Greek islands and Israel, a seasonal turnover that saw hundreds of young lads flocking back and forth across the Mediterranean. Chris found himself in the 'Eilat trap', as it came to be known, and became the latest one to cop for an unexpected bed and breakfast.

'One morning, I was hungover-drunk in a supermarket and put a piece of cheese in my pocket for a laugh, even though I had money on me. It was just a bit of fun with another Manc I was with. I fully intended to place it back on the shelf, but the owners saw me, dragged me into a back room, tied me up and started giving me a right hiding. The police arrived and joined in! Then they took me off to the local jail and locked me up for a week. No ifs or buts about it. After a couple of days I was taken to a court, where everyone spoke Hebrew, and I had to swear on about six different Holy Books, there in the navel of the world. I saw the coppers who twatted me, still looking disgusted. There were six to a cell, three sets of bunkbeds, and we were locked up twenty-four hours a day. My fellow inmates gave it the let's-have-it routine the first day, but they must have decided I was alright after that, because they were no bother. I'd recently had both my eyebrows shaved off and a skinhead Mohican, during a boring night on the moshav. I got a bottle of vodka for each eyebrow and a case of beer for the head. I was in a cell with three Israeli drug dealers and an army deserter who'd fucked off to visit his bird and got court martialled. The sixth guy wasn't in long – they dragged him off to another cell after he threw a total wobbler one night. To be honest the food was alright, and if I'd had some books it would have been great.

'One day, the lads in my cell took all the mattresses, including mine, piled them up against the door of the cell and set them on fire. The guards didn't give a shite. There was an inferno raging in one half of the cell and we were all clustered at the other side. The scene was mental. English lads regularly came to the barred window that looked out on the street to bring me cigarettes and other treats. One time, someone passed a Stanley knife through the window of the cell, and the leader of the drug dealers slashed all their arms with the blade. It was a trick they employed to get sent to the hospital, where they stood a better chance of escaping. They told me they'd all managed to escape before by doing that in other jails. There was a shower in the corner. The hole for the water was also the toilet. It's not very nice, having a shit in front of four blokes in a small room. Taking a shower wasn't much better. I went days without having a cack. Finally one afternoon, the guard called me out, handed me my passport, and a banana, and let me go. I was relieved because I'd just finished paying for my flight home when I got nicked, and wasn't sure I would be out for the day of the flight. It wasn't an experience I'd like to repeat, but it was certainly an experience.'

A small travel agent on the main drag put up an interesting sign one day in October, as Yorkshire Pete recalled. 'The Israelis apparently laid on a special cheap flight once or twice a year to get the English home who were skint. It was probably a thank you for all the hard graft we did for the bastards. This was our ticket out of Israel, the only way, cos we were all broke. One lad, Stuart from London, had a rope holding up his jeans, he'd lost so much weight and couldn't afford a belt. He could afford vodka, acid and herb though. We took off from an Air Force base in the desert, for a flight to Gatwick, in an unmarked plane, I swear to God. It just shows you what a situation the mental English created; actually catered to by the militaries of other countries, to get us the fuck out of there, after we'd drink them dry and build their cities in the sun.'

The plane was full of nutters: Mick from Sunderland, Mick and Pete from Yorkshire, Tim from London, Chris from Surrey, Dave from Bournemouth, Gary and Stuart from Salford, Chris from Stockport, and a load of others. I arrived back a few days before my twenty-first birthday, and my parents had no idea I was coming home. They didn't even recognise me, as I'd put weight on and lost the skinny scally appearance of old, not to mention the shaved head replacing the long hair of yesteryear. They threw a party for my twenty-first, and it was great to be back with my family and friends. Kenny and Dave-B- turned up, and we laughed our arses off, riding the rails of memory, recalling all the mad adventures we'd got away with. We danced all night, to the old-fashioned sounds of Tony Christie and Engelbert Humperdink, just like in the 70s when my folks used to host big parties. It was a far cry from a mad frontier town in a desert. I'd been gone for a year, but I'd acquired the travel bug, and was already plotting my next sojourn. I was another fish on the line, hooked and ready for a life on the road.

18

LIVING THE DREAM

Whatever happens, happens.

—General Tony O'Neill

Launching off on a jet became the thing to do overnight, and ever-more young men and women were jumping aboard the iron bird. Sometimes it might be a month in Turkey and Italy, spending your savings, or else a few months in Germany, working on building sites. But there was always the desire to go home and find out what you'd missed while you'd been lying on a beach on the edge of the world or working up trees in the middle of a desert, and the lads inevitably returned from their voyages after a while, as the Manchester chemistry drew them back, like water into salt. Being back would be a novelty for a few weeks. Everyone heard about your adventures, whether they wanted to or not, and many would brand you a lying twat, such were the tales (and their closed-mindedness). But there were still plenty of good lads who knew the score, and things were shaping up for the rest of the 80s to be a grand old trek around the globe, wreaking havoc everywhere we went. Domestically, we had nowhere left to go, did we?

A lot of the boys had been steaming through Europe for the past few summers, returning with stories and clothes, ragged from designer shops in Munich and Nice, and this was a logical extension of that. One of the earliest Perry Boys, Matt-H-, was rumoured to have been living in a cave on a Greek island, eating fish and seaweed with some locals, and lasting for months like that. Corky had embarked on a tour of Scandinavia, having already conquered Israel the year before I did, with Hursty, another psychedelic nutter. Sean-W- went to Greece and spent the summer playing his guitar and being educated in the ways of the world, and a host of others had rampaged across the continent, with predictable consequences: jail cells, mayhem and eventual return to the shithouse shores of Blighty.

Manchester was entering the Golden Age of clubs, after several years on the edge of the known universe. Upon returning for a few weeks, many would go down to London to live in houses with others they'd met on the road, sharing hazy times. We'd only ever been to London a few times before, usually as part of a United mob intent on getting smashed and misbehaving, and this was the first time we'd seen the place properly, in peacetime, as it were. The day I arrived, I sat on the National Express bus, watching the city reveal itself, as we headed through the northern outskirts towards Victoria. I was impressed. There were huge apartment blocks everywhere, with nice lawns and elaborate wrought iron fronts, their gratings and grilles describing a regal history, full of parades, bugles, Union Jacks, soldiers and Empire. Immense buildings, housing all manner of history and technology, space age- looking fixtures and signs, bristling from the facades, and beautiful glazed shop fronts, shining bright and clean, under the weight of yet more apartments above. There were squares and lawns with statues and fountains in the centre of them, and long roads packed full of hotels, both old and new, with stone balconies and rich wooden doors with large brass handles.

The atmosphere in London was as different from the rest of England as New York is from the rest of America. It's a combination of intensified English reality and large foreign influences. The cockneys had such a different way of expressing themselves they might as well have been from another planet. It was like they'd taken the English proclivity for talking nonsensically, massively enhanced it, and then formatted it through some complex technical language, with the result that they said things you could barely understand, but which sounded informative, intimidating and intelligent, simultaneously. The fish and chip shops were too healthy for north-western tastes, though. Saveloy was a piss-poor alternative to steak pudding and gravy back in the heart attack capital of England. Cockney mates would constantly nick our clothes to wear, and thought it was dead funny; these 'lads' from up north who for some strange reason had all these really good clothes. Many still hadn't been educated on the history of the Nameless Thing, in 1987. They were just accepting the styles and wearing them, blindly, without questioning where it had all come from, assuming they were the product of London. But the City had me hooked, and if I could make a bit of money I'd be all set. The fact that a lot of young fellers had started travelling, and returning to work for employment agencies temporarily, meant that these job agencies were full of lads all up to the same thing, so a synergy was created; the network expanded, and boys from all over the country would agree to go off on an expedition together, as they worked shoulder to shoulder on some cabbage mentality assembly line.

Tez-H- worked on several: 'Sometimes the foreman at the factory would offer you the opportunity for a fulltime job there, and it was hard work not laughing in their faces. They'd say things like, "Y'know, this is a good solid job here, and you'll likely be wanting to settle down soon, eh? Have you got a girlfriend? She'd be well chuffed if you came home and told her you've got a fulltime job." Little did they know you already had a plane ticket bought for your next voyage, and every day was just another dollar towards it. The wages at these places were utter shite, and you had to be signing on the dole, and probably up to no good all at the same time, just to get a decent wedge together.'

People started bringing others that they'd met on the road to Manchester for the weekend, for some good times. Brought up in the south as they sometimes were, they couldn't accept the notion that there might be a city north of Birmingham that was of any consequence. One lad, Dave from Bournemouth, sampled the scally welcome in the summer of 1987. 'After the Friday night, pub-crawling in taxis, I was amazed at the size of

Manchester, and I hadn't even been to town yet. On the
Saturday night we settled in a pub on the main drag into town
in Prestwich. The acid was strong as fuck and we were buffeted
for hours by the effects and the people, who were all in the same
condition, and determined to get to a club in town for some
dancing. I'd never seen anything like it, the number of joints
being rolled, the characters, and the acid. Of course, I'm a south-
erner and proud, so I didn't betray too much amazement to the
bastards. Every one of them was utterly convinced that they'd
invented the modern world, and that anything anybody outside
Manchester did, ever, was simply a copy of their thing.
Unfortunately, it appeared to be true.'

Manchester was definitely changing into something else at
that point. It was as if all the people suddenly wanted to live the
way we had been living. Anything you had in England, you had
to fight for, and you had to invent it yourself. In other words,
you *really* had to want it to happen. The invention of those styles
back in 1979 had been a major plot twist in the history of our
country, literally an evolutionary endpoint; people simply
couldn't come up with anything better, and consequently
continued to wear what became known as 'casual' fashion. But
we were still peasants when it came to giving ourselves cultural
choices, even as late as 1987. The new café culture in Britain was
just about rearing its head. Euro culture was what it had all been
about for a long time, but America was looming impressively all
the while.

America was an unknown lump of possibility in the late 80s.
A few weeks and a couple of jobs into the New Year of 1988,
Dave Leckie and myself travelled to Gatwick on a National
Express mobile shithouse. A big bottle of whisky from duty free
came out during the flight. In February 1988, not too many
British tourists were heading to America, so it was uncharted
territory. It was a couple of years before the Orlando Disney
World boom hit, when everyone and his dog went there. We had
one-way tickets and some flash money for the customs officials.
I was actually skint. Somehow, they let us in. We had been
unable to find a flight direct to our target, Miami, so were flying

to Newark, New Jersey. We didn't expect to get anywhere near New York City, as we had no idea where Newark actually was in relation to the Big Apple. The next move would be to get a flight, or a motor, and head for Miami. We jumped on a bus outside the airport, with 'Downtown' on the front of it, thinking we were heading for downtown Newark. At some point, we entered a tunnel. Dave was sat in the seat in front of me, talking to a girl. As we emerged from the tunnel, we were greeted by the sight of the glorious Manhattan skyline, blazing away in the night, framed in the window. Dave slowly turned to me, with a big smile on his face.

We arrived at the Port Authority Bus Terminal, near Times Square. It was already dark. The scene was exotic and strange. Neon signs protruded from every surface at every possible angle, the streets swarming with people, on their way home from work. This was the real Times Square, in early February, 1988, long before they cleaned up its act and turned it into Disneyland meets Warner Brothers. Every few feet, someone would try to sell you drugs; walking home from work and there's blokes all over the sidewalk offering you smack and angel dust. The shops all seemed to sell transistor radios, enormous fake gold necklaces, porn videos, or else were peep shows. It was a Lou Reed song come to life. We found a place to stay right in Times Square. It took us about ten seconds. Everything was happening at twice the speed it normally did. We saw a big, shiny truck on fire, right on 42nd Street, blazing away. We went in a bar, and ordered Guinness. It took an age to arrive, but when it did it was the most beautiful pint of Guinness I'd ever tasted. We spent the rest of the night wandering around the streets, exploring the concrete canyons of Manhattan.

The next morning we were out bright and early, and straight to the World Trade Center. The rooftop was total marzipan; we felt we could see almost to England. It was bracing, not unlike the air at Skegness. We took the subway everywhere, and went up the Empire State Building just as the sun was going down. At some point, we booked a flight to Miami, and one of us had to go first class. We were due to fly out early the next morning, so we took a bus back to Newark, and slept at the airport. We drank the rest of the big bottle of whisky, and crashed out on some window ledges. We shared the booze with a homeless tramp, who was almost pissing himself laughing at the stories we told him. The next day, I was woken up by Dave; apparently, we were about to miss our flight. We hoofed it through the terminal, and were soon on a flight bound for Cleveland, Ohio, where we would change for Miami. I went first class to Cleveland. The steward had me in stitches, asking me questions about soccer and George Best and Rodney Marsh. He kept shouting 'You bloody wanker!' across the cabin at me in a fake English accent. On the Miami leg, Dave was in first class, and I was sat next to a white rapper from Manhattan, also travelling down there for spring break, which was a big deal for the Yanks. He told me, 'With that accent, man, at spring break, you've got it made!' As the plane arced out over the blue Atlantic, I could see the waving palm trees and backyard pools of Miami. Something special was in the air. Twenty-two years old and chomping at the bit. We had no idea what spring break was, but we were about to find out.

We took a taxi from the airport to Fort Lauderdale, to the north. The driver took us along A1A, the coast road, and yellow-green tropical plants slipped by, as well as girls in bikinis on roller skates, old women with dressed-up dogs, big boat-like automobiles, and plenty of bars and restaurants. The song 'The Heat Is On' was playing on the radio.

The taxi-driver told us, 'If an American sees a fifty-foot pile of dogshit in his neighbour's backyard, and his neighbour tells him it's the latest fashion, he'll get *two* fifty-foot piles of dogshit in his own fuckin' backyard. That's how dumb Americans are.'

At the time, I thought he was joking.

Miami became a city in 1896, home to just a few hundred people, mainly trouble-causers and dreamers. Massive waves of immigration, particularly from the Caribbean, had since pumped the population into the millions, and conferred a wild, Latin flavour on the city. Corruption was rife, as was drug smuggling. The Everglades, a ridiculously gigantic area of swampland, held innumerable alligators as well as the body parts of those instrumental in attempting to obstruct the South Florida expansion across the lower tip of the peninsula. The concrete and neon competed actively with the wetlands for domination of the tropical playground. Unfortunately for the rare Florida panther, crocodile, environmentalists and Seminole Indian, the concrete and neon was winning. Only the gators could cope with it.

The ocean was to our right, turquoise and spangling in the afternoon sun. Dave directed the bloke to a hostel he'd stayed at the previous year, the Sol-y-Mar, on Vista-mar Street, a block from the beach, and the infamous Fort Lauderdale Strip. The Sol-y-Mar was nestled among giant palm trees and other dense foliage, with a courtyard and a swimming pool. There were people sitting around the balconies, chilling out, drinking beers. The rooms were clean, with hardwood floors. Fucking marzipan. All the buildings were stucco, painted in pastel shades of pink, yellow and blue. There were hotels and motels everywhere, apartment blocks and bars, among the palm trees. At that point, I was almost skint, and we'd only been away a few days. For the next few weeks, I don't think I had more than fifty dollars to my name at any stage, except once. The best things in life are free, they say. In South Florida, they said it a different way; looking up, I saw a small plane, trailing a long banner. The banner said, 'THE CANDY STORE, FORT LAUDERDALE STRIP'S GREATEST PARTY ZONE. FREE DRAUGHT BEER ALL DAY.' *Free beer?* We were sceptical, to say the least, but that's what the sign said.

Initially home to just 70 deranged alcoholics and gamblers, Fort Lauderdale was later named for a major who led an American volunteer force into the area in 1838, but who left after a month. Somewhere along the line, boozing and living it up became a major component of its character, as the city merged with Miami to the south. In early 1988, it was packed with alcohol-crazed young people, mainly college students on spring break. Every hotel room was booked, and it was chaos. All the clubs along the strip were offering great deals, trying to make their place the official headquarters for the college crowd.

There was the Days Inn bar, a glassy shining place, right in the middle of the strip; there was the Tropic Cay, with its cheap chicken wings, down a side street; and there was Penrod's, a large club that sold five-cent draughts, one of the main contenders for spring break HQ. But the Candy Store took the biscuit. During the day, beer was indeed free. Every night, they had a special: six dollars to get in and all you can eat and drink for two hours. The first time we went there, we had a fight. With each other. I was going to the bar, ordering nine tequilas at a time, and downing the lot in five minutes flat. There were whole chickens on offer, turning on spits behind glass, in an orange glow, not unlike the chickens in Greasy Joe's chippy back home – but these bastards were *free*. It was like ancient Rome. Dave fell off his chair trying to chat up some girl. I got thrown out, leaving my passport inside. I didn't even bother to look for it, and indulged in weeks of mayhem with no ID. Back at the hostel we knocked the living shit out of each other, for some reason. I know Dave's a blue bastard, but it had nothing to do with football, just pure drunken chaos. We were walking around with shiners and fat lips for weeks afterwards. You can't offer the English free anything without there being trouble.

I got a job working on yachts at the marina. The big yachts were full of antique furniture and beautiful trophy wives. For an old scally like me, it was easy-peasy, and I had some decent booze away, not to mention a couple of nights with lonely ex-beauty queens whose husbands were off on business trips. I worked for a guy from Kentucky for a while, and then started working on a large yacht that belonged to a flower importer, or so he said, along with two Aussies from the hostel. We worked on that boat for weeks, waxing and painting and varnishing it. One day I saw a blonde-haired girl in a star-spangled bikini, signwriting the side of a yacht with the name 'Wild Goose'. That was when I decided to go back to Manchester and learn signwriting. There were manatees living in the Intracoastal Waterway, which was Lauderdale's canal network, and large fish swimming about. One day, I remember watching some medium-sized fish being pursued by a large fish, thrashing about and churning up the water. Just as the large fish was closing in on its prey, a pelican swooped down and had it away. It was all just happening, right before your eyes. Sometimes, big fish would jump out of the water, onto the dock, wriggling about. Pete, one of the Aussies, joked that the sexual organs of female manatees were identical to those of human females. He said, 'A lot of blokes are leaving their wives for them, eh?'

The Miami Grand Prix was on at the time, and I worked on *Big Eagle*, Budweiser's yacht. It was massive, 175-foot long, with plastic trash cans packed with ice and beer everywhere. This was the southern tip of a former tropical paradise. The once lush jungle of mangroves was now bristling with skyscrapers, airports, apartments blocks, sharply intersected by the extensive canals of the Intra-Coastal Waterway, all shimmering in green and pink neon advertisements for booze, cigarettes, and good times. The *Big Eagle* staff told us to help ourselves; you can probably guess the rest. We worked our backs off, wet-vacuuming all the carpets, dragging the long electrical leads around the boat, emptying the dirty water into the quay every few minutes. The beer flowed, as did the pizza and everything else that wasn't nailed down. When I stumbled back to the Sol-y-Mar that night, I was weighed down with souvenir trinkets, food, bottles of Scotch and cans of beer. The guy gave me 100 dollars. That was the most cash I had all the time I was there, but cash was never my thing.

This abominable, moulded concrete intrusion into the ancestral lands of the Seminole Indian was typical of developments generally, be it in Salford, Sao Paolo or Sydney. The world was under assault from asphalt and a traditional form of existence was everywhere being eclipsed by moneymen and their earth-moving machines. It was the story of my life. Immediately behind the Sol-y-Mar, there was a little forest, with monkeys living in it. Sometimes they would venture into the hostel for a look around. There were even parrots in the area. Aside from us, and a gang of Aussies, there were also a few English, from London, Staffordshire, and one or two other places. There were girls from Holland, Canada, America, France, Germany and

Sweden. The Staffordshire lads were from Newcastle under Lyne, and they sounded like Scousers. The rooms of the hostel became one big party, and if we weren't working or sleeping, we were having it, big time: Sex 'n' drugs 'n' rock 'n' roll. Everyone was constantly taking the piss out of each other, and you ran the gauntlet 24/7 without a minute's peace.

For several reasons, Dave and I both had to be back in England soon. We had no idea how we were going to get home, until Dave found an old, expired credit card in his wallet. I went and bought two tickets on Virgin Atlantic there and then. Fuck knows who the card belonged to. Fortunately, a cop came to the Sol-y-Mar one day to inform me my passport had been handed into a police station somewhere in Lauderdale. I find they do come in handy sometimes, so I went right down there with an Aussie and picked it up. The last day we were there, we had a flight out of Miami at something like four o' clock in the afternoon. At two o' clock we were still in Penrod's, legless. We were entering belly-flop competitions, and limbo competitions, anxious to make it past the qualifying stages. We should have been sitting at the gate, and we didn't even know how we were going to get to the airport. They were giving away Marlboro merchandise, as they, too, were in town for the Grand Prix.

'We stumbled back to the hostel, where we persuaded a guy from Corsica named Tony to give us a lift into Miami,' remembered Dave. 'On the way, Ian started throwing up, so he kicked us out of his car, and we were clueless at that point. Ian passed out on the side of the road, and I was trying to wake him up and thumb a lift at the same time. A bloke came up and told us to get our shit together, as the cops would do him for vagrancy in that condition. Finally, two massive black guys stopped and drove us into Miami. They made a detour into the city, and dropped someone off first, then took us to the airport. How they let us through I do not know, but through we went, and we waved goodbye to fantastic Fort Lauderdale, to the girls and the sunshine and the mayhem. They told me to take Ian to the café for a few coffees before we got on the plane. You'd never get away with that these days.'

I regained consciousness somewhere over the mid-Atlantic. We'd been raving it up with a couple of the stewardesses earlier in the week, but we were still denied drinks, beyond the initial free one. I was utterly potless. I put my hand in my pocket, to see if there were any moths in there, and felt something strange. I pulled it out, right in front of a flight attendant; it was a bag of weed. He turned a blind eye. Someone at Penrod's had given it to me, and I'd forgotten all about it. I slunk back to my seat with my discovery. We ate it all, there and then, and spent the rest of the flight silently watching old episodes of *Porridge* on the screen. Riding that turbulence with glazed expressions, neither of us was there for the fun of it, believe me.

19

THE PROMISED LAND

All men should strive to learn before they die, what they are running from, and to, and why.

—James Thurber

ANYBODY WATCHING THE FA Cup semi-final between Liverpool and Nottingham Forest in 1989 remembers that day. Those that attended the match have been forever altered by what they witnessed; the gravity and scale of the death was more than enough to bend all of football out of shape. For those not at the game, watching on television, the Hillsborough disaster unfolded live on screen. Immediately, what had happened was obvious to anyone who'd been to Hillsborough in numbers. The Leppings Lane End, where the disaster occurred, had a fearful reputation as a potential death-trap. United had played at Hillsborough just a few weeks earlier and at half-time we'd moved from the uncovered corner section to try and enter the more central section, through the oversized tunnel in the middle of the away fans' end. A lot of other United fans must have had the same idea, and we all pushed through the tunnel. All of a sudden, I realised my feet were off the ground, and I was caught in the middle of a clash between an immovable object and an irresistible force. The incoming flood of bodies down the tunnel could not be accommodated by the two small sections that the tunnel led into, as the segregation fences were focussing all the people straight down the middle of the terrace and preventing an even distribution of pressure. I swear I knew at that moment that something irregular was going on, and I was well used to being in crushing crowds at Old Trafford week in and week out.

When the police opened the gates at Hillsborough that fateful day, the entire influx of bodies was directed down into those centre sections, but this time the source of the pressure was coming all the way from out in the street. It's no surprise that people were crushed to death in those little sections. The tunnel was too big and its catchment sections too small and it was a death-trap waiting to be realised. It is known that policemen were sometimes posted at the end of the tunnel to direct supporters to left and right once the centre section was full, itself an indication that something was wrong with the layout; grown men don't need telling where to go when entering a football ground. Maybe the average crowd at Hillsborough just didn't provide a decent enough illustration of what might happen. If it were Old Trafford or Anfield, where capacity crowds were the norm, something might have been done to rectify the structural problem sooner. I know I complained to people that day, including police, as they were the only interface between 'us and them' that existed. That said, Manchester and Liverpool had stadiums that were the best designed in the country, and a tunnel of those proportions emptying into a section that small was unlikely to have been a feature of stadiums in those cities.

So South Yorkshire Police were the scapegoats this time, possibly because of their sluggishness to respond to events on the day. Policemen were observed forming a cordon along the centre line, to prevent Liverpool fans from reaching the Nottingham Forest fans at the opposite end, in the initial belief that it was a pitch invasion. Even after people were pulled from the carnage and carried on make-piece stretchers fashioned from advertising hoarding, some police continued to hold the cordon on the halfway line. When it became common knowledge that a South Yorkshire policeman had deliberately leaked the 'pissing on and pick-pocketing their own dead fans' myth to *The Sun*, nobody in Liverpool felt sorry for that particular Force, and the newspaper was boycotted for its part in the outrage.

The English disease is caused by the fact that shit rolls down-hill. It was a shocking wake-up call, and one that eventually created the Premiership, by ridding the country of terracing and bringing in a higher level of economic dynamism. We all like to slag off the prawn sandwich brigade, but they had a hand in making the Premiership the most attractive league in the world, with their middle-class pay-scale. It's ironic that the people sitting above the corpses of the crushed turned out to be the ones who had been rewarded with larger seating sections, which only they could afford.

There were two very eventful years from 1988 to 1990. This was the true rise of Madchester, the days when it was happening. Everybody seemed to be connected to some form of skulduggery, often via several simultaneous conduits, each a maximised channel for the throbbing energy of our incredible party. Slowly, people were realising that the attitude and clothing invented by a few thousand teenagers in Liverpool and Manchester around 1980 was actually becoming an integral component of those cities' character.

Sometimes we'd be in a club in town on a Tuesday night and we'd be the only people in the place – nature's way of telling you you're overdoing it, maybe? Little scallies would pick you up in stolen cars and give you a lift home, billowing smoke and laughter. Local pubs became GCHQs for innumerable neigh-bourhood crews, each intent on providing refreshments and entertainment to varying degrees. Weekends were fantastic, as we went into town and sampled the light shows at every place going. There'd always been plenty of grafters in Prestwich, doing markets, selling, kiting, dealing, the full issue, and it reached a peak now. Many simply worked nine-to-five jobs. It was nowt to be ashamed of. We were all earning, one way or the other: myself, Dave-B-, Andy-M-, Howard, Dave-G-, Bowie, Mesmerizer, John McCann, Tongey, Mike-G-, the good ol' boys. One night, as we stumbled out of the Ostrich to go to town, Howard lit an air bomb, and aimed it at me and Dave-B-. I heard a whizzing sound, and was struck in the eye by what felt like a small folded packet of powder, with an elastic band around it. It bounced off my eye, and a split second later, it went off, about four feet above my head, with a mighty BOOM. If things had been different, I might have lost an eye. As it was, we just laughed.

Both United and City fans crammed the clubs, and there was an absence of the hatred and violence with which the teams' relationship had been previously stained. It was all about getting high and tripping on the music and the light shows. The new, smaller Manc Casual mobs were still going at it, but even though we wanted to see each other liquidated as an entity, United and City got along. The previous few years' battles and jibbing into Maine Road, where we took over their sections, was over anyway. The big meet-up and walk down to the ground from the Grey Parrot pub in Hulme, or wherever, still happened, but little blue resistance was met. When I went to the Maine Road derby in 1991 with Tongey, the police had erected barriers and were checking for tickets, just like everywhere else by then. We ended up in a pub in Moss Side, and later roamed drunk round the hotel bars in Piccadilly, singing 'Native New Yorker' and winding the ladies of the night up for a laugh. There were some nasty goings-on back then with City sniper squads, but I knew very few people involved in that sort of thing at that point, as it was all about clubbing and having a laugh.

Travelling was becoming an obsession among the stoney-broke tribes of Albion, a moonlit exodus, a rolling convoy, composing every Tom, Dick and scally from every major city, market town and suburb. Many from the scrapyard of the Industrial Revolution became willing émigrés, deserting the rusting machines, brickish mills and sickly polluted waterways for experiences far away. The foreign panoramas were assaulted by rivers of Perries, all intent on having a riot every day. These lads had progressed beyond infection by the Nameless Thing into the world of expanded consciousness: psychedelia. They were in the process of acquainting themselves with the new form of spiritual transport – the music, chemicals, and light shows behind the exploding phenomenon of Acid House and Rave. In places like Cairo and Istanbul, the ethnic music blasting

from the Eastern amplifiers bespoke something unearthly, reve-
latory, and not unlike the stuff pumping into the clubs back
home. Ignoring sensible advice from *The Travel Show*, many
curiously ate things they shouldn't from street vendors, and
ended up lying in their hotel rooms, shivering and feeling like
they were dying. They would vow to sort themselves out. But,
once cured, it was back onto the mad boulevards of these exotic
cities, to hunt, to drink, to find other English lads who were also
on the case, for the Nameless Thing has no cure – it merely
mutates and pushes the host into ever more elaborate forms of
fun and games.

The variously changing popular holiday destinations of the
distant 90s were all being visited in the 80s by the adventuring
Perries. These lads witnessed the destruction of much of
Europe's infraculture, that ancient web which had supported
trade, travel and communication for millennia. They were the
last to see these locations in their unspoiled form. It was the
expanding frontier of so-called progress, wherein traditional
modes of existence were obliterated and replaced by glossy
concrete versions of that more authentic, previous medium.
High-rise hotels popped up on premium real estate, to house
the holidaymakers from the north. It was Salford in the sun.
Snide Lacoste and Adidas had replaced the ethnic trinkets of
old, and the saddest thing was, people thought it was great.

By 1991, Eilat was populated by a new breed of English. They
were of the Ecstasy school, and they knew it all. Little bastards.
While most of the boys from the mid-80s were of the Perry or
later Casual breed, this lot had had the way paved for them. They
had no idea of the way Israel used to be, before an army of
British style-boys had built it up from the sands. Israel had seen
several years of mad dogs coming and going, and the welcome
was wearing thin. The irony was that, if anything, the original
wave of English were the ones who themselves had been
displaced by the bulldozers, back home in their various British
cities. They were the ones who'd transformed Israel, as their own
authentic working class worlds had been 'improved' similarly. In
the Moshav office, the farmers were refusing to take British

volunteers because of all the drunkenness and attendant lunacy over the past several years. Chris from Stockport was one of the victims of this discrimination:

'Other nationalities were coming in the door and getting sent straight out, to the Promised Land. The English were all sat there, with long faces, knowing we had more work in us than the lot of them put together. We just enjoyed a drink, was all. As a result of this situation, we tended to be assigned to regions that were undesirable. Four or five cockney skinheads in Lacoste and Fila came in one day, and after being stuck there a few hours, they lost their rag totally. They persuaded the Israelis to sort them out with a moshav, or else. There was a couple there from Wales trying to point out on their passports that they weren't from England, but the Israelis were strict; no British or Irish for the cushy places. Send them to the frontier, where the only thing to do was work or drink, or go insane from heatstroke.

'The English boys were sent to moshavim right next to trouble spots, like the Gaza Strip. Attacks from the Intafada were common. Farmers had their guns taken from them and were murdered by Palestinian workers who they'd employed for several years. Another was knifed to death the week before I arrived, by a worker who'd also been with him years. There were Palestinians everywhere in the area, as the Israelis used them for labour, along with the foreign volunteers. My farmer told me you cannot trust a Palestinian, even one you know well, as they might be sleepers waiting for the signal to kill, or fresh converts to radicalism.

'I was given the job of driving across the border into Gaza every morning at five o' clock, to pick up the Palestinian workers. As I approached the border, there would be hordes of Palestinians along the sides of the road, the numbers increasing as I neared the customs area. The funny thing was, most of these Palestinians were wearing Adidas and Nike, and they looked like a crew of lads paying into a football ground. So they'd had their biblical town knocked down, replaced with concrete apartments, and now they were all done up in labelled sports-wear! It was a sick fucking parallel to many of us in England.

The only difference was they got into it after Adidas relocated to the Far East, and most of what they wore was snide from Turkey or somewhere.'

And still the British came, running in rivulets down the slopes of Europe, into the blue otherworld of the Mediterranean basin. Greece was a favourite stopping point, before catching the ferry to Haifa. Some drug-induced shenanigans in the islands, with naughty girls and bottles of Raki and plenty of Abo (Arrack, brandy and orange). In Tel-Aviv, in September 1991, many were working for builders, mixing sand and cement all day by sieving the pebbles through a wire mesh screen and using the shovel the old-fashioned way. Palestinian plasterers were our masters, and they worked at lightning speed. I was up for the challenge, and lost about two stone in three weeks. I ate one meal a day, and slept soundly at night. Slowly, I earned enough to buy a ticket home. This was the first time I took my Bundle with me, the signwriter's kit, but I didn't write any English. It was all Hebrew and Arabic, going from right to left, and it was a joy.

The day I flew home, I met two English lads in the customs queue, a big Geordie-type from Hartlepool and a cockney Millwall supporter who had a massive tattoo of a butterfly across his body. He was going cold turkey, and said his mate was meeting him at Gatwick with a big bag of smack. The Israeli security staff were giving everybody the usual drilling. The Hartlepool guy took out a black and white PLO head-scarf right before he went for questioning, and the Mossad were not amused. He explained he planned to wear it at the football back home, and they just stared. We all got smashed in the bar and swapped tales of recent mayhem in the Holy Land. Back in London at Victoria Station, we ran into a Chelsea lad who'd just arrived back from a cup match at Tranmere. His boat-race was scuffed up, and he looked well sick. Tranmere Scousers had battered the fuck out of the cockney supermen, and this poor bastard's wallet had been nicked. He was asking us for money, and we laughed in his face — we didn't have a penny between us, having spent our last coppers in the bar at

Tel Aviv airport. We had to jib all the way from Gatwick to the cold north that night.

Even as they exited the city in search of ancient wonderlands, the mature Perries were returning to Manchester in droves, more outrageous and demented than ever. It was a feedback cycle, as some arrived, some left, and so on, mixing and merging our new experiences together in the bricks and mortar matrix of Mancunia. We were half-man, half-creature, and weren't able to feel comfortable in the civilised world anymore. We wanted to run amok and drink and generally be out of control, preferably somewhere subtropical and somewhat lawless. Anything else was a bore for graduates of the Liverpool–Manchester class of 1980. Many lads were bored by life and unsure what the hell was going to become of them. We had seen too much and done too much, and the prospect of eking out an existence with the rest of the nine-to-fivers was terrifying. We'd rather die.

The name of the game, to us, was remaining beyond the curve, ahead of the biological constraints of being an animal born on a planet of this type, with its dynamic load of environmental chemistry. Genetic processing of those chemicals had formed plastic cells that mutated strangely over billions of years, finally becoming this present moment, where the questions confront you: when you walk out of those high school gates forever, aged sixteen, are you the captain of your own destiny? Will you make it up as you go along? Are you going to remain that same sixteen-year-old, becoming fatter and balder, or are you heading for self-realisation? Self-education? Or will you just get your childhood sweetheart up the tub and resign yourself to job, mortgage, kids, two weeks in Esparantos, and finally death? It was no contest.

United were gathering pace, and their glory years were about to begin again. A lot of the lads had never stopped attending games, and they made sure they were there to see the reds by any means necessary. Martin-X-, a loyal supporter, described the way they obtained tickets for the 1994 League Cup Final against Aston Villa. 'A couple of weeks before the match, a certain group of reds from Wythenshawe went to Villa Park. On the

ticket office counter was a stack of token sheets, left there for
anyone to pick up. I don't think they expected someone to pick
up a hundred of them in one swoop though. Then it was straight
into the souvenir shop, and every programme from that season
was available. We bought one from each game, took them back
to Manchester, and sought out a friendly printer. He copied the
tokens – just the face side – and it was off to Villa Park again
with a stack of full token sheets to pick up the tickets. After a
few spins through, the knock-backs come on. Nothing to do
with the tokens, just the same faces that kept coming back raised
the alarm. The Villa fans there didn't want to know, so we
enlisted the help of every taxi driver in Aston. Each was given a
"fare" and all he did was walk in and get us the tickets. Right at
the death, one of the lads goes in, and all the staff started getting
busy, giving his token sheet a good looking at. Was it on top?
The Brum bloke's immortal line in that comical accent, "He
looks a bit black!" pointing at one of the tokens that hadn't
copied too well and was moody as fuck, got us right at it. I think
it was Dalian Atkinson. You couldn't make out his face at all. It
was now well on top, and the magic "Police!" shout went up and
a sharp exit was made by all. One of the lads jumped in a taxi
and went to Witton Station, but the daft fucker never realised it
was only used on match days. He spent hours waiting on the
platform. I jumped in the motor and was off to Highbury for
that night's 2-2 draw with Arsenal, in which Eric Cantona was
sent off. Great days indeed, and I could tell a million stories
about them.'

The European Championships of that year were won by
United goalie Peter Schmeichel, when he saved van Basten's
penalty. The atmosphere in the city was on the turn, like a
chemical reaction, the catalysts being individuals like ourselves,
coming and going with stories and artefacts of our many plun-
ders across the oceans. Where Liverpool had gone into Europe
and returned with designer gear, Manchester was going everywhere and returning with colourful mementoes; each was added
to the strangely growing jigsaw of cultural and gastronomic
fusion permeating the city, turning it into something new.

United finished second, behind the sheep-fondlers, before winning the league in 1993. It was the start of a fabulous run, one that I was to miss due to absence in foreign climes. It was ironic, given that I'd faithfully attended the matches during the shite years, when many others were giving it a miss. I remember Eric Cantona playing for Leeds, scoring a hat-trick against Liverpool in the Charity Shield. Even though I detested Leeds, Cantona was a heroic figure. When Alex Ferguson scooped him up for a song in November 1992, it was sensational news. The King had come to the castle.

* * *

Three months prior to Eric Cantona's arrival, the interconti-nental flow of scallywags continued as ever. Orlando in August 1992 was simply catering to the vast Disney complex in the city. Florida was at the crest of the wave, with Brits travelling to the States in greater numbers than ever before. The Sunshine State was as big as England and Wales combined, providing a lot of space for children like us to romp around in.

The name Orlando allegedly came from a time during the Seminole Indian wars (like much of Florida's historic names) when it was discovered carved into a tree by a crew of idiots on the run from the villages of America – and the rest is history. Air bases, citrus groves and aerospace companies all contributed to the growth of the city, but after one Walt Disney secured use of the area in the mid-1960s for his vast theme park, the place evolved into an utter joke – sorry, major tourist attraction – as a result.

In 1992, the city had a huddle of new glass buildings and roadways dissecting its centre, and the bars and clubs were everywhere, amid the bushy palms. There were lads and girls from all over Europe arriving from all directions, having worked on Camp America for the summer. The days were hot and humid, with the monsoon every day at around three. The city's youth hostels were full of trendy geezers, products of the Nameless Thing without knowing what the Nameless Thing even was. What had been a tiny trickle of Perry pioneers in early 1988 had become a steady flow. The look was now totally universal among the English: polo or tennis T-shirts, Levi's, Adidas trainers or stylish hiking shoes, and a bit of the old Lambeth walk thrown in for good measure. We had harnessed the power of the lightning, discovered the difference between 'acting' and 'conducting yourself'. He Who Has His Wits About Him knew to keep up the energy levels and seek adrenalin on tap in this changing world. It had truly spread, this inferno, from deepest green Devon to the Heart of Midlothian, from the quietest bays of north-western Scotland to the grey continental supply routes of Kent. The pandemic had claimed all in its stead, and the new generation were swarming across the globe looking for laughs. Lads were arriving with thirty-day, anywhere-in-the-USA airline tickets, and giving them away to other lads when it was time to leave and they had days left on their pass. Back then, you could fly anywhere within the States and not even show ID. People were flogging their return tickets to other people and accompanying them to the airport just to check them in. These thirty-day passes and international return tickets were changing hands as fast as people's changing fortunes. Everyone wanted to stay in America, and the game was on to find a way to do it.

This was the time of the Auto Driveaway, the fabled American Dream come to life. Unkempt English scallies would stumble into an office somewhere among the strip malls, palm trees and tinted glass, and were given somebody's car to drive across America. It made no difference whether you were intoxicated or emitting the reek of a compulsive masturbator; good Americans needed their cars transporting across this grand continent, and they were too lazy to do it themselves, which left only oddballs, weirdos and other assorted drifters to do the job for them. The amazing thing was, it worked. A small deposit, refundable upon delivery, was paid, and off you fucking well went. Some shot off to New York, some to Chicago. And some went truly west, to California, the Golden State.

The journey was executed in legs, stopping at major cities for fun and games along the way. California began for the white man as a Gold Rush target, and was filled solid with every drunken idiot prospector and crooked millionaire in America around the mid-1800s. Indians, who'd lived there for thousands of years, were displaced first by the gold miners, then by the farmers, who arrived in vast numbers on the newly-constructed railroads, where they drained the aquifers and dragged as much green stuff from the parched desert as humanly possible. Large numbers of East Asians arrived, establishing San Francisco's amazing Chinatown, the first of several large influxes from Asia. California became the world capital of entertainment in the twentieth century, and a distinctly cosmetic character encroached upon the regional personality, a tidal wave of super-ficial arseholes who became the laughing stock of the country, despite the state generating the world's sixth largest economy.

Chris, from Eccles, lived in San Francisco for a few months, working as a carpenter. He described the shady Manc pioneers that were quite well-rooted there on the west coast, in 1992. 'They were drug dealers. About fifteen of them. San Francisco was developing something of a rave scene, and they'd been drawn to it. They were definitely a naughty bunch, and were moving in all the trendy circles, knocking out E, acid and pot. There were Storm Rave nights and The Gathering, at clubs like Toontown and Fantasia, who were the first in the States to make it happen. Both San Fran and LA had rave clubs going at this point. I remember people talking about going off to some mad electronic night out in the desert to watch the moon. These Mancs were in there, doing the business.'

Surprise, surprise...

I slept on a staircase for a week or two, then decided to get the fuck out. I caught a ride with a Glaswegian who was working concerts all over the country. He was a good lad, but we differed on one major point: he was disgusted by those who sold their passports for a bit of beadage. I personally would've *given* my passport away to any worthy cause. The Pacific Coast Highway is littered with the burnt-out shells of Englishmen who plunged into the unknown without a safety net. They stand as an inspiration to other intercontinental jibbers not to falter,

to just do it, and balls to the consequences. The sunset over the
Pacific is like nothing you've ever seen: immense orange and
purple sheets of light smudged across the entire horizon, topped
by a gigantic juicy blush, like the world had been kissed by the
electric-pink lipstick'd mouth of the American Dream. It
destroys all rational thought of being careful, and inspires in the
minds of young men notions of gold and jewels, romance and
violence. The usual shite. There are ragged palm trees everywhere, cacti, and big glassy futuristic mansions tucked away in
the hills to your left, while the blue ocean sparkles to your right,
if you're heading south, which you fucking well should be.

At some point you will collide with The Big Orange. The
road junctions become larger, and the lanes in the road multiply
with each mile, until you are driving along a vast palm-lined
boulevard, with funky looking shops and people driving by in
convertible Rolls-Royces. Everything is concrete, metal and
glass. The architecture assumes a cartoon-like appearance,
blended with an ineffable quaintness. Malibu and Santa Monica
roll past, and eventually you hit Venice Beach, little sandy paths
with bungalows along them, full of heads who are game for
some fun. Perry Boys, both old and young.

Here are the nutters. Spread thinly but numerously across the
wildest and most unique city in America, the British lads are
everywhere you go, smoking spliff and talking shit. The freeways
penetrate and flow over the rocky canyons into mansion neighbourhoods wherein dwell the Billy Idols, and any taste you may
have is screwed up and left in a bin by the door. In Hollywood,
the streets are lined with thick, bushy palm trees that shade the
ornate apartment blocks of old town. Off in the distance, up the
hill, the actual 'Hollywood' sign can be clearly seen. It's surreal,
deja vu constantly, as a result of all the films you've watched in
your lifetime. These were the very streets where a lot of those
films were made.

It takes six months just to get a reasonable feel for LA, to
understand why things are where they are, and the quickest way
to get to them. Downtown Los Angeles towers in a yellow haze
created by the exhaust fumes, which stacks against the moun-

tains behind it, held there against the rocky trap by coastal breezes coming in off the Pacific. Angelinos live at the bottom of a vast column of gas, through which tons of nitrogen dioxide twist upward, reacting into photochemical smog and eclipsing huge numbers of skyscrapers. You can be close to a major centre and not realise it for days, as the buildings are engulfed in nitrogenous poison, all the way to the crippled ozone. In 1992, England was well used to the idea that young people liked to dress well and attend huge parties full of blissed-out trippers, many of whom headed for the beaches of Spain in summer, where English rogues patrolled the towns, supplying the product. The rogues patrolling the boulevards of Los Angeles weren't quite so well known. Simon, from Salford, met several Mancs there that year, and became part of a slowly galvanising little Manc mob.

'It was all borderline criminals, merging with the big permanent British population on one side, and with the Perry-type lads passing through on the other,' said Simon. 'There's always been a big community of British musicians here, and they were quite busy with the sex, drugs and rock 'n' roll. We weren't gangsters, but we had connections enough to be able to deal to our own here on the west coast, and make a reasonable living from it. We'd all been through the eighties and it was ancient history. We didn't give a toss about Spain or even watching United anymore. LA was a massive place and it's cheap to live there. Being one of the Boys was as much a part of life as breathing. You'd have to live in the Outer Hebrides not to know that by then. We had cars and loads of girlfriends, and even decent apartments. It was like, *fuck me, I have arrived*, every minute of every day.'

Rental charges for apartments in LA were notoriously inconsistent, and it wasn't unusual for someone to be paying top dollar for a crappy hole with no view, while five miles away someone else enjoyed a spacious wonderland with massive panoramas out of the window, all the way to the Pacific. One guy arrived from Failsworth on a two-week fly-drive from Manchester Airport. He picked up his rental car, and on the first day reported three thousand dollars in traveller's cheques lost or stolen, which were then replaced by the company. In hours, he had doubled his money. He decided to sell his return flight to another English guy, who he accompanied to the airport and checked in under his name, and proceeded to drive the rental car for another three months, before dumping it at the airport when he flew home. The car was a wagon of madness, a ferry for drugs, girls, booze, stolen goods and Manc lunatics. It was probably never even listed as missing. This was how these people lived, how they wanted to live, and they got away with it for years. Only in America.

Fortunately a guy from London paid for me to spend my first night in the hostel in Venice Beach, as I literally had thirty-five cents in my pocket, barely enough to make a local payphone call. He was a crackhead, and was trying to stop smoking the rock after his mate had been killed in a crackhouse a couple of weeks earlier, his skull smashed with a large blunt object. Once in the hostel I concentrated on finding a way to make some money, and felt extremely grateful to this generous guy. He was one of the many who had been sucked in and spat out by the giant funky town, but he had a heart of gold.

I had the Bundle with me, and started to write signs and banners for the hostel and other places in LA, advertising raves organised by the English lads. I was an artist, as integral to the scene as the DJs, and was quite proud of some of the psychodelic work I did. Rodger, the Aston Villa Villain I'd travelled from Orlando to San Francisco with the previous month, had plenty of suggestions, being something of an E monster. LA sports some pretty decent graffiti, and I was only too happy to contribute at times, covering some of the walls in Venice Beach with monstrous illustrations of hybridised animal-things, fusions of insects, humans and birds, that clawed their way up the sides of the beach walls.

Some of the lads went to Las Vegas to look for work in the hotels and casinos. Vegas is a few hours drive from LA; set off at midday and at dusk it appears as a huge agglomeration of multi-coloured lights in the distance, blackness all around it, like it's floating in space. The Strip is a ridiculous and abominable assortment of themed monuments to hedonism. The brightness of the lights makes it seem like high noon. There's Caesar's Palace, famed host of boxing matches, the erupting volcano outside the Mirage, the Sands, the Desert Inn, the Sahara, and a funny little casino called the Tam O' Shanter, that has an illuminated green and black tartan titfer revolving at the top of a long pole. There's the Stardust, Silver City, and, of course, Circus Circus. They gave away free drinks in the casinos, which was a bit more interesting. I spent a few weeks wandering through these twilit grottos, but I wasn't sure if it was worth the free drinks, just to sit and watch dozens of people make absolute cocks of themselves, washed in neon. I was using the Bundle to give a facelift to the Hotel Casablanca, the seediest motel on the Vegas Strip, bought by a guy we knew from LA. I left Rodger the Aston Villa Villain there, as he was running the Casablanca. The place was besieged nightly by local street gang members, trying to use the telephones in the foyer to set up deals. There was a lot of crack and Ecstasy being thrown about as bargaining chips, but the Ecstasy was mostly Jekyll shit. The sensible option was to stick with the crack, and plenty of it. It was all good fun, but I was broke, and that was getting boring, not to mention staying up all night going completely mental most of the time. I remained there for a couple of months, painting signs, but eventually decided to push the eject button on my seat, as money was hard to come by without a Green Card. I spent a day hitching from Vegas back to LA, ready to leave America behind. At LAX airport, I managed to cop for a connector from London to Manchester at no extra charge, and off I ran to the gate. I was returning to Manchester again, and must admit it was a relief, after several months skidding across the USA on the seat of my pants.

20

BEYOND THE FRINGE

If you don't know where you're going, any road will take you there.

—George Harrison

BACK IN MANCHESTER in late 1992, things were jaded. The culture that had developed over the past twelve years was now thoroughly entrenched. It had become a mainstream lifestyle for many, and it entailed a strange overlap between tradi-tional values and a new chemical-fuelled ability to think outside of the box. The large percentage of people making interconti-nental missions to places distant, had contributed hugely to the veins of spicy foreign influence that swirled about the city; we were bringing back our experiences and recreating it in Manchester, as accurately as we could. Second-city status had always been contested, as many in the south believed Birmingham to deserve the title, but the truth was that many natives of Brum regularly visited Manchester for a night of clubbing, or a day of shopping, as it offered more than their own city. We didn't feel inclined to return the compliment. Londoners didn't want to hear about this, they just wanted to keep anything worth a toss as close to home as possible, as ever, even if it was a lie.

A good-sized little crew from Prestwich and surrounding areas had been regularly winging its way back and forth between Manchester and Sydney, Australia, for a while. Kenny, my long-time mate from school, was one of the Pommies who made the trip. He disappeared for years. 'I flew on this mad non-stop airline, Manchester-Vienna-Kuala Lumpur-Sydney, direct, no stopovers. When I got there it was night-time. Corky picked me up and took me straight down to the Eastern Suburbs, at Coogee Beach. I was knackered but they took me out for a drink. We walked into this bar, and there was a band on, playing Doors and Stones music. I thought, "This is fucking brilliant." We were in there till five the next morning. There were loads of English there, so many I couldn't believe it. The next day I was walking down the street, admiring the beer gardens and the pubs, thinking the hilly neighbourhood looked like San Francisco, when I hear, "Oi!" I look inside this pub and Churchy's sat there, one of the lads from back home, and a bit of a character. He introduced me to a lot of the places to go around there. It was kind of a mixed neighbourhood, with apartments, private homes, shops and the beach.

'I moved into a flat with an Irish lad and a girl, and started bricklaying. The Sydney to Hobart Boat Race was on at the time, and I flew down to Tasmania with Churchy and this cockney who we called Aunt Sally, cos he looked like Aunt Sally from Worzel Gummidge. It was Boxing Day. We were knocking out snide sunglasses to the race punters, Gucci, Armani, Oakley and what have you. They were all in cases and looked sorted. One woman even let us set up our wallpapering table inside her boozer, which was sound, cos it was a major watering hole for sailors coming in from the race. They had this big bell, and every time they finished another bottle of Bundaberg Rum they'd ring it like fuck. It was an impressive piss-up from these sailing merchants. Everyone was completely leathered, including us. We had loads of decent sailing gear away off the pissheads. We scored a bag of herb that was outlandishly powerful. We had to wrap it in plastic, put it in a sock, and hang it out of the fucking window in the hotel, but still you could honk it. You could smell it outside in the effing corridor! We booked a stall on Launceston market to flog more shades, but just me and Aunt Sally went, as Churchy was bollocksed with all the tackle. The worst thing was, we had to lob a load of herb down the shitter when it was time to fly back.

'Hammy came over from Manchester, and he said it was like a secret place in England that nobody tells you about, there were so many English there. He fucked his ankle up in Kuala Lumpur on the way over, and arrived in Sydney in a wheelchair. The hills wouldn't have it, and he had to go home and have it all pinned together, the poor bastard. But plenty remained. There was the Thompson Twins, who spoke to you in fucking stereo, and both got deported together. Ady also got deported. Ants lived in Melbourne, away from the Sydney antics. Brass, Kev White, Lee and Ken Collins, and Corky's cousin, Eddie, who worked on the bricklaying with me, all came on down for a long or short spell. Eddie had his visa running out right before the World Cup in Japan and Korea, so it was an opportunity to go to the World Cup. We landed in Nana Plaza, Bangkok, and were having a drink, when who should come traipsing down the fucking road with suitcases, but three of the lads from home, on a World Cup voyage. It was Hammy's brother, Skez, and Mike-C-, Eddie's brother. We got straight on it then, and one thing led to another, and Eddie ended up marrying this Thai girl. He's since had two kids with her, plus one of her own that came with. I was in Bangkok the night she had their first kid. He phoned me from down on Pattaya to come and be there with him. I met a lad from the old neighbourhood who owned a bar named after the building society he robbed to get the money to relocate. There were about fifteen of us, all from home, on the piss in his bar, admiring how he'd come up in the world. You couldn't make it up.'

The Mancs in Oz were many, and they remain to this day. They are just another example of how unemployment and poverty breaks up working-class families and scatters them to the winds. But, by heck, it's fun, lad.

By now, anywhere was fair game for an adventure, and everywhere you went there were English lads steaming about. Spain fell victim to probably the larger fraction, though, and along the length of the Costa there stretched untold numbers of lads on the run, on the rob, on the make and on Ecstasy. Working the clubs and pubs, selling timeshares, flogging stuff on the beaches, or simply dealing drugs to the British over on holiday, were among the modes of survival practised by the victims of the Nameless Thing. For the Thing was not just about dressing smart; it entailed jibbing, thieving, using one's napper like a cockney wideboy, and being able to get by with some verve and satisfaction. We came from the nation that invented the modern world, but we wanted to live like savages, to re-ignite the fires of the ancient stone circles, and pull that pagan energy from inside our souls.

After a very short stint in Spain and a few months in England, I went back to the States. It was a great magnet at the star-spangled Western extreme, pulling, always pulling, like the shiniest apple at the top of the greenest tree. I returned to Fort Lauderdale once more, the boats and the beauty. Dave-B- came along for a fortnight's holiday, and we stayed in the fabled Sol-y-Mar. The place was no longer full of gangsters from New York, Sicily and Corsica; things had changed. This time it was different from 1988, or even 1992. At the end of 1993 there were many more English everywhere, looking to score drugs and get fucked up. Disgraceful.

After Dave-B- went home, I moved into a yacht I was working on at the marina, a million-dollar beauty. It was a nice place to chill on and crash at the end of the day, drifting into sleep with a red sunset and the towers of apartment blocks and luxury yachts all around. I even went to work on Christmas Day, I was so happy just to be there. I felt like I was living in an episode of *Miami Vice*. I met three guys, from Oxford, Liverpool and Manchester, who were constantly flying into Miami with their coat pockets full of Ecstasy tabs. They said they expected to be caught, but they were pushing it to the limit. Everywhere they giggled and winked, nudge, nudge, nudge; the products of our generation.

Rob, from Oxford, was working in a T-shirt shop on the Lauderdale strip, but making his main money at night. 'There were a good few clubs in Lauderdale, and people wanted E off us, as ours was so much stronger than the shit you could get in the States. I met this Scouser and Manc in Spain, where we were all working, and because there was a lot of air-traffic between Spain and Miami, we took a little trip. The security was non-existent, so we just said, "Fuck it, let's start bringing it in in our coat pockets and acting casual." I think because we genuinely didn't care about getting caught we never stirred up any suspicions. We were coming through customs at Miami wearing these jackets. Our

pockets were bulging with hundreds of capsules. Rhubarb and
Custard, it was, the one that made you see a big smiling sun in
your mind every time you closed your eyes. The reggae band
Inner Circle played a free concert on the beach for Superbowl
weekend of 1994. The beach was packed with ravers, dancing and
drinking at bars set up on the beach. We made a killing.'

I worked for about three months on the boats, whipping up
and down the south Florida coast on speedboats, yachts and sail-
boats, before fleeing in another Auto Driveaway, this time bound
for Salt Lake City, Utah, in a pick-up with monster wheels.
Ready to take on the American continent once more, I made
1,100 miles in one hit, all the way to Shreveport, Louisiana, right
on the Texas border. The towns of Alabama and Mississippi had
whizzed by, looking sleepy and often strange. I rose early the
next day and gave it plenty again, right across Texas, where there
is often fifty miles between gas stations in the middle of baking
Mars-scapes and vast plains. That night I was in the New
Mexico desert. At one point I rolled down my window, and saw
something I could not fathom; the night sky appeared to be
brighter than the silhouettes of the desert hills framed before it.
This was because of the vast number of visible stars. I pulled
over to the side of the road and admired the view. There was a
shooting star every ten seconds. Only in these desolate regions
are we able to experience the view from Earth in all its glory,
away from the light pollution. The uniform spray of starlight
seems to soothe the battered head, a warm physical connection
to the unknown cosmos. Everywhere else we are condemned to
the ignorance of industrialism, born in Manchester and
colonised across the poor globe. We are faced with apparent
darkness, and we don't give a shite. So much to answer for, eh?

From Salt Lake City I flew to Orange County, California, just
south of Los Angeles. It was March 1994. There was something of
a music scene in Hollywood, with plenty of English psychedelic
bands passing through. The smoke was flowing and the good
times were had by all. The Satisfied Customer spent time in
Hollywood around this time, and was hanging around with the
English buccaneers. They were big on foam, apparently. 'Some lads

were using upholstery foam to rob banks; stuffing it up inside the
overhead dispenser to block the dollar bills as they came out.
Punters just assumed a malfunction had taken place, and moved
on. The lads came back later, and harvested the green stuff. One
guy used to hang a sign at the deposit box, informing the punters
that it was broken and to use the "safety letterbox" in the main
door for their envelopes of cash. Inside the letterbox was a basket,
and he'd lob a piece of foam into it, bringing the level of the
basket right up to the slot in the door, where he could grab the
envelopes. Each time someone put cash into the slot, he'd be
there, rescuing it for the cause. There was enough random opportunity in West Hollywood to keep you in food and beer for the
rest of your life. They knew every major hotel and youth hostel
in Hollywood, and every corridor and room in them. If there was
something worth having they had it. These Yanks just left money
out everywhere, and never locked their cars. The place was a
wonderland. It was like everyone just took drugs and tripped their
time away, on the proceeds of a couple of hours graft a day.'

I wasn't there for the fun of it, and I dug trenches for an elec-
trician for a few weeks, to install pool lights in the big back yards.
One day, we had three after-shocks from the bad earthquake of
a couple of months earlier, the Northridge Quake. It was a truly
unsettling sensation, being moved back and forth through space
by the earth's crust, as it shook itself free of pressure. The electri-
cian asked me if I'd be interested in driving his ex-wife back to
Illinois, as she was moving there. I agreed, and found myself on
the road again, driving a big rig with a chimney on top and a car
on a trailer behind me. I'm sure you needed a special licence to
drive the thing, but I asked no questions. We did Route 66, backwards, from LA to Chicago. Flagstaff, Arizona was a nice little
mountain town, and it looked like the Wild West. Gallup, New
Mexico, and Amarillo, Texas, I'd driven through before. The
deserts gave way to mid-western humidity, as we drove through
Oklahoma City, Saint Louis and into Illinois. I dropped her off
in Decatur, Illinois, and took a Greyhound bus to Chicago,
where I had urgent business; Manchester United were playing
Chelsea in the 1994 FA Cup Final the next day.

I arrived in Chicago in the wee hours, watching the city grow like a wall of fire on the horizon. It looked even bigger than Manhattan, with its many skyscrapers, ablaze with lights. I phoned an Irish pub in the *Yellow Pages* in the Greyhound station, and they said, 'Come on down.' A taxi delivered me there, and there was actually a pint waiting on the bar for me when I walked in. Excellent people, the Irish. A bloke called John let me kip at his house that night, and we returned to the pub the next morning at half-eight, as kick-off was at nine with the time difference. I watched the match, which United won 4–0, and had a few with some cockneys who watched it in the Irish pub. They were Chelsea hooligans, and were giving it the Hitler salutes and everything. The older Irish blokes looked bewildered by the antics of these cockneys, and were shaking their heads in disbelief. One of the Chelsea supporters was travelling on a fake passport, after being previously caught in Maine with counterfeit money and deported. He was a well-known head among the lads across the States. We all got thoroughly pissed, and myself and a cockney red among them celebrated the latest addition to the trophy cabinet, while the others put out the fire of failure with lashings of ale. They offered to let me stay at their place, out in the sticks, and drive back to Fort Lauderdale with them, but I declined, though it was tempting, as they were sound lads.

I went to Auto Driveaway again, and this time copped for a Chevrolet, bound for Boston, Massachusetts. As I drove around the city one last time, I found myself on Lakeshore Drive, looking at the posh hotels and blue Lake Michigan. It was the nicest thing I'd seen there since I arrived. I figured I'd get back to the East Coast, and meet up with an Aussie from Lauderdale on Martha's Vineyard. Little did I know I was about to meet my future wife, the woman who would turn me into a human being. Almost.

★ ★ ★

Massachusetts, New England, is a funny place, with funny weather and even funnier people. Unfortunately, it is not funny in the 'ha, ha' sense; it is funny in the 'what the fuck is your problem?' sense.

They are assholes, as Americans say. The part of the brain responsible for empathy appears to have withered and shrunk,
surrendering the reins to a darker, savage urge. New York City has
a reputation for rudeness, but it is undeserved, in my opinion. The
epicentre of American arrogance lies in Massachusetts, with the
exception of the people at the universities and colleges, fine
research institutions, and certain parties living down in the
Southampton woods who like to shoot guns and get fucked up.
Massachusetts is a state littered with Manchesters and Bedfords
and many other English-sounding place names. Boston is known
as 'The Hub', and is home to some great fast-paced bars, where
the locals roar on their various sports teams. The rivalry between
Boston Red Sox and New York Yankees baseball fans is comparable to the Manchester-Liverpool thing, with one big difference:
Red Sox are complete shite and have won the World Series just
once in the last eighty years. New England is comprised of six
states directly north of New York City, and outside of summer the
sky is often grey, the drizzle persistent, and the trees plainly decid-
uous. You might as well be in England. Head south-east and you
hit Cape Cod and the Islands, Martha's Vineyard and Nantucket.
The ferry takes two-and-a half-hours to get there, if you take the
slow ferry, which I did.

Arriving in Oak Bluffs harbour on Martha's Vineyard with
$60 to my name, I decided to rent a moped to get me to the
youth hostel. Mopeds were $45 a day, so that was ruled out. It
had to be a bicycle, and the hostel was ten miles away. I hoisted
my holdall onto my back and started pedalling. It was hot and
there were dips and gullies, but I got there, sweating and knackered, in the end. I paid to stay at the hostel and started asking
people about work. I got a few numbers from the *Yellow Pages*,
and started phoning through the list, knowing I only had a day's
money left, and I still had to get that bike back down to Oak
Bluffs. I was lucky. I found a housepainter who needed
someone, and he knew my Aussie mate from Lauderdale. He
said he'd pick me up the following morning at seven o' clock. I
was put on a job in some massive millionaire's house, being
constructed right on the ocean. Back in the high life again. It

had its own lighthouse, a guest house, and fabulous views of a
channel running from the sea. There was a large sailboat
anchored in the channel, which belonged to the owners. I
wanted to climb aboard and ride it up and down the coast, but
they weren't sailors; it was for show. A lot of things are for show
in this part of the world. The whole island was forested except
for the towns, kind of a gigantic Prestwich Clough, our psychedelic stomping ground of old.

The Vineyard is a millionaires' playground, but it is a small
island, twenty miles by seven at the most, and housing is almost
impossible to find. Lads arriving from the mainland spent days
scouring the island, ending up in virtual closets, often in the
'gingerbread houses' in Oak Bluffs. Gingerbreads were extremely
frilly, decked out with miles of elaborate Victorian trimwork, and
painted in a riot of gaudy colours, a total tourist lobster-pot. In
summer 1994, the gingerbreads were full of Irish kids who had
come over for the summer. Half were from Cork and the other
half Dublin. The World Cup of 1994 was about to begin, right
there in the USA, and England weren't invited but Ireland were.

The island was home to a mad lot of painters, builders and
roofers, a bunch of cokeheads, with lots of action after work in
the pubs and clubs of Oak Bluffs and Edgartown. The Irish were
delirious when they beat Italy in their opening game, talking
about winning the World Cup and other nonsense, and some
great all-day sessions were had with the Cork boys. The Dublin
lot were referred to as 'the Cockneys' and they were a loud,
confident bunch, kind of like real cockneys. I met a few English,
but not many. It seemed everyone was on the rob here too, as
most of the shops were staffed by Yank kids there for the
summer, and they didn't really have a clue or give a toss. If you
paid for anything you were doing yourself no favours.

I worked three jobs at the same time, in between mad
benders with the Irish and the Yanks. Finally, the money started
rolling in. One night I met a young American girl called Kim, a
beautiful cherub with a face surrounded by waves of dark hair.
We shared a few words, and I didn't see her for a few weeks.
Then, one night after work, there was a knock on my door, and

when I opened it she was standing there, with a smile that I can still see plain as day every time I look at her. We arranged to meet for a night out the following week. By now, I actually owned a moped to get to work on, so I was really coming up in the world. We went out a few times, and pretty much moved in together right away. We lived in a bungalow up a sandy path, overlooking the ocean. Deer would come into the garden, and we could see boats sailing by. There was an island out to sea called No Man's Land, where the US military dropped bombs for target practice. Once, it was lit up by gigantic sheets of orange fire, when they used live ammunition by mistake.

Kim provided a stability I hadn't had since before I went off the rails, and I began to feel a new sensation – relaxation. I realised I had never relaxed before I met her, and within a month or so I was starting to write stories and memoirs in an organised fashion, the type of organised fashion lacking when you're living on a post office roof or a staircase. She is of Italian descent, and I can definitely vouch for the claim that the way to a man's heart is through his stomach. Kim created aromas in our kitchen that were addictive, via combinations of vegetables, garlic, meat and pasta, while she had several pans on the go at once, flying about among the steam. That said, I'll never lose my taste for a good chip butty or a fry-up.

We were married in the Registry Office in Bury, England, at the end of 1994.

I relaxed, but I didn't slow down. The Vineyard was a summer island, and its population plummeted after October, then rose again in May. People worked the summers and hit the road for the winters. I met a great cockney lad called Chris in the summer of 1995. He was a West Ham boy, and the following year his cousin came over, another Hammer. They had a load of interestingly colourful 'merchandise', sent from London Town, in their freezer. They were dishing it out like candy. We went to see Lou Reed play on the Vineyard, totally fired up, along with scally Greg-H-, all of us completely bollocksed. We shared plenty of hilarious nights on the beach, in the clubs, hitching down the roads, totally off it, and laughing at each other's spiel.

I warned them about the dangers of drugs, but of course they wouldn't listen. The missus took a while to get used to the English habit of heavy drinking, and we had some major ding-dongs. Her Italian temperament ensured she gave as good as she got. Every chance I had I was off getting pissed with the cockneys I worked with, and I spoke in a London accent all the time I was around them, just for a laugh. They said by the end of the summer I sounded more like it than they did. I've always found that the ability to affect different roles and accents is a good way to manoeuvre yourself out of a corner, so I welcomed the opportunity to master the tongue of the supermen. Chris was the best cockney I ever met. He was brilliant.

The next few years saw more of the same: we went to Europe on Eurorail tickets, and travelled through France, Belgium, Germany, Austria, Hungary, Italy, Switzerland, Luxembourg, and back through France to England. The highlight for the Yank wife was visiting the ancestral homeland, Sicily. In England, we drove all over the place and gave it a good coat of looking at, especially the important stuff west of that vertical line through Birmingham.

Subsequent winters were spent in one place or another. We just did it; working all summer, then blowing all our money but not caring. I always managed to attend at least a match or two when we were in England, thanks to people giving me tickets. But the best trip of all was the one we made to Barcelona in May 1999. When United beat Milan in the first leg of the quarters, I said I wouldn't drink alcohol again until they were knocked out of the European Champions League, or until they reached the final. By the time we'd made it, I was gagging for a sesh.

Barcelona was as beautiful as I remembered from my stint in Spain selling oil paintings a few years earlier, when a vanload of us went to Catalonia and tried our luck on the beaches. We stayed in Sitges, twenty minutes south on the train. The first morning we headed to the Nou Camp and bought match tickets off a Spanish kid who'd taken advantage of his nationality to make a few quid. We paid £150 apiece for them and it was worth every penny. We found a little crew of lads off Las Ramblas, and got on the lash. Some of these fuckers had been going round, asking other United fans to show them their tickets, as they were worried they'd bought counterfeits, and then snatching the tickets and doing one. One youngster had about ten tickets, all snatched, and he was on a killing.

I was a bit pissed when we arrived at the Nou Camp, after the cafes of the city, but I soon got my act together and was leading all the sing-songs in our section of the ground. We were up on the top tier of the uncovered side, towards United's end, and we were in splendid voice. The United contingent was awesome, and I mean that in the old-fashioned sense of the word, no understatement. By the ninetieth minute my singing was over, and I sat watching the seconds tick by on the big screen. Then it happened, and the rest is history. We didn't get in till half-five in the morning, and had been hammering free beers all night, as the bar staff couldn't keep up with the madness. All those years since childhood were suddenly crowned with the biggest prize of all. We were on Cloud Ten.

The following morning I went for a walk and ran into Corky, one of the lads from Prestwich, now living in Sydney. I couldn't believe it. He led me around the corner into a café, and Churchy was sitting there, one of the original Perry Boys, another Prestwich lad, and literally the first to make it to Australia. I couldn't believe it again. Churchy had been a Roxy Music nut in the early days, and when he wasn't decked out in original Perry gear, he was dressed smartly in a suit, like Mr. Ferry himself. These were with a load of other Manchester lads, and they had been selling snide replica United shirts in the subways of Barcelona to finance their trip. They'd flown from Sydney to Bangkok, picked up their merchandise, and hoofed it all the way to Spain for fun and games. Kenny, my longtime best mate, was with them, as he lived in Sydney at the time, but I failed to locate him. There was a fair-sized crew of Prestwich lads all living in Sydney, all mental, always having it. They said they were going on to Ibiza, for more of the same. Spain's lax marijuana laws saw us utterly bollocksed, boozing and still unable to believe those final seconds of that epic match. We were confirming it in the newspaper as we couldn't believe the evidence of our own senses.

I was surprised by the attitude of certain United fans I met in
Barcelona. When they found out I was living in America, they
would come back with sarcastic comments, like, 'Oh, so you go
every week, then?' I gather it was a response to the bandwagon
jumpers of the 90s. These lads were always United shirt-wearing
types, wannabe-one-of-the-boys. When I got talking to the proper
lads, those wearing no colours, just out for some fun and games
and a lot of beer, they didn't miss a beat, and recognised someone
who'd been there. I wonder where the replica shirt brigade was in
1989 and 1990, the days of the 38,000 crowds, when City beat us
in the league standings, and 5–1 in a league match? They probably
bought some of the snide stuff my mates were selling, so I'll thank
them here for financing the trip for some real reds.

This is an interesting point, the wearing of replica sports gear.
If you follow the entire course of the Nameless Thing, then you'll
see it emerged from a hazy beginning, in which a lot of replica
football kits were worn. It was all about having the club badge,
and of course the designer label, even as far back as 1975. We all
remember the posers who brought footy boots to the park to play
in when the rest were content to wear trainers, which were
already passé by 1977. But when the label-less quality clothing
craze started in Manchester, a discontinuity was created, unbeknownst to those of us who participated in it. Of course, we wore
all the designer stuff, but we also wore the other stuff, too: lambswool, cashmere, suede, leather. When the sportswear companies
moved to the Far East, the quality of the gear went down, and
suddenly it was almost embarrassing to be seen in some of it, as
everyone now saw it as a load of shit. The standard of living went
up, and people could afford better clothes, and the label-less thing
actually became dominant for those with taste who could think
for themselves. It is ironic that those replica kits of the mid-70s
are still something of a craze – but a craze among the bandwagon
jumpers and divvies, for the most part. I believe that the fall of the
Scousers came when this move to the Far East occurred, and the
Mancs took on the mantle, pressing forth with their euphoric
philosophy, casual styles, and effervescent music.

21

SOUND AND VISION

I'm not really sure what it was, the best moment. You always hope it's to come.

—Bryan Ferry

THERE'S A BRAND new talk but it's not very clear. It is the noise the human animal makes when it reveals its thoughts. Being the only type of ape that can speak, we're at a huge advantage. Language, with the aid of memory, enables us to communicate and preserve complex information, and facilitated the advent of data storage via cave paintings, papyrus scrolls, cartouches, arabesques, calligraphy, books, records, tapes, CDs, computers and mobile telephones. All of these are products of language, be it in the form of an image or the binary code in a computer. Language is the weapon that enabled us to survive the Ice Age and come screaming out of the traps into the Holocene, slaughtering and poisoning and generally shitting all over the planet and everything on it. It's a wondrous thing.

Animals such as us use sound and vision to threaten, attract, warn, confuse, frighten and disappear, as the occasion demands. We use all our senses to negotiate the world, but it is sound and vision on which we most rely. And it is these two that people have always employed when going into battle with other tribes, the war paint, designer labels, original styles, and hardened regional accents wielded as effectively as any weapon.

Some of those animal skins we wore as cavemen must have looked fabulous. Our monkey hands and minds were able to

manufacture a splendid array of different styles, and whittle a
variety of fasteners. The tusk of a mastodon, the horn of a yak,
or the mane of a horse, led to some excellent little buttons,
toggles and ties with which to bundle ourselves against the
winds. But did fashion emerge way back then? Was the sight of
Ug, standing proudly outside his cave, wrapped in sabre tooth
tiger skin, enough to stir Mrs Uck next door into nagging her
long-suffering husband into going out and slaying a similar
beast, so they could keep up?

When the Ice Age ended, things moved up a gear, and
humans charged themselves with the task of doing the business.
These prehistoric peoples were exposed to rapidly changing
landscapes and ideas, their vocabulary adapting to accommodate
the strange new nouns and expressions coming into use, as
humankind pressed north into newly-exposed valleys, following
the big game, the mobile food and clothing. The vocabulary at
the end of the dinosaur 1970s was also forced to adapt, and
expressions such as 'composite rubber', 'cushioned arch-
supports', 'ribbed skiing sweater' and 'cashmere-cotton elastic
blend' tripped excitedly off the tongues of youths in north-west
England. The end of the Ice Age was a more significant event
than the birth of the Perry Boy, but the same excitement was of
its essence; we are destined to repeat the cycles of our distant
fathers, and the molecule called adrenalin is as good for you
today as it's always been. The more adventurous no doubt
acquired the rarer pelts and were first to familiarise themselves
with the language, while the more imaginative produced the
better styles. Tribes possessing these qualities were the ones that
survived and became present-day humans. The sight of a large
fire, roaring in the middle of a vast frozen plain, surrounded by
well clobbered-up numbers of people, was an advertisement:
come and join us – we're simply the best. And so did the march
towards northern civilisation begin, with Old Trafford the
biggest campfire of all.

Clothing has been fashioned from animal and plant material
since the beginning, because that's all there was; anything else was
rock, or air. Animals and plants produce their fibres via DNA-

expressed proteins, which function as structural or connective tissue. Proteins and biopolymers such as collagen, elastin, and cellulose have proved among our greatest allies in the fight for survival. Once people were agriculturally static, and the bowls with the stripes had been accepted, people began to specialise, and some specialised in clothes and shoes. Through the ages, the style of clothing has mutated, from the thousands of years of robes – Sumerian, Mesopotamian, Babylonian, Egyptian, Greek and Roman – to a more recognisable form of skirt, which itself persisted for hundreds of years, to the late 1700s when a new form of attire emerged, one which more resembles the styles of today. All the while, the same few materials were used, because they were unbeatable. And all the while, people tried to keep abreast of the fashions. Clothes, footwear and jewellery were all major cargo along the trade routes of the prehistoric world, as people wandered purposefully from place to place, over desert and plain, to exchange their wares. Fashion, both sartorial and linguistic, is as ancient as the Pennine Hills.

But proteins can be counterfeited, just like everything else. Plants and animals provided an inexhaustible source of high-quality natural fibre, and many were artificially selected or bred for their physical properties, in the same way certain fruits, nuts and pack animals have been bred for theirs. The year 1940 ushered in what scientists and others refer to as 'the chemical society', a sudden shift from natural materials to human-synthesised compounds, many of which were heralded as the wonderstuff with which we would fix all our ills and live forever as a superior creature. Modern advances in chemical and genetic engineering have enabled a remarkable specificity to emerge, a manufacturing process whereby shirts, trousers and shoes are designed to functional peculiarities demanded by a particular sport or occupation.

Without doubt, the products of the chemical society have secured advances in public health, architecture, law, forensics, engineering, medicine, and much more. Pesticides have ensured that millions avoided malaria. High tensile steel has enabled humans to bridge chasms in their environment that once

seemed unsurpassable. Plastics alone signalled a new and fascinating era for virtually everything they touched. Footwear and
sporting attire were forever transformed, and the dawn of the
'designer' label was upon us. Some time in the mid twentieth
century, a small handful of sportswear designers, sporting figures
and clothing manufacturers conspired to invent a whole new
industry around the articles of clothing worn by famous athletes
during play. People everywhere slowly realised the ability to
emulate their heroes – especially those with a few quid to spare.

European culture has always tended towards the casual, the
laidback, in the face of colonial rampage and bloody slaughter;
European aristocrats and other imperial somebodies were the
beneficiaries of this unique style. The tennis shirts and cricket
jumpers of olde were as much aesthetic as athletic to the toffs
and nobs who could afford them back in those all-smoking
days. But as the physical condition of humans has improved over
the past hundred years, along with the chemical society, the
streamlined and ultra-expensive tackle has evolved and come to
dominate our lives. We are once more preoccupied with
pouches, toggles, ties and waterproofing, like the cavemen of
old, as designer companies convince us of the necessity for attire
with which we may assault a mountain or traverse rapids. The
shoes we put on to walk to the corner shop for a newspaper are
of a type championed by last year's decathlon winner or Everest
conqueror. The name of the material our buttons are made from
is no longer 'tusk from big hairy thing' or even 'wood'; the hardware dangling from every corner of our jacket is manufactured
in mysterious plants full of men in white coats, and its name is
nine syllables long. The coat itself is likely a super-adapted fabric
synthesised by organic chemists. As ever, the media of advertising has us in its tentacles, and is sending mixed messages. We
are receiving Ice Age red alerts, while simultaneously being
informed we are heading into 'global warming' caused by the
chemical society. One thing is for sure – you must be prepared,
and the way to do that is via your sporting and outdoors shops,
where the tools for the job are freely available. It appears that the
Perry Boy culture arrived at a time when environmental disrup-

tions were becoming more explicit, and perhaps their insistence on the wearing of quality goods sprang from a subconscious realisation that we were entering an evolutionary endpoint, for which we provided the uniform. It surely was the timeliest of 'trends'. It certainly triggered a mass-market demand in Britain for specialist attire, much of it designed to protect against cruel and changing conditions. And so the men in white coats continue to produce their wonderstuff to protect us from the rising tide that yesterday was locked up in the North Pole.

The Native Americans have a saying: *when the last Indian dies, the water will come down from the north and everybody will drown.* This sounds hauntingly like climate change. In the United States, Indians have been pushed onto reservations. In the rest of the Americas, they are engaged in outright warfare with their governments or else standing paralysed as the great Amazon rainforest is ripped to pieces all around them. A way of life is under assault, and is disappearing forever. Like those ancient brick Salford streets that were crushed by bulldozers, the habitats of indigenous peoples around the globe are being vaporised to make way for the mass-produced solutions of the chemical society. Where ten years ago, a tribe wore hand-crafted sandals, they now wear Nike. Instead of intricately woven natural tunics, it is synthetic Adidas. Traditional headgear has been substituted by baseball caps, and durable wooden bowls of vegetable shoots and rice are now Big Macs and Coca-Cola in throwaway containers. When The Fall from Paradise and the Big Surplus happened, the clever monkey needed space to expand. And so brother slew brother, the farmer slew the herder, and watered the forecourts with his blood. Humankind is obliged, like all living things, to repeat the patterns of the past, in an endless cycle of ever-more healthy or pathological behaviour. The spread of agriculture 10,000 years ago led to the Industrial Revolution, which in time led to the Nameless Thing, which rendered all people everywhere uniformed doppelgängers, walking adverts for sportswear companies.

Football hooligans did not cause global climate change, and farming is not by itself an altogether bad idea, but when a moth flaps its soot-blackened wings in Salford, who knows where it will lead? Since those first farmers used the Euphrates and Tigris rivers to irrigate the fertile plains of Western Asia, the food has been plentiful and the population has expanded. But a vicious circle was created; when brother slew brother to make space to grow food for the exploding population over ten millennia, the last of the Indians became a possibility. Today, at the end of all the fun and games, indigenous people remain in shrinking little pockets here and there, and the water surely comes down from the north any day now. When that water finally arrives, driving the cockneys shrieking upland from their hovels, the north-erners will be waiting.

It is currently fashionable to blame America, not football hooligans, for the fact that native peoples are wearing Adidas and Nike (symptoms of a larger catastrophe), but there is at least one silver lining for those who hate Uncle Sam and his bastard culture: when confronted with a Stone Age hunter-gatherer in Papua New Guinea, wearing a New York Yankees baseball cap and a Manchester United shirt, ask him who the Yankees are. You'll be lucky if he is even aware of the word 'baseball'. Ask him who Manchester United are, and he'll tell you their rank in the Premiership, previous six results (and scorers), and possibly even the attendances. This, my sons, is the language of true Empire, true Religion and true Worship.

Those young lads from the early 80s are now entering middle age and dictating much of the media take on life. This also means that they are dictating which eras people should feel nostalgia for, and it is now truly our time. Adidas and others recently began releasing retro editions of their golden oldies from the late 70s and early 80s, which are being snapped up by young as well as old. Shirts and shoes not beheld for decades have appeared on people, and they still look good today. There is no end to the possibilities inherent in this masterstroke executed by the designer companies. Perhaps the rare *purple* Fila Bjorn Borg tracksuit top will be reissued, once the source for the unique colour is rediscovered somewhere in the Amazon rainforest.

Sound and vision. From the posturing, to the chanting, to the clapping and the different regional accents themselves, all have evolved over vast time scales, to crystallise in the crucibles of Albion. Mancunians today are a well-known and well-copied species, but it wasn't always the case. Through the 60s, 70s and 80s we watched as cockneys, Scousers and Glaswegians established themselves as the boys. Their accents came to symbolise a type of stylish toughness, a lovable roguishness that bespoke verve and cleverness. Mancs were portrayed as dim-witted Albert Tatlocks, muttering 'Eh oop' as a prelude to everything they said. In the 80s, *EastEnders*, *Brookside* and even *Emmerdale* had its urban-tongued villains and slippery eels, while the Manchester (now renamed 'northern') soap continued to wow audiences with its completely unrealistic cast of slobbering idiots. That The Street was named after a real street in Ordsall, the national epicentre for toughness, verve, cleverness and style, was immaterial to its producers; bullshit sold, and that meant more than any authenticity. We Mancs were forced to sit and whinge and moan, while the Scousers and Glaswegians took the piss. We knew we were the real McCoy, so why weren't there any real Mancs on the telly? Why couldn't actors from elsewhere do a decent Manc accent? And as for the amusing and novel Manc slang, well, words failed us; never a single solitary 'radio rental', 'Dolly Dimple', 'radar', 'nice one', 'town halls', or even 'Dibble'. Our spiel remained in the dark, while the residents of Albert Square gripped the nation with their shitty old houses and depressing pub.

In his book *Red Army General*, Tony O' Neill states that, although United had the biggest crew of boys, none of them had ever written a book about hooliganism because they were too busy doing it to bother writing about it. This sums up Mancs perfectly; we really were not cultured enough to conceive ourselves as media objects, as that would be 'poofy' and dead wrong. But how we suffered for our authenticity! It never occurred to us, as we bemoaned the pretenders, that it was up to us to do something about it. The Mancunian accent still struggles to come through a lot of the time, but it's getting there. It was only when Madchester exploded that the rest of the

country woke up to us, despite years of indications that something was going on in Manchester. The Perry Boy movement
was an underground phenomenon, but the gangs, the music and
the drugs were hot news, and finally people got it.

Today's youngsters appear mired in a nightmare landscape
where knifing somebody to death for a mobile phone is
common and generally being an evil little twat is cool. The football grounds, bombarded with CCTV like a meteor shower,
have become lifeless craters, and the hooligans rendered extinct,
like the dinosaurs. But, like the dinosaurs, we don't half love to
revisit that era, to read about it and make films that portray those
monsters in all their glory. What is the next stop on this weird
sleigh-ride? Indigenous English eco-tourism? Will organisations
similar to the Pike and Musket Society spring up, in order to re-
enact famous battles between rampaging firms of clobbered-up
geezers, at the sites where they occurred? I shouldn't have said
that. The cockneys will be all over it: Johnny Smith and three
hundred ICF taking liberties at Millwall, anyone?

Things are different now from how they were in 1980.
Technology has blossomed, and previously unusual artefacts and
behaviours are commonplace. Any young scally with half a brain
can isolate (pseudo) ephedrine from common cold medication
and cook up a passable batch of methamphetamine. Young kids
are walking around in vests made from Kevlar, an aromatic
polyamide long-chain molecule which possesses intermolecular
bonds and interactive stacking, creating a flexibility and
strength-to-weight ratio far beyond that of steel. It's bulletproof.
Polymer science is predicting an array of new materials that will
transform our lives, including unbreakable and ever-sharp
ceramic knives with which to prepare a gourmet meal. People
make videos of weddings, christenings and even births. Chavs
film themselves on mobile phones murdering people with
ceramic knives for more mobile phones, presumably while
wearing ceramic-impenetrable Kevlar vests, and high on home-
made speed. It's no laughing matter.

As the years have worn on, I've often tried to plunge back
into the maelstrom, to dredge up some bones and pottery from

that Golden Age. Maybe because I'm scientifically inclined, I have always believed that a linear approach to analysis is the only way, so I started at the beginning. The first time I ever set eyes on a Perry Boy I cannot say; there was a lot going on, and all of us, even thirteen-year-old me, knew in our bones what constituted the real McCoy, and what didn't. It's this real McCoy that I began to hunt for, late on a Friday or a Saturday night, clutching a cold beer in front of the computer. I would spend hours patrolling the internet, searching for articles about the Perry Boy culture, about the Merseyside scallies, and about the clothes and other accessories of the early 80s, but most of what I found was inaccurate and written by people who hadn't been there.

I am a daydreamer, and do not spend enough time in the 'present', as they say, because my mind is full of memories. I can still see Andy-M-, surveying the pub through hooded eyes, his cards close to his chest, his betting slip in his shirt pocket, sparking one up and merging into the woodwork like a camouflaged reptile with the tattoos on his hands and throat. I can see Dave-B- in his birthday clothes, ragged and rattled by the Scouse day out. All the boys, like Kenny and Dave-D-, who went jetting around Israel, Spain, Australia and America, are in my head, and they make a lot of noise. Hopefully writing this book will shut the fuckers up.

From the Fred Perries and Hush Puppies of 1979, to what emerged from the tunnel at Old Trafford when the Liverpool boys were in town in early 1980, full circle back to Hush Puppies again, to the rave phenomenon, to today's incredible internet access where a person can join discussion groups such as *80s Casuals*, this thing of ours has never died. In fact it's as popular as ever, but that's why the good stuff is difficult to find; it's buried under an avalanche of bollocks from glacial retreats both irrelevant and unoriginal. I apologise to those from outside the north-west, but it was *these* valleys, *these* glacial retreats, that exposed the country of the Nameless Thing. Anything else is simply a counterfeit. When I read Dave Hewitson's contributions on the web during one of my forays, and his *The Liverpool Boys are in Town*, I finally felt that at last somebody was characterising the thing from an objective standpoint. I suggest you obtain a copy of that important little book before it becomes a collectors' item. A late-night drunken email to Hewitson, and an instant reply, told me I had finally made contact with a kindred spirit, and a Scouse one at that. Hewitson was primarily in it for the excitement, like most of us who were there.

Another bleedin' fool, Kenny, described the thrill: 'Anybody who was there will never forget the pumped sensation of seeing hundreds of lads, all wearing quality tackle, with those strange effeminate haircuts, all worked up, all excited fit to burst, knowing there was a train coming in any minute. It made no difference if you were on the train, or waiting for it; the important thing was it was coming, and it was carrying a full crew of boys.'

Boys. That's the word, the name we had for the Nameless Thing. What started as Perry Boys was reduced in time, the prefix dropping as the Thing became uniformly established. We were *Boys*, eerily appropriate, as most of us were indeed around the fifteen-to-eighteen age group. Photographs from the period reveal how our skeletons were unfinished; the telltale faded line, where the jeans had been let down, says it all. We were growing lads. It's been a long and eventful journey for those inventive Liverpudlian-Mancunian spores of yesteryear, as they chuffed along the tracks, gaining momentum and morphing into new forms, finally infesting the rest of England and triggering Phase Two; when the culture collided with certain psychoactive molecules, it triggered Phase Three, and when that new generation came of age and began exploring the outside world, it triggered Phase Four. Whether England is a better place today than it was in 1980 is a whole new discussion. One thing is for certain – if we hadn't taken the reins and jumped outside the box, we might still be wasting time trying to shock the previous generation with outrageous clothes, instead of trying to change our world and our fortunes. We have matured, those of us who participated in the creation of those new attitudes, over a quarter of a century ago. We sing a different tune and we dance a different dance, all night long, in a combination of tradition and technology. Places are shaped by the peasantry – the food, the architecture, the drink and the humour – and it is an honour to have been part of the generation that made the greatest strides in bringing home the bacon.

The powers-that-be in Britain are convinced that the changes under way will erase forever the tendency to jog along in a mob, chanting and searching out a rival tribe to slaughter. I am not so sure. CCTV may seem to have solved things, but people are people. The emergence of chavs, of kids in hooded tops who will knife you to death as soon as look at you, may well be a symptom of the repression of the more diffuse football hooliganism. Whenever you interfere with the energy in a system, that energy surfaces elsewhere, sometimes in a more concentrated form. Perhaps in this case that form is a multiple stab wound inflicted by an instinct crammed into a window of opportunity far too small in spacetime. The English genome must find its own comfortable place to be, instead of trying to be a carbon copy of some others. It is true that we are Europeans, but Europe contains a variegated sprinkling of specimens; we are not all the same. Perhaps the Government should allocate large private spaces for young men to engage in their tribal differences. Make them wear boxing gloves and training shoes, search them for weapons, and even charge them money to do it. Some form of insurance would be required, to cover any medical costs. It would be somewhere for John Smith to go and get it off his chest on the morning of the game, leaving time for him to have a few pints with his adversary later, like a rugby player. Just a thought.

From the beginning the greatest rush was always the feeling that you were somehow out on a limb, living on a thin line, sharing your experience with a small number of like-minded souls. This is the essence of a frontier mentality. America was founded and built by such people. So was the Industrial Revolution. Anything new must represent some form of growth, an annexation of a dark and unknown territory. The extremes, the tails of the bell curve, are where the action is, and where you'll find those that are different. The middle of the bell

curve, fat and packed as it is with those seeking security in the
centre of the herd, is a tedious and unrewarding place. There is
only the grind, the nine-to-five of normalcy, the slow death of
the respectable. It is a useless realm, and its distractions are plentiful and mediocre. Without challenges we wither and die, and
it is towards the challenges you are drawn, if you have a shred of
life left in you. You must head out to where the people are rare
and the conditions unpredictable and unknown. You must avoid
the Football Special and take the service train. There you can
breathe easy.

From the early days of the Perry, through Casual, to the
dispersal across the continents, nothing has really changed.
Those of us who emigrated are faced with our own set of
issues, as we merge into new cultures on strange continents.
These days, I live at least two hours from a big city, but there
are health food stores, universities, bookstores and decent cafes
to eat and drink in. I am often very uncomfortable around my
middle class friends, as they think so very differently from me.
The American attitude towards alcohol consumption is frankly
ridiculous, and even intelligent people here believe you to be
at least partly evil if you like a regular skinful. It is a polarised
country, with the health-conscious, ultra-liberal Europhiles on
the one side, and the more conservative, boozy, Nature-
conquerors on the other. For relief, I sometimes turn to these
coarser elements in the population. These 'uneducated' people
know a good cheese and a good wine, but they also like to get
outdoors. They enjoy riding the million-acre woodlands on
snowmobiles and quad bikes, a goodly supply of strong spirits
in the saddlebags. They chop down trees with chainsaws in
anticipation of the sub-zero nights of winter. They have nick-
names like The Master, The Crusher, The Gimp and The Stiff.
The natives of this forested zone wear labelled brands of
outdoors gear such as Carhart, and Timberland or Rockport
boots. It's like a uniform here. They kill large beasts, skin,
butcher and eat them. They like to shoot big guns, silly guns,
because they can, and gather around the woodstove on cold
winter nights, swilling tequila and losing themselves in the haze

of the frontier. It is a different life, and I miss Manchester like crazy a lot of the time. But the frontier, the *edge*, is where it's at, kids. Don't ever let anyone tell you otherwise.

So, it's breakfast in America. A land of too many choices. Is it bacon, proscuitto, serrano, ibérico or is it simply West Ham? Whatever you eat for breakfast, make sure you wash it down with a decent drink, and may you always have the good luck and common sense to overface yourselves repeatedly, *for the path of excess leads to the well of wisdom…*

ACKNOWLEDGEMENTS

To Pete and Chris at Milo, for believing that a thing like this could be allowed into the gang. Without your being there to recognise the worth in my ramblings I'd still be howling at the moon. Thank you a million times over.

To Dave Hewitson, for caring enough about the subject to be scientific in his own book, and urging me to write this thing, which I might not have but for him.

To Jane for editing mercilessly, and watching my back by bringing out the knife when required.

To the many contributors, anonymous and otherwise, who literally made it all possible and real.

To the 80s' Casuals mob for keeping me interested and even getting me back in some decent gear!

To all on the United discussion forums for keeping me up to date and letting me live through you.

To everyone, friends, family and enemies alike, who I spent time with from 1979–1999, and I hope you're all as sane as can be expected, under the circumstances.

To Gary Beluzo at HCC for introducing me to ecological stoichiometry and the Gorilla.

To my blood brother Aaron Hellem, for sniffing me out, bringing me back to the dark side, and feeding bourbon to the devil on my shoulder.

To John Clark at UMass for the toxicodynamics, beer, chicken wings, etc.

To all close friends: Kenny Lewis, Sean Whittaker, Uncle Silverback, etc, who read it and provided feedback.

To Kim for always being there to encourage and convince me I could be something more than I believed I was.

To Mum and Dad for throwing me at that world and that world at me, thereby qualifying me to actually write this thing. You're my best friends, and I love you both more than you'll ever know.

And lastly, to that cauldron of noise and excitement, and everyone who ever pulled on the red shirt and headed down that tunnel, into the bright lights. May you live forever.